The Last Day

An Exploration of Humankind's Spiritual History and Destiny

by

Walied Jassat

GR
GEORGE RONALD
OXFORD

George Ronald, *Publisher*
Oxford
www.grbooks.com

A catalogue record for this book is available
from the British Library

ISBN 978–0–85398–559–4

For my mom and dad

The true test of love
is what we are willing to
sacrifice for our beloved. Your
sacrifices have paved a beautiful path
for me, which I can never fully
return to you, but I will try
to honour you and this
journey that God
has given us
to share.

CONTENTS

ACKNOWLEDGEMENTS

Thanks to my sweet, understanding, forgiving, loving wife Varkha for her support and never ending love and belief in me, and for being by my side through everything, helping, appreciating me and my work. To my Mom for her deep faith and open mind and ever selfless and giving nature; my Dad for his sacrifices and big heart; to my sisters: Wasi for her adventurous spirit, boldness and excellence; Shai for her supportive, sweet, loving nature; Rara for her creative musical soul, strong faith, wisdom and maturity beyond her years. To Aadamo, the human dynamo, who is crazy like his uncle! And little Zaidu who is a blessing and joy, whose deep eyes have yet many mysteries. To my bro-in-law Hussain who is an ever reliable, kind friend and other bro-in-law Asrat . . . a diamond in the rough. To my mum-in-law Anita and bro-in-law Vimal, whose courage and sacrifices have earned my deepest respect. To my other big sister Sonja who looks after me and always uplifts my spirit and gives me hope and strength; and my other big sister Nasheetah who always puts a smile on my face and who is a comfort and shoulder to complain on; and my other other big sister Hailey who is a shining star and inexhaustible servant of mankind. Thanks also to Uncle Lowell, Aunt Edith and Uncle Ata Rouhani for advising and encouraging and for reviewing my manuscripts, and Leyla, Sam Lyle, Golara, Gomolemo for support and appreciating my work. My Aunt Sabera (other mom) who made learning fun when we were kids and who always takes a keen interest in my creative exploits and adventures. To my high school English teacher Reyhana for persevering with me and nurturing my gift even though I was a most troublesome and irritating punk in the class. My aunt Zaheda (my other other mum) who constantly advises me to pray and submit to the Will of God. To my other Aunt Hajoo and cousin Nauman who are on the other side of the world but always supportive of my work.

To my high school buddies, Shaker, Moosa, Aadilez, Muazzam and Yunus: I really value and treasure your friendship and all the fun, crazy times we shared. To my crew the Urban Legendz: Bongz, Mo, Hlezi (another sister from another mother), Siya Masiyah, James, Luna, Rameez, Brian, Musa, Trouble, Thuto, Timothy, Eugene, Conor, Dexterz, Grae, Ivy, Africa, Space-KG, Sku and the rest of the gang. Your love and support is legendary and you really make me believe in myself. To my colleague Mariaan, you are radiant and I'm glad to be your son number 397; and Willem van Rijn for always encouraging me. And to my DRC crew, Raphael, Dolf, Jerry, Eddie, Badi . . . you guys are amazing. To Lynne, Leon and Ghazala, and Shane for interesting conversations and sharing ideas. To Fariba for her friendship, advice, inspiration, books and engaging conversations; James Manning for his appreciation of me and my work, and to Maciek, my quality friend, for unfailing support and valuable input. To my friend Nicola Brescia whose dedication and determination have been an enduring example and inspiration; my cousin Naseem who introduced me to the beauty and wonder of nature and cousin Samiya Apa who showed me how someone could overcome personal tragedy and emerge radiant and loving, and her lovely kids Ta'seen and Tazkiyah. To my cousin Reza for the gift of creative expression and the far more valuable gift of his freedom and independence of spirit, which broadened my horizons. To my grandfather Goolam-Bhai, Papa, whom I loved a lot and who was truly humble and

The Last Day

caring. And to my other grandfather Checker whose legacy opened many paths and doors for a whole generation. To my cousins Uwaiz and Luqman whose spirit of adventure and will to succeed taught me a lot. To my brotherhood Tariq, fatherhood Hamid and motherhood Nazreen, Aunty Banu, Uncles Nisar, Mohsin, Baboo, cousin Fayaaz Kajee, my friends Ivy, Shaka, Ntswati, Xola, Anisa, Kabengele, Nelson, Chris Songok, Kully, Mokone, T-bo, Cassius and Outlwile, Ryan and Leyla, Anis and Hannah, Johnson, Cornelius, Michael (Aussie), Ebrahim, Zolani, Mamutseki, Martin, Sina, Farzam, Omid, Aryan, Luvuyo, Nabil from Cameroon, Latoya, Dominique, Nicky, Oupa, Sbu, Philile, Charles, Denny and Mary Pat, Nondwe, Mojdeh Mutale, Denny and Beth, Roya, Mary, Mpunki, Hailey, Balram, Kiran and also little Nirvan, Chana, Devina and Avid. To my 'kids' Jabu, Mimi, Gugu, Subz, Elmon, Johnny, Zaza . . .

I could write a book about how amazing each of you is. If I have left anyone out please forgive me. Thanks for everything my friends! Also thanks to all the critics and haters who helped me to refine my work and better understand the task ahead of me.

Just as this book was going to press, our daughter, my little princess Jasmine, was born. She has changed our lives in the most wonderful way, showing us a whole new world and an ocean of love . . .

Finally, thanks to God and His Messengers . . . the ultimate source of my inspiration and creativity . . . my Light!

In the Name of God the Most Gracious the Most Merciful

1

RISE AND SHINE

Introduction

For some time I was accumulating books, translations of scripture, compilations and other sources, fascinated with the concept of prophecy and the spiritual destiny of humankind. I cannot say that I was researching it with a view to writing a book on the subject, but early one morning after returning from a family holiday to the coast I was inspired . . . inspired by the magical experience of camping on the beach, the unfathomable majesty of the ocean and the delightful starry expanse. Crossing borders and encountering a very different place and culture also has the tendency to open one's mind and expand one's horizons. Interwoven with these ineffable feelings were my dreams, yet deeper and harder to describe. I have always felt this difficulty in articulating my thoughts and feelings, partly due to my own inhibitions but also because there never seemed to be words, no matter how well arranged, that were ever able to capture what arose in my heart. Perhaps it is this that makes me a writer, this mixed with awe and wonder at the beauty of God's creation and hope for inner tranquillity and outer peace. In a sense there can be no inner peace for me unless there is peace in the world, and similarly there can be no peace on earth unless there is tranquillity radiant in the hearts of each of us. It is this lonely longing for love that is my real inspiration, longing for the love of God and the unity of humanity.

My family and I had just returned from an amazing

adventure-holiday to the coast. We had camped out on the beach for a few days and on our last day decided we would all get up early to watch the sunrise. My mum, being the only one with the self-discipline, rose early and stirred us all to come out of our tents. I had to convince myself that it was worth it, then picked myself up, stumbled outside and climbed into a hammock overlooking the dark, gloomy ocean with its chill morning breeze, wet and salty. The sky was a deep dark violet with stars twinkling between the wispy clouds and over the ocean the sky was aglow with ever-lighter tones of cerise as the earth slowly turned. The whole sky was gradually changing. Dimly luminescent clouds drifted aimlessly, and the stars disappeared one by one until there was only one star still left in the sky, the morning star they call it, or the planet Venus, I think. It was like being drawn into the melancholy heart of a rainbow, watching the moving colours chasing away the deep dark blue to the far reaches of the world. The sun itself was not yet visible but the whole sky was displaying the effects of its effulgence.

So utterly beautiful was the way in which the sun announced its arrival. Then, peeking over the ocean horizon, a bright glowing golden flame appeared and slowly grew and rose to show its spherical shape and radiant pulsing disk, which reflected on the ocean and glimmered off the rolling, crashing waves. Gradually and gracefully it rose, such that it was not damaging to the eyes for so powerful a source of energy appearing out of the darkness. I was able to look directly at the sun for a little while and it was like a beating heart. Something in my own heart rose with a prayer or a song of praise silenced by the splendour. So radiant was the sun that it transformed the sky completely and lit up the clouds with its pink golden flames, eclipsed all the stars and filled the sky with light and the earth with clarity. It climbed steadily up and made the horizon glow with a glorious shimmering hue. And climbing higher still, its disk was obscured behind clouds but its effect on the sky was not diminished. Rising still higher, it was now so bright that I could not look upon it anymore. The sky became its familiar blue and the clouds became the usual white, and everyone came out and went about their business. The fishermen strolled by and boats went out to sea. The tourists came out with their cameras and took photos of each other, and we sat watching the dawning of a new day.

> By the Glorious Morning Light, and by the night when it is still, Thy guardian Lord hath not forsaken thee . . . (Q 93:1–3)

Thousands of days the sun has risen over each of our lives but how often do we ponder the splendour of God? Countless gifts and blessings surround us, even life itself is a blessing we will never fully comprehend, but very seldom do we thank and praise our Creator. Often we worship out of cultural habit, just going through the motions we were taught; sometimes we have moments of inspiration, or desperation, when we are drawn to commune with our Source and Sustainer; but most days we live on autopilot, mindlessly playing out the role in our routines, moving like the sands of the hourglass from one empty chamber to another. For me, the ocean and glorious sunrises and meaningful dreams are inspiration to enkindle my faith and to reconnect with the soul-stirring Words of God.

But honestly speaking, sometimes I do feel forsaken, lonely and sad. Maybe I get so caught up in analysing the past, fearing the present and worrying over the future that I cannot recognize what I have. Maybe I'm always wanting, always craving, always searching, but never finding . . . never at peace. Maybe I cannot connect my seemingly meaningless life with these exalted words revealed by my guardian Lord through His Messenger. Maybe the pain and suffering of my life have blinded my mind and closed my heart. I struggle to see the miraculous in the mundane and purpose in the profane and beauty in the banal. I struggle to trust in God and submit to His Will, not in the vague cosmic, mystic sense, but in the day to day of every day.

Every new day, however, represents an opportunity to learn, to awaken, to draw nearer to God, and to begin to live in His presence, to be moved by a higher motivation, thus gradually changing the why and what and how of all the things we do and think and feel. The Creator of all things has fashioned the physical reality to furnish me with these potentialities, to give me these powers, to give me freedom and to give me choice. He has given me sunshine and shelter, food and health, abilities and talents, love and laughter. He has given me education to develop, work to serve humankind, sleep for rest and dreams to guide me. He has given me prayer as a means to commune with Him and to enter into a loving relationship with Him. Most importantly, He has illumined my heart and world with His Word and the life and legacy of His Messengers, which lead me ever forward and upward.

On the night of our return from the holiday I was very tired after much exertion and long driving, and so I fell into a deep sleep. In the early hours of the morning I dreamed a lovely and memorable dream. I found myself in a home from olden times. The room was aglow with a warm gentle light and before me was a door. A feeling of reverence and awe filled me and I realized that I was standing in the home of the Messenger of God. It was a feeling at once exhilarating and enchanting. I reached for the doorknob, not knowing what I would find on the other side of the door. As I touched it, the realization that his hand had touched the very same spot and that he might be standing on the other side overwhelmed me with such a feeling of the sacred and sublime as I cannot explain, and I awoke. Lying in my bed with the gloomy glow of a city sunrise creeping into my room, I stayed for a while reflecting on the dream and enjoying the feeling of love for the Messenger of God. Then I sprang out of bed and began with this work, or rather this adventure. I could not have known then all the wonderful things I would discover in the process of writing this book . . . for to explore this theme of the Last Day is to lose yourself in the timeless and placeless love of God and to find yourself again in the times and places of His Revelations.

Recently at a gathering of youth from different religious backgrounds the theme of progressive revelation was being discussed. People were grappling with the truth that every Messenger of God was rejected and persecuted in his time. So I asked them a question to try to put it in a more personally meaningful way:

'OK, we know that God is the greatest and most powerful and can do whatever He wills, right, so why does God choose to give His message in this way, through a single human voice, in the immensity of space and time? He could give His message in many other ways that would make all people obey Him instantly in whatever He commanded, so why does He choose a way that is so painfully hard and slow?'

They thought about this for some time. One young man raised his hand and said that it is 'fear'. If God were to take on a booming fiery voice from the sky then everyone would be full of fear and He doesn't want that. A girl said that she often wondered why God could not just make everyone understand. It was an interesting conversation and in the end they asked me what I thought. I said that God is self-sufficient and almighty. He loves us very much but He doesn't need our worship or our support. He created this reality to help us, so we need Him. We need Him to survive, to live, to grow and most importantly to change, to become better than we are. And the only way to improve is to understand, to realize or to choose.

And so God sends Messengers. They are people born on this earth just like anyone but are pure and loving and radiant. And these people through their actions and sayings inspire a revolution in human thinking, doing, knowing and being. They release into the world new ideas that will inspire good thoughts and actions, and which people must themselves think about and decide whether or not to align themselves with, not out of fear or force but out of understanding and personal experience. The Messenger is the perfect example of all the goodness that God loves, and just by being himself he attracts the hearts and souls of the spiritually minded. But he also arouses the suspicion and hatred of the worldly and those in power, who feel threatened and destabilized because the Messenger reveals to them their ignorance and arrogance. He captures the love and allegiance of the people and this releases a primal animal egoic[1] instinct in the established politico-religious leaders until they descend into complete savagery and reveal their true colours.

The persecution of the Prophets, the fall of wicked nations and the rise of religion are inseparable processes, very prominent and pervasive in the Qur'án and Bible, so we shall explore these as the story of the Last Day unfolds. But what we can note for now is that God is not far from us, nor is He hiding away from us. He is helping us to understand and transform ourselves so that we stop creating misery and start creating peace and joy. In order to independently evaluate these transformative ideas we must be free to choose, and that is the purpose and nature of this physical reality. The flip side of being free to choose divine ideas is that we are also free to express our animalistic, primitive or egoic selves. Submission to the Will of God is a long and painful process.

> Let there be no compulsion in religion: Truth stands out clear from error: whoever rejects paganism and believes in God hath grasped the most trustworthy handhold, that never breaks. And God heareth and knoweth all things. He brings them out of the depths of darkness into the light. (Q 2:256–7)

Paganism can be defined as belief in and worship of idols. There are material idols and there are mental idols. A material idol is a physical object to which a person gives his devotion while a mental idol is a thought, condition or thing to which a person gives his attention and devotion and in which he puts his trust. The world today is in the depths of darkness. While the light of faith has virtually prevailed over material paganism there is yet an overwhelming immersion in and preoccupation with the pleasures and treasures of the world. There is at the root of it a great greed and need to satisfy the lower self, resulting in a world filled with division, war, crime, poverty, disease and suffering. These very conditions have been foreshadowed in all the Books of God, in which He describes a 'future' time of great suffering and darkness in the world.

The Prophet-Founders of the world's great religions have revealed the signs and conditions of the Last Day. The beloved Prophet of Islam, Muhammad (peace and blessings of God be upon him and his family and *ummah*) similarly revealed many verses and also spoke often about the 'Last Day' or the 'Day of Judgement', as it is more commonly known. Since then many centuries have passed and the matter has become very complex and nebulous. When we were children what we were taught about the Last Day was very frightening and confusing: great calamities will be followed by the appearance of terrible monsters; the words of the Qur'án will disappear; giant trumpets will be blown by two angels; the world will come to an end; and everyone will be raised from the dead, judged and given to eternal heaven or hell. It was all contradictory and fantastical. However, when we explore the Qur'án and *ḥadíth*, Bible and other world scriptures a picture emerges which is truly consistent and logical. It cannot be described or summarized from where we are but in order to arrive at that vista we have to walk many paths and unravel many mysteries, clear away much confusion and cultivate a symbolic imagination to appreciate that prophetic picture.

We will see later that many other signs have come to pass as well. This compilation or exposition is made entirely for the sake of unity and the love of God. The point is not to criticize and break down others but to sincerely and objectively try to connect prophecy with reality. If I have erred then I pray that God will forgive me and guide me and the respected reader towards truth and right understanding. What I hope I will be able to achieve is to allow the scriptures to tell the true story and it is my role simply to clarify the pattern so that the pieces of the puzzle may be brought together. The Last Day is, indeed, one of the most puzzling matters and the greatest mystery facing the modern mind. May God guide each one of us so that we will come to an appropriate understanding of the Last Day.

The symbol that has been used most frequently and effectively in all scriptures is that of revelation as a light in the darkness.

Light and Time

Our learning is cumulative and as we grow, our powers and abilities develop. A young child attends school and progresses from one grade to the next, learning more each year, entering into deeper study and new fields of knowledge, always building on what she has learned. In the life of a child, every year there is a new beginning, a new teacher and new things to learn. The child cannot learn higher things without first learning the basics, but once they are learned, then they are applied automatically or intuitively and the child can progress to higher levels.

This is how it works in the life of an individual and so it is not difficult to understand that the education of humankind must follow a similar pattern. We, as collective humanity, are being educated through successive revelations to ever higher and higher levels of human development. We cannot teach ourselves about the important things in life – how to be virtuous, how to live together, how to overcome suffering and achieve true happiness and true love – any more than a child can teach itself higher mathematics. We need a teacher who has that knowledge and who lives out those qualities. The teachers of humankind are those pure souls whom God chooses to bring love and truth, to teach and guide, to be a light in the darkness. These are the Messengers of God. Religion educates humanity according to our circumstances – where we are, when we are, what we are able to accommodate, what we can understand, according to our capacities and abilities. Religion enables us to progress. Revelation brightens the world and shows us the way, one divinely guided teacher after another.

In nature there are many cycles. There is the great annual cycle in which the earth completes a circuit around the sun passing through four seasons. There is no real beginning or end, for the cycle is continuous and there are variations depending on where in the world you are. In my part of the world the summer is hot and it rains quite a lot and everything is green and flowery and flourishing. Then we go through autumn when the weather cools, the rains dissipate, it gets a bit windy and the leaves turn golden brown and start falling off the trees. Then we go into winter when it gets really cold and dry and many trees shed all their leaves. But winter eventually yields to spring and it slowly warms and rains again and things return to life and become fresh again. Leaves grow again and flowers blossom and then summer returns. All things depend upon the sun for their sustenance and growth and all are fashioned by God in such a way as to enable them to adapt to changing conditions. Consider the tree. It manifests great beauty and bounties – leaves, flowers and fruit – during the summer months of sunshine and water, and conserves itself and its energy during the harsher months of winter.

We co-exist in harmony with nature's cycles and the daily cycle of the sun is the one that we are most conscious of. It affects our lives the most and we pattern our lives according to it. Our sense of time and conception of reality is governed by this cycle described by the rotation of the earth on its axis giving us day and night, giving us consciousness and sleep, light and darkness.

> It is He [God] Who beginneth the process of Creation and repeateth it, that He may reward with justice those who believe . . . It is He Who made the Sun to be a shining Glory and the Moon to be a light (of Beauty), and measured out stages for it, that ye might know the number of years, and the count (of time) . . . Verily in the alternation of the Night and the Day, and in all that God hath created, in the heavens and the earth, are Signs for those who fear Him. (Q 10:4–6)

God's design is perfect, from its boundless infinity down to its minutest detail. The earth is perfectly located in relation to the sun. It is exactly where it must be in order for life, as we know it, to exist here. Any closer to the sun and all the liquid on earth would vaporize and life would be impossible. Any further from the sun and it would all freeze on a cold desolate surface and, again, life as we know it would be impossible. The movements of the earth are not arbitrary and meaningless.

> God is He Who created the heavens and the earth . . . and maketh the sun and the moon, constant in their courses, to be of service unto you, and hath made of service unto you the night and the day. (Q 14:32)

The word 'day' in general use refers to a full rotation of the earth on its axis. From the cold darkness the sun rises into the sky from the East, gradually providing light and warmth, till it reaches its maximum height and radiance at midday and then declines towards the West. It loses its brilliance and heat till it sets and the world is again plunged in gloom and then utter darkness. The earth cools, the moon glows with the reflected light of the sun and the stars twinkle again. The moon and the starry expanse also seem to move across the sky and at midnight the earth has turned completely away from the sun. It continues to turn and once again the sun dawns on the horizon, the moon and the stars disappear and are replaced by the splendour of the sun. In reality the sun is ever-present and radiant but the earth turns continuously and so, for fixed alternating terms, the sun becomes manifest and hidden.

We awaken, climb out of bed, freshen up, eat something, go about our work or education or whatever it is we do. We see by the light of the sun; we are warmed by the heat of the sun; our food comes ultimately from the energy of the sun – carbohydrates built up by photosynthesizing plants. The sun is the source of all energy on earth. Through the food chain all creatures and organisms on the planet are sustained. We drive our cars and operate our machines and computers and electrical appliances all fuelled ultimately by the energy of the sun; mainly through the use of hydrocarbon fossil fuels but increasingly also solar, wind and water or gravitational power as well as nuclear fission or fusion power – but all still directly or indirectly dependent on or arising from stellar fusion. We manage our affairs according to the time of day. Date and time are very important to us and these are dependent on the movements of the earth. In the evening we retire to our homes, relax and then settle into bed. We become drowsy and we automatically know that it is time to sleep because our bodies shut down and we lose consciousness according to this natural rhythm of the sun embedded into our biology. It gets dark, and it gets colder, and it is not a time for work, play or study, it is a time for rest, reflection and restoration. Some people, however, are not able to follow this pattern, such as those who work night shifts and those who suffer from insomnia. So while it is possible to step out of this natural pattern, all such people experience significant negative effects on their health and well-being after a while. This is because our bodies and minds are attuned to this cycle. This natural cycle governs our lives on earth and establishes a pattern within which we grow with balance.

> And we shall surely show them of Our signs in the world and within themselves . . . (Q 41:53)

In this cyclic repetitive process we are given a symbol by which to understand other great processes that are beyond our contemplation.

> To God belongeth the dominion of the heavens and the earth and God hath power over all things. Behold! In the creation of the heavens and the earth and the alternation of Night and Day, there are indeed Signs for men of understanding. (Q 3:189–90)

In the life of humanity the revelation of God's Word has been likened to a great teaching, an outpouring of heavenly showers, to the flowering or springtime, to a wellspring or oasis in the desert, to a glowing lamp and the rising sun in the darkness of the world. Revelation has repeatedly been likened to a light in the darkness:

> O Mankind! Verily there hath come to you a convincing proof from your Lord for we have sent unto you a light (that is) manifest. (Q 4:174)

> Say: I but follow what is revealed to me from my Lord: This is nothing but Light from your Lord, and guidance, and mercy, for any who have faith. (Q 7:203)

> Can he who was dead, to whom we gave life, and a light whereby he may walk amongst men, be like him who is in the depths of darkness? (Q 6:122)

Among the titles of the Prophet Muhammad are 'Raḥmatan li'l-'Álamín' ('Mercy unto all Mankind') and 'Sirájun Munírah' ('Shining Spiritual Sun').

> A Messenger, who rehearses to you the signs of God containing clear explanations, that he may lead forth those who believe and do righteous deeds from the Depths of Darkness into Light. (Q 65:11)

> O Prophet! Truly We have sent thee as a witness, a bearer of glad tidings, and a warner, and as one who invites [a caller] to God's (Grace) by His leave, and as a Lamp spreading light. (Q 33:45–6)

> I call to witness . . . the Dawn as it breathes away the darkness; verily this is the word of a most honourable messenger. (Q 81:15–19)

Hafiz Ghulam Sarwar in his detailed and thorough book *Muhammad the Holy Prophet* confirms that:

> Muhammad is the Spiritual Sun or star by whose light all mankind are to be guided, not because he is a deity (God forbid) but because his light is the Light of God and his path the Path of God.[2]

> Darkness is ignorance, unbelief, and iniquity, which is the natural condition of man without divine guidance and revelation.[3]

It is clear then that faith, love, truth and the knowledge of God are as light and the absence of these is like darkness. And so the Apostle of God is an emissary of Light. As an ambassador of the heavenly realm he is a radiant star that rises over a dark world and illumines and warms, enkindles and brings to life. He is a glowing lamp around which the faithful gather and seek warmth and illumination. He is the radiance of love, within which the children of men may grow, and work and play and progress.

The Surah of Light (An-Núr) opens with clear explicit instructions for the punishment of transgressors of religious law and elaborates the theme of practical guidance and laws but it also contains the following verses:

> God is the Light of the heavens and the earth. The similitude of His Light is as a niche wherein is a lamp: the lamp is in a glass: the glass is as it were a shining Star. [This lamp is] kindled from a blessed Tree, an Olive, neither of the East nor of the West, whose oil would almost glow forth (of itself), though no fire touched it: Light upon Light! God guideth unto His Light whom He will: and God speaketh to mankind in allegories, for God is Knower of all things. (Q 24:35)

The last verse tells us that 'Light' is a symbol or allegory that God uses to help us understand. Faith is for me a small fire burning deep inside from where I draw my inspiration and meaning, my direction and purpose. It is where I take my sorrows and fears and burn them. It is where I warm myself and find peace and tranquillity. Without this faith, this Light, this knowledge, inside my heart I would be lost, lonely and cold, and this is for me the Light of God and His Revelation. I cannot see God nor do I hear Him speaking but when I read the Word of God then I know that God has spoken because I see in the lives of Muhammad and Jesus and Buddha and all the Messengers, those examples of all that I wish I could be, and I discern in their words all that I wish for the world of truth and love. This Light that I cherish in my heart comes from the Messenger . . . the Lamp.

God shines His Light of love and truth for all to see. Truth that we personally connect with makes our lives meaningful and beautiful; and in the same way that the lamp illumines the room or the space around it, so the Messenger of God illumines the lives of his loved ones and makes things clearer, helps thinking minds to understand and those who are lost to seek redemption and all to transform their lives towards virtue. Later in the surah the following verses help us to understand the contrast between light and darkness, faith and disbelief:

> But the Unbelievers – their deeds are like a mirage in sandy deserts, which the man parched with thirst mistakes for water; until when he comes up to it, he finds it to be nothing: but he finds God (ever with him), and God will pay him his account: and God is swift in taking account. Or (the Unbelievers' state) is like the depths of darkness in a vast deep ocean, overwhelmed with billow topped by billow, topped by (dark) clouds: Depths of darkness, one above another: if a man stretches out his hand, he can hardly see it! For any to whom God giveth no light, There is no Light! (Q 24:39–40)

In another sense, darkness is that condition of suffering characterized by emotions and feelings of inadequacy, fear, anxiety, anger, hatred and suspicion. We can understand this from our own experience of being in a dark room or place. We are afraid because we do not know if we might stumble and fall and hurt ourselves, or perhaps some beast or wicked person means to harm us. When the light shines everything becomes clear and fear vanishes with the dark shadows. Similarly the Word of God dispels anxiety but, more especially, it transforms suffering into tranquillity.

Abdullah Yusuf Ali draws on *Mishkat-ul-Anwar*, the work of the respected and renowned scholar and mystic of the early 12th century CE Imam al-Ghazali. In his summary of the Surah of Light (Núr) in Appendix 8 of his translation of the Qur'án, Yusuf Ali explains that:

> . . . the physical eye sees by the sun; the spiritual eye sees by Revelation (the Qur'án [Word of God]). There is a world

> invisible, with a Light of its own, quite different from the world visible, with its own physical light. The former, the spiritual world, is far above the physical world: not in space, for there is no question of space, but in grade. Yet the World of Sense is a type of the World of the Realm Celestial. All the Prophets are Lamps, and so are the Learned: but the difference between them is incalculable. If the Prophet of God is a Lamp Illuminant, that from which the Lamp is itself lit may fitly be symbolized by Fire . . .
>
> That Ultimate Light is the final Fountain-head, Who is Light in and by Himself, not a light kindled from other lights. The term 'light' as applied to any other than this primary Light is purely metaphorical. But these metaphorical lights have various gradations. So there are gradations in their opposites. There is no darkness so intense as the darkness of Not-being. A dark thing is called 'dark' simply because it cannot appear to anyone's vision; it never comes to exist for sight, though it may exist in itself. But that which has no existence for others *nor* for itself is assuredly the very extreme of darkness. In contrast with it is Being, which is therefore Light. Thus God Most High is the only Reality, as He is the only Light.[4]

Sometimes it is not so easy to understand these deep philosophical and mystical matters. But what is achievable for all of us is to have faith and to believe with all our heart and soul in what God has given us. So whether or not we can connect with such lofty spiritual truths from the Qur'án, we should hold firm to the basic belief that God loves us and that the Messenger is His lamp shining His light of guidance.

Shaykh Abdul Qadar Gilani was a teacher in the grand old city of Baghdad around the early 12th century CE and many people came from far and wide to hear his discourses and *tafsír*. In one of his discourses he counsels his listeners:

> Close all the sides with your realization of the unity of God

> and with the effacement of your self, then with your fading away and your own effacement and that of your knowledge. Then will be opened to the eye of your heart the countenance of God, the Mighty, the Great, and you will see it with the two eyes of your heart when it comes with the rays of the light of your heart and your faith and your settled conviction. At that time there will appear a light from your inside and manifest itself on your outside in the manner of the light of a lamp which is in a dark night . . .[5]

Jalal ad-Din Muhammad Rumi, the 13th-century CE Muslim poet and mystic whose spiritual devotional poetry has won the hearts and admiration of people across the religious spectrum, wrote:

> There is a Water that flows down from Heaven
> To cleanse the world of sin by grace Divine.
> At last, its whole stock spent, its virtue given.
> Dark with pollution not its own, it speeds
> Back to the Fountain of all purities;
> Whence, freshly bathed, earthward it sweeps again,
> Trailing a robe of glory bright and pure . . .
> God's balm on the sick soul; and then returns
> To Him who made the purest light of Heaven.

The world famous Lebanese artist, poet, writer, mystic Kahlil Gibran echoes these sentiments in his writings:

> Beloved, the fires of love descend from heaven in many shapes and forms, but their impress upon the world is one. The tiny flame that lights up the human heart is like a blazing torch that comes down from heaven to light the paths of mankind. For in one soul are contained the hopes and feelings of all mankind . . . Heaven fills my lamp with oil and I place it at my window to direct the stranger through the dark.[6]

The Light of God has inspired countless philosophers, mystics, poets, intellectuals and every other kind of seeker. We are illumined with that Light and we are enlightened and we brighten the lives of others. Gradually we begin to shine with the light of virtue, with the light of love. If in the commonplace material reality the rising of the sun is the most significant event, then in the history of humankind the most significant events have been the appearance of those ambassadors of the Kingdom of Reality, who are the appearance of God's love, mercy, beauty and wisdom.

These blessed beings, the Messengers of God, have been the prime moving forces in human affairs and have reshaped the entire human reality in every place and time that they have appeared. They are loved by their people and followed because of the beauty and glory with which God has invested them. The Messenger brings wisdom far exalted above the ways of his people and he humbly begins a career in love and revelation that attracts the hearts and minds of true seekers. In time his humble teaching is embraced by millions, even billions, for thousands of years after. The only men to have had this immense impact in the world and history are the ones who have revealed the Word of God. They replace the old and generate a new standard for human thinking, doing, knowing and being.

This renewal of humankind by the forces and influences of Revelation is the most important cycle in the life of humanity or in known human history. Revelation becomes ritualized into distinct religions, the positive effects of which bring about marvellous developments in social, economic, scientific, artistic and, most importantly, moral and spiritual progress. But in time the Light of God (the positive influence of the Messenger) fades and people again descend into darkness. Their religious practices become mere cultural habits and the words of the scriptures are read without meaning or sincerity. The quality of leadership deteriorates from the absolute purity and infallibility of the Messenger and his enlightened and pious disciples and companions, to the much later scholars and priests. The light of the Word fades, scriptures and prophecies are misinterpreted, people are misguided, laws and principles are disregarded, and immorality sets in. It is at this point that once again Revelation must return to brighten the lives, enlighten hearts and societies, to inculcate moral and virtuous practices and to generate physical and social progress, religious structures and worship.

So if Revelation is a 'Light' and the Messenger is a 'Sun', then how are we to understand 'time'?

> He created the heavens and the earth in true (proportions): He makes the Night overlap the Day, and the Day overlap the Night: He has subjected the sun and the moon (to His law): Each one follows a course for a time appointed. (Q 39:5)

> Praise be to God, Who created the heavens and the earth, and made the Darkness and the Light. Yet those who reject Faith hold others equal with their guardian Lord. He it is Who created you from clay, and then decreed a stated term (for you). And there is with Him another determined term; yet ye doubt within yourselves! (Q 6:1–2)

God appoints a time for the sun and the moon, for waking and sleeping, for life and death. Everything has its determined measure and proportion, its appointed term and time. This appointed term is mentioned many times in the Qur'án.

> To every People is a term appointed: When their term is reached, not an hour can they cause delay, nor (an hour) can they advance (it in anticipation). O ye children of Adam! Whenever there come to you Messengers from amongst you, those who are righteous and mend (their lives), on them shall be no fear, nor shall they grieve. (Q 7:34–5)

> For each period is a Book. (Q 13:38)

Every people, prophecy and Revelation similarly has a period of time or duration. This is how we come to understand the appointed term and the cyclical nature of Revelation.

> Neither too soon, nor too late, shall a people reach its appointed time. Then sent we Our Apostles one after another. Oft as their apostle presented himself to a nation, they treated him as a liar; and we caused one nation to follow another; and we made them the burden of a tale. Away then with people who believe not! (Q 23:43–4)

This mystery will unravel as we go along but it is best illustrated by the lives of the Messengers and the suffering they endured at the hands of their own people. The final appointed time is the Last Day, when all Messengers and all people will be gathered:

> For every Prophecy is a limit of time, and soon shall ye know it. (Q 6:67)

> He gives them respite for a stated time, and whenever their time comes, God has been watching His servants. (Q 35:45)

> . . . when the stars become dim, when the sky is cleft asunder; when the mountains are scattered (to the winds) as dust; and when the messengers are gathered unto their appointed time. For what Day are these (Portents) deferred? For the Day of Sorting Out. (Q 77:8–13)

The Days of God

> It is God who has created the heavens and the earth and all between them in six Days, then He established Himself on the Throne. (Q 32:4)

Yusuf Ali in a note to his translation of the Qur'án explains:

> God's creation is not a simple act, once done and finished with. It is continuous, and there are many stages . . .[7]

And in a further note says:

> The 'Day' does not mean a day as we reckon it, *viz.* one apparent course of the sun round the earth, for it refers to conditions which began before the earth and the sun were created . . . These figures 'as we reckon' have no relation to 'timeless Time', and must be taken to mean very long Periods, or Ages, or Aeons.[8]

Furthermore God explains His creation and the process of Revelation:

> Not for idle sport did We create the heavens and the earth and all that is in between! . . . Nay We hurl the Truth against falsehood, and it knocks out its brain, and behold falsehood perishes. (Q 21:16–18)

We are also warned:

> O mankind! Fear your guardian Lord, Who created you from a single soul [self, living being, person], Created out of it, his mate, and from them twain scattered (like seeds) countless men and women. (Q 4:1)

Creation in the Qur'án is a vast and fascinating topic but since it is not the focus of this work we shall not explore it in depth.

We are introduced to another 'Day' of God in The Ways of Ascent (Al-Ma'arij, Surah 70):

> The Angels and the Spirit ascend unto Him in a Day the measure of which is (as) fifty thousand years. (Q 70:4)

This statement is beyond human contemplation, let alone explanation, because we are as yet only vaguely aware of what is meant by 'the Angels and the Spirit' and what it means to 'ascend'. Also, our entire recorded history fits into some five thousand years, so we cannot unravel the meaning of such an exalted verse. In ordinary usage the word 'spirit' means essence or innermost reality, the fabric or character of a thing. It is also used to describe the deepest essence of man that is his soul. But 'the Spirit' as discussed in the Qur'án and the Bible is far more than we can ever hope to understand. The Qur'án explains *Rúḥ* or Spirit:

> They ask thee concerning the Spirit (of inspiration). Say: 'The Spirit is of the Command of my Lord [*al-Amr*]. Of knowledge it is only a little that is communicated to you, O men!' If it were Our Will we could take away that which We have sent thee by Inspiration . . . (Q 17:85–6)

So the Spirit is of the command or decree of God. But also it is written in the Qur'án of those who believe in God and the Last Day:

> Say: the Holy Spirit has brought the revelation from thy Lord . . . (Q 16:102)

> For such He has written Faith in their hearts, and strengthened them with Spirit [*Rúḥ*; proofs, light and true guidance) from Himself . . . (Q 58:22)

So *Rúḥ* also describes the quintessence of truth and mercy that is the revelation and inspiration of God to humankind through pure Messengers, but also the inspiration or guidance to the individual, simple souls who believe in the Messengers. Furthermore we are told that:

> Verily this is a Revelation from the Lord of the Worlds: With

> it came down the Spirit of Faith and Truth [*Rúḥ al-Amín*], to thy heart and mind, that thou mayest admonish. (Q 26:192–4)

God's command or decree is also synonymous with 'the Spirit', which is often used to refer to Gabriel (the bearer of God's message or Word) and to Ḥaḍrat 'Ísá, known in the English-speaking world as Jesus Christ, often called Rúḥ Alláh (Spirit of God).

> To Jesus the son of Mary We gave clear Signs and strengthened him with the Holy Spirit. (Q 2:87, 253)

Because our understanding and language is limited, it is inappropriate to attempt to unravel the meaning of the 'Spirit' and also the preceding verse concerning the 'Day of God', which is as fifty thousand years to man, for its purport is known to God alone. Some interpreters have sought to reduce such a lofty verse to the level of human imagination and they use it to describe the wingspan of an angel, as the distance a man would walk in fifty thousand years (at least, that's what we were taught in the *madrasah* or Islamic school when we were children). This is an example of people of limited understanding trying to explain things that are beyond them. The Qur'án warns us about such people, as we shall explore later.

God teaches us about creation and evolution in proportion to our capacity for understanding such things. God also teaches us about His decree and Revelation in yet another 'Day' of God. Here is a very significant verse of the holy Qur'án, central to this exploration:

> He established His Decree [*al-Amr*] from the heavens unto the earth; then it ascends unto Him, in a Day, the measure of which is a thousand years of your reckoning. (Q 32:5)

Yusuf Ali again explains in his commentary to the Qur'án:

> How could the immense mystery of Time behind our ideas of it be enforced on our minds better? Our Day may be a thousand or fifty thousand years, and our years in proportion. In the immense Past was God's act of creation: it still continues, for He guides, rules, and controls all affairs: and in the immense Future all affairs will go up to Him, for He will be the Judge, and His restoration of all values will be as in a Day or an hour or the twinkling of an eye; and yet to our ideas it will be as a thousand years![9]

'*Al-Amr*' taken literally as 'His Decree' or '*Amru'lláh*', meaning 'the Decree of God' is used on several occasions in Qur'ánic verses that describe previous Revelations and the judgement or retribution meted out to the unbelievers. It also refers in other instances to the appearance and authority of the Messenger of God, the holy Book which he brings and the path he establishes in the name of God. All of these meanings are simultaneously applicable in the above verse. God establishes His decree through His Messengers. His Messengers are a shining light in the darkness, and the Revelation they bring is like the break of dawn after a long dark night. But every Revelation has a limit of time, an appointed term, and so it declines and sets, and ascends unto God after an appointed term and darkness sets in once again, and once again a Messenger is sent to light the way and renew religion.

The Qur'án introduces us to these immense cycles as the 'Days' of God that are like days within a week, within a year. There is the 'Day' that is a very long aeon, of perhaps billions of years, in which some aspect of the physical earth takes shape. Then there is the 'Day' that is as fifty thousand years in human experience in which the 'Angels and the Spirit ascend', and then there is the 'Day' that is as a thousand years in human experience in which the decree of God is established or His Revelation renewed.

The symbols allow us to appreciate the process of the creation of the earth and man, and there are distinct periods for each process. There is the formation of the earth and all its wonders and creatures that is accomplished in unfathomable ages or cycles; there is the development, civilization and education of humankind, and there are the Revelations of the Messengers and their religions which follow in cycles of roughly one thousand years. It is like a calendar with which we may reckon the passages of history and evolution.

For the purpose of this discussion we must confine ourselves to the exploration of the last 'Day', the Day of His decree. We find this idea of a Day in the sight of the Lord as a thousand years confirmed in the Old and New Testaments:

> Lord, you have been our dwelling place throughout all generations. Before the mountains were born or you brought forth the earth and the world, from everlasting to everlasting you are God. You turn men back to dust, saying, 'Return to dust, O sons of men.' For a thousand years in your sight are like a day that has just gone by, or like a watch in the night. (Psalms 90:1–4 NIV)

> But do not forget this one thing, dear friends: With the Lord a Day is like a thousand years, and a thousand years are like a Day. The Lord is not slow in keeping his promise, as some understand slowness. He is patient with you, not wanting anyone to perish, but everyone to come to repentance. (II Peter 3:8-9 NIV)

This is confirmed by a *ḥadíth* in which the decline of the *ummah* (people or followers) of Muhammad is also prophesied:

> 'How long shall your religion endure?' Muhammad was asked. 'If my *ummah* (followers) becomes righteous, it shall last one Day, if corrupted, it shall last half a Day. And a Day

> of your Lord is the equivalent of a thousand years of your accounting,' he replied.[10]

Again we are told in the Qur'án:

> Verily a Day in the sight of thy Lord is like a thousand years of your reckoning. (Q 22:47)

This time the verse fits in with the theme of the destruction of previous peoples who had rejected a Messenger of God. The rise of Revelation and the decline of the wayward are parts of the same process. A 'Day' of God is roughly a thousand years in normal earthly experience. This Day refers to the rising and setting of the Sun of Truth. Just as the sun governs our reality in physical or material terms during the course of a day, so too does the teaching of the Messenger of God govern the reality of the life of people and nations. Revelation becomes manifest and then hidden in alternating periods. Nothing is ever the same after the Chosen One of God has arrived somewhere because he is invested with such power and wisdom that he awakens the slumbering souls and they describe a new reality, a new earth and a new day.

The renewal of religion or the regeneration of humanity and its period is given as roughly a thousand years. It is roughly this period of time, give or take a few hundred years, that separates the missions of the Messengers of God entrusted with a 'Book' (Religion) from Adam to Núḥ (Noah) to Ibráhím (Abraham) to Músá (Moses), 'Ísá (Jesus), and to Muhammad (and, as we shall see later, there is a similar period of time between Muhammad and the Mahdi and Masih or return of Christ). Each of them in his own time and way experienced the ignorance and depravity of his people and was persecuted and oppressed by the authorities of his day. Each Messenger presented a clear and bold challenge to his people who, despite professing to be the followers of 'true religion', were unable to recognize the manifestation of God's light for their time. But the Word of God always prevails to establish the true religion, to renew faith in God, to revitalize humankind and to resurrect the spiritually dead to new life.

> By the Sun and his (glorious) splendour; by the Moon as she follows him: By the Day as it shows up (the Sun's) glory; by the Night as it conceals it; by the firmament and its (wonderful) structure; by the earth and its (wide) expanse; by the Soul, and the proportion and order given to it; and its inspiration as to its wrong and its right; truly he succeeds that purifies it, and he fails that corrupts it. (Q 91:1–10)

Yusuf Ali suggests that the beginning of the above verse can be understood metaphorically as expressing deeper truths concerning Revelation:

> The first pair is the glorious sun, the source of our light and physical life, and the moon, which follows or acts as second to the sun for illuminating our world. The moon, when she is in the sky with the sun, is pale and inconspicuous; in the sun's absence she shines with reflected light and may metaphorically be called the sun's vicegerent. So with Revelation and the great Prophets who brought it; and the minor Teachers who derive their light reflected, or perhaps doubly reflected, from the original source.[11]

It is said in the Qur'án that God is the:

> . . . Lord of the Easts and the Wests. (Q 55:17)

Abdul Haq Vidyarthi explains in his work *Muhammad in World Scriptures*:

> God, being the Cherisher of the Worlds, cannot ignore any

> of His creatures. He is the Lord of the Easts and the Lord of the Wests. Just as the physical sun travels from the east to the west giving light to every people and place, similarly the Sun of Spiritual and Divine Light also equally sheds light on all people and all countries. Every nation has got its own east and seeing the sun rising from there thinks that it has risen for them alone, there being only one east and west. But anyone who knows the shape of the earth can understand that every point from where the sun rises is the east for the people on its one side and the same point is the west for another people on the other side.[12]

This is a wonderful metaphor for understanding Revelation and the various religions of the world, and how they misunderstand each other and become arrogant in their knowledge and reject the faith of other people. Every place and people have seen the Light of God's Revelation and progressed according to their own conditions and capacities. Religion makes possible true civilization and true education, and sets in motion the spiritual, material and technological advancement of humankind. This process is cyclic and progressive.

> So I do call to witness the ruddy glow of sunset, the Night and its Homing [going home], and the Moon and her Fullness: Ye shall surely journey from stage to stage. (Q 84:16–19)

We are told in Surah 14 (Abraham/Ibráhím) that Músá (Moses) was commanded:

> Bring out your people from the depths of darkness into light. Remind them of the Days of God. There truly are signs in this for every steadfast, thankful person. (Q 14:5–6)

Revelation and the Last Day

Surah 70 (The Ways of Ascent/Al-Ma'arij) tells us:

> By the Lord of every sunrise and sunset, We have the power to substitute for them others better than they are – nothing can prevent Us from doing this. So leave them to wallow in idle talk, until they come face to face with their Promised Day. (Q 70:40–4)

Every people have come face to face with their Promised Day. Every wayward nation that rejected Revelation has been replaced by a 'better' people. Every rotting fruit is replaced by a fresh fruit when the season comes. Revelation means to make known what was previously unknown, to bring to light, to make manifest, to reveal, to unravel, to bring forth. It is the transformative power of Revelation that stirs up the world and changes it. Through pure souls who are born in this physical reality, God is able to speak to mankind and diffuse His knowledge into the human collective, essentially as guidelines and ideas, which people must themselves evaluate and with which they must align themselves. These pure heavenly souls are inspired with the knowledge of God, and self-realized in God consciousness, and so they have earned, and have been given, the authority to reveal truths about human existence and the spiritual reality. They are the Chosen Ones and they live pure lives and love equally all people. They bring inner peace and unity, and they reveal through their actions and teachings those good qualities and behaviours that are deemed suitable for all people. They describe our individual and collective destiny and the path to success, dazzling and dissolving the worldly pretenders who oppose God:

> Fain would they extinguish God's light with their mouths, but God will not allow but that His light should be perfected, even though the unbelievers may detest (it). It is He Who hath sent His messenger with guidance and the religion of truth, to cause it to prevail over all religion . . . (Q 9:32–3)

Destiny does not mean that everything is predetermined and we have no free will; rather it means that God is Almighty to achieve what He wills. He guides us through our free will and leads us into the light. If God wanted to show us how great He is, it would be very easy for Him. But He has mysterialized the magical into the material so that the minds of men may yearn and seek and eventually find truth in the words of His chosen Messengers and thereby transform their lives and, slowly but surely, the world. These Messengers of God, these manifestations of His mercy, are revelations of something much higher than the people that surround them are able to comprehend. The Messenger replaces the people's existing knowledge and institutions like the sun replaces the stars at dawn. The Messengers are opposed and persecuted by their people but eventually the beauty, power and truth of their teachings persist and overcome the worldly ignorant and set a new standard. It is important to note, however, that there are always people who recognize the Messenger of God and join him in his mission and continue his work after his passing. There would be no religion without them.

Revelation builds upon previous or existing beliefs but comes to enhance them, to cause people to release what is false and superstitious and to develop and build on what is essential and true. If a Revelation appeared which was utterly foreign and did not allow people to link with what they have known for untold generations, then it would be incomprehensible and as alien as a foreign language. On the other hand, if the Revelation were not new and challenging then there would be no point because there would be no need to change. Revelation must clothe the future in the language of the past. Revelation is always new and always presents a challenge but at the same time it is, in a sense, always the same essential outpouring. The love that God has for us is always perfect and never changes. The challenge for mankind is the same each time: 'Here is the Word of God. Can you recognize it or are you too attached to the imitation of ancient outdated rituals? Are you too afraid to open your mind?' This is the challenge of every new Revelation. Many are bound by fear to stick to what they have been conditioned to believe:

> When it is said to them: 'Follow what God hath revealed,' they say: 'Nay! we shall follow the ways of our fathers.' What! even though their fathers were void of wisdom and guidance? (Q 2:170)

But some, very few, can transcend aeons of cultural conditioning to rise to the challenge with the courage and understanding to seek something better and higher. This is unacceptable and dangerous to the majority, who will not stand to have their cherished heritage challenged and overthrown, to have the socio-economic status quo shaken and destabilized. The more the Messenger awakens the true seekers, the more the leaders of the pack want to tear them down.

Just as in nature, with a troop of chimpanzees for example, power is still perceived in the old animal sense, where the most aggressive, physically strong and cunning rise to power to control people and resources and to have their will expressed over the will of others and, unfortunately, even over the Will of God. When God speaks to mankind He wants to transform our ways. After the initial resistance of the established authorities against His Messenger and his followers, God eventually overcomes these egocentric, self-exalted impostors and establishes Himself on the throne of earthly power, but only for a time. Again that same controlling, competitive, greedy, power-hungry animal impulse gains the ascendancy, and while leaders (kings and shahs and tsars) appear to profess faith in God and appear to follow His teachings, they are actually worldly pretenders, usurping power and controlling people and resources for their own benefit and exaltation. The *ḥadí<u>th</u>* make mention of such wolves in sheep's clothing, as we shall see.

The corruption, arrogance and personal ambition of these despoilers make them the least suited to serve humanity, which requires humility and selflessness. Apart from these powerful internal forces there are also external forces, such as conquering empires and nations, which not only deepen the extent of the power struggle but also infuse fresh waves of ignorance, arrogance and religious innovation into ecclesiastical and political bodies. While the religious texts and the observance of rituals may seem to remain unspoiled, the authorities who determine the course of their nations and congregations, and assume the right to interpret and apply divine law, become a pale shadow of what they are meant to be. The spiritual force of the original Revelation loses its grip on the minds and hearts of people, who descend into their instinctive self-serving inclinations. Religion becomes a form of exercise or entertainment and the core which is moral and spiritual growth and the practice of virtue fades away and is only dimly glowing in the hearts of some. It is when this cycle reaches its nadir and the night lights grow dim that God revitalizes the dark world with fresh Revelation, attracting true followers; and the Revelation again presents as a threat to the established authorities and the cycle repeats itself.

The Prophet challenges the iniquitous political and religious authorities. They resist and persecute and try to kill him but his message persists and gathers a following and, in time, transforms their reality. This is a sad condition which virtually every Messenger of God has had to endure. Revelation is a story that stirs emotions. It is at once shocking and heartbreaking, inspiring and liberating. We lament that these beauteous beings have been so sorely mistreated but then we remember that their earthly lives have been but the blinking of an eye in the view of eternity. So though they appear to suffer while on earth and make great sacrifices for our progress and freedom, after their release from their physical cages they return to their sublime abodes of glory in the gardens of paradise. They make the ultimate and supreme sacrifice so that we can begin to live happy, loving lives within peaceful orderly societies. God has full authority and power to change the world of man through Revelation:

> Any revelation We cause to be superseded or forgotten, We replace with something better or similar. (Q 2:106)

> When We substitute one revelation for another, and God knows best what He reveals (in stages) . . . (Q 16:101)

And He warns us that we will find no change in His ways; that is to say, in the process of revelation or in the education of humankind:

> (This is Our) Way with the messengers We sent before thee: thou wilt find no change in Our ways. (Q 17:77, 33:62, 35:43)

> So set thou thy face truly to the religion being upright, the nature in which God has made mankind: no change (there is) in the work (wrought) by God: that is the True Religion: but most among mankind know not. (Q 30:30)

'Submission to the Will of God' is the true and eternal religion, even before Adam, even before the creation of the earth, the true meaning and practice of which become developed and refined and made that much more pure and full with each successive Revelation from the glorious heights of infinite knowledge. The Qur'án is thus more radiant than all that has gone before it. Apart from the essential moral code that is common to all religions, it recognizes all other Prophets and religions and enhances the idea of the brotherhood of humanity and the unity and oneness of God, and establishes laws for right living. We are still self-centred and desire-driven and so our motives and behaviour are not yet ruled or controlled by our intelligence or understanding minds. Thus God reveals firm laws to protect us. Through reward and punishment, and fear or shame, our behaviour is regulated and we can progress towards higher understanding and love.

The way of God in educating mankind has been to send His Messengers. While the followers of the Messengers of God generate distinct religions, with different social and ritual laws as befit the times and people, the essence of true religion does not change. Revelation is progressive, a gradual unfolding of God's plan for us. This means that there are no individual or separate books that God sends as such. Rather He reveals precisely what humanity needs at a particular time for its moral, social, intellectual and spiritual advancement, like successive chapters of one book. This is what is meant by the following Qur'ánic verses and *ḥadíth*:

> And dispute ye not with the People of the Book, except in the best way, unless it be with those who do wrong. But say: 'We believe in the Revelation which has come down to us and in that which came down to you; Our God and your God is One; and it is to Him We submit.' (Q 29:46)

> O ye messengers! . . . verily this *ummah* (following) of yours is a single *ummah*, and I am your Lord and Cherisher: therefore fear Me and no other. But people have cut off their affair of unity between them, into sects . . . (Q 23:52–3)

> Those who deny God and His Messengers, and (those who) wish to separate God from His Messengers, saying: 'We believe in some but reject others' and (those who) wish to take a course midway. They are in truth (equally) unbelievers; and We have prepared for unbelievers a humiliating punishment. To those who believe in God and

> His Messengers and make no distinction between any of the Messengers, We shall soon give their (due) rewards: for God is Oft-Forgiving, Most Merciful. (Q 4:150–2)

> The prophets are brothers (in that they diffuse the light of Sharí'ah from one single lamp). Their mothers are different, but their religion is one. And I am nearest of men to Isa ibn Maryam (Jesus) because there has been no prophet between him and me. He will descend. When you see him do recognize him . . .[13]

This confirms that the Prophets shine the same light of revelation and also that Jesus will return to shine that light once again. Each Revelation, or decree, is a 'Day' in the reckoning of God and the 'Last Day' is associated with the return of Ḥaḍrat 'Ísá (Jesus Christ or Rúḥ Alláh, meaning the 'Spirit of God') and his earthly mission which will last for 40 years and which will eventually bring abiding peace, harmony and true religion to all the people of the world. Of course, this is putting it simply and briefly as the essence of the Last Day but there is a lot more to it. There are signs – lesser and greater signs – and the appearance of certain figures, the details and interpretation of which we will go into later as this exploration develops.

The Promised One and the Last Day

If you were to ask people what the Last Day refers to, most would tell you in sketchy, broken accounts about the violent catastrophic end of the world and the collective resurrection and judgement of all people. The mountains will be scattered, they would say, and the sky will be cleft asunder; the stars will fall and Jesus will return and bring peace and prosperity and unity. True religion will disappear; true religion will appear. There will be stories of beasts, marauding cannibals and one-eyed monsters. The world will be destroyed by an angel blowing a trumpet. How do we reconcile these apparent contradictions, fantastic signs and events that people describe?

The aim and focus of this work is to explore the prophecies of the end times and to achieve a consensus between the Qur'án, *ḥadíth*, and other scriptures, an accord between past, present and future, and a distinction between the symbolic and the literal. For me, the most outstanding feature, which shines brighter than any other, is the promise that Rasúl Alláh (Messenger of God: Muhammad) gave us: that with the return of Jesus there will be peace on earth like it has never known before and that all people will believe in him (that there will be one common Faith). Very importantly, the Qur'án does not suggest that the earth will come to a violent catastrophic end. Rather it says that:

> One Day the earth will be changed to a different earth and the heavens also . . . (Q 14:48)

It is said of Jesus in his second coming that:

> There is not one of the people of the scripture but will believe in him before his death and on the Day of Resurrection he will be a witness against them. (Q 4:159)

In his first coming Jesus, like every other Messenger of God, challenged his people with fresh revelation and new laws and teachings, but yet presented the same eternal faith in God. So what will be the nature of his second coming? When will it take place? Why will he come again? What will happen while he is here? What will he do? Where will he go? And what will happen after this? And what about all the catastrophes and commotions on the earth and in the heavens? We will explore in greater detail these questions and the answers from the Qur'án and *ḥadíth* and other scriptures as well, but by way of prelude we can quote the Qur'án about itself, in a marvellous verse which weaves together our themes with the power of the Word of God:

> If there were a Qur'án (Divine Message) with which mountains were moved, or the earth were cloven asunder, or the dead were made to speak, this would be the one! But truly the command is with God in all things! Do not the believers know, that had God so willed, He could have guided all mankind? (Q 13:31)

The Glorious Qur'án

The Prophet Muhammad – peace and the blessings of God be upon him and his family and followers – was well loved and respected by his people. They knew him also as al-Amín, the 'Trustworthy'. But those whose hearts were closed and minds were veiled could not understand the meaning of the Qur'án and after his declaration they made accusations calling him, who was the essence of mercy and truth, a poet and a soothsayer, a liar. God, however, testifies to his authenticity:

> So I do call to witness what ye see and what ye see not, that this is verily the word of an honoured messenger; it is not the word of a poet: little it is ye believe! Nor is it the word of a soothsayer; little admonition it is ye receive. (This is) a Message sent down from the Lord of the Worlds. (Q 69:38–43)

> By the Pen and by the Record which men write, thou art not, by the grace of thy Lord, mad or possessed. Nay, verily for thee is a reward unfailing, and surely thou hast sublime morals. (Q 68:1–4)

The Qur'án is a book of surahs revealed by God over a period of some 23 years through the Angel Gabriel through the Prophet Muhammad for the instruction and guidance of humankind. It is a compilation made by the trusted *Ṣaḥábah*, the companions of the Prophet Muhammad who undertook the immense task of verifying and authenticating the surahs that they had together memorized or written on parchments, leaves and bones. The Qur'án is written in the most excellent Arabic in lofty and moving language. It has a unique style and an exquisite beauty of prose and poetic imagery. It was proclaimed by one who could neither read nor write.

At the time, poetic eloquence was much valued and poets travelled and competed to recite their poems publicly and to publish their words. Most poems were witty odes to the sensual lifestyle of those steeped in darkness and ignorance, in the times of darkness and confusion known as Jáhilíyah. God chose to reveal His Word in the finest Arabic such that it eclipsed all these worldly values and 'pop stars' of old and set a new and higher standard, not merely in poetry but in life and love. At the same time, the masterful use of imagery and symbols wove layers of truth and meaning into the fabric of the Qur'án.

The knowledge of God is far exalted above the perception, mind and consciousness of even the most enlightened of human beings, let alone the general public. Far exalted are His material reality and the endless universe above anything that we can comprehend, how much more so the secrets of existence, the mysteries of creation and the unknowable essence of His being. Much that is in the Qur'án is easy to understand and clear because it pertains to events, people and the Prophets of the past and things concerning our everyday lives, practical aspects of righteous behaviour, morality and purity. But many things that refer to spiritual truths that transcend the material reality must be explained by metaphors or analogies, which describe spiritual truths, or the things unseen and unknown by relating them to the things that we see and know.

Hafiz Ghulam Sarwar explains in his book *Muhammad the Holy Prophet*:

> If everything mentioned in the Qur'án is to be taken literally, then there would soon be an end to our appreciation of its subjects and its beauties. Those who insist on the literal interpretation of the Qur'án are reducing its allegories to something worse than human composition.[14]

The Qur'án itself testifies to this:

> We have put forth for men, in the Qur'án every kind of parable (similitude), in order that they may receive admonition. (Q 39:27)

> See how we explain the Signs by various symbols . . . in diverse ways. (Q 6:46, 65)

> God guideth unto His Light whom He will: and God speaketh to mankind in allegories, for God is Knower of all things. (Q 24:35)

Symbolism is part of the power of the Word of God. It paints images for our imagination and thus draws us beyond the literal into the higher awareness and spiritual intelligence which are latent faculties of our consciousness. This very capacity of symbolic imagination enables us to transcend the material and the literal, something which is important for spiritual progress. It is also essentially the language of translating worlds and realities unseen and unknown into human language. Certainly, the Qur'án is not a book of magical melodic incantations to be read without understanding. But, sadly, this is a common thing these days and is among the signs of the Last Day. As the *ḥadíth* says:

> There will come a time upon the ummah when people will recite the Qur'án, but it will not go further than their throats (into their hearts).[15]

> When the Qur'án is read as if singing a song, and when a person is esteemed for reading in that way, even though he is not knowledgeable.[16]

It is not a certain pleasant combination of sounds that gives the Word of God its power. It is when those sounds combine to convey meaning which results in spiritual growth and virtuous behaviour that we realize its power and beauty. Prayer is a dynamic process in which we learn what to seek and then strive for what we seek with God's help. The Qur'án is a message meant to be read and understood and put into practice but we are many times removed from the true beauty of the glorious Qur'án.

We lose something in the translation from Arabic into English, apart from the lyrical melodic flow and periodicity, the textural and tonal diversity, the depth of expression in the way Arabic engages the voice, the tongue and palette, the lips and the deeper throat, the lungs and nostrils, involving the speaker or the reader very much in what he is saying or reading. But more importantly, we lose many subtleties of meaning and allusions, which, despite the sincerest efforts of translators and commentators, is impossible to fully convey. The eloquence and majesty of the Qur'án are not reproducible in any other languages. Its brevity and profound simplicity cannot be conveyed in any other form. We can extract the general substance of meaning but we cannot fully appreciate the Qur'án other than in its original form and language. But that is not to say that translations into other languages are unreliable. The true meaning can be captured and subtleties and nuances interspersed within the text or appended as notes and commentaries. Deeper or subtler meanings, may, however, be lost.

Also, we find ourselves in a different time and place and must project ourselves into the culture and mindset of the people who were the recipients of this Revelation. If we are to fully appreciate the parables, similitudes and signs of the Qur'án, we must know the meaning that the symbols and imagery had for those people and we must not judge it by our standards and our day. In addition, the Qur'án has many cascading layers of beauty and meaning, and the metaphors and imagery are extended over many verses and surahs, linking ideas and themes. Often, by taking out verses as fragments from a whole, we lose some of the Qur'án's contextual depth of meaning – a bit like a flower plucked from a lovely garden. We can still appreciate the loveliness of the flower and its aroma but we cannot take the beauty and tranquillity of the garden with the flower. The Qur'án's message is timeless and universal but our understanding of it is limited:

> We have put forth for men, in the Qur'án every kind of parable (similitude), in order that they may receive admonition. (It is) a Qur'án in Arabic, without any crookedness (therein) in order that they may guard against evil. (Q 39:27–8)

> Is one whose heart God has opened to Islam, so that he has received Light from God, (No better than one hard-hearted)? woe to those whose hearts are hardened against the remembrance of God! They are manifestly wandering (in error)! God has revealed (from time to time) the most beautiful Message in the form of a book, consistent with itself, (yet) repeating (its teaching in various aspects) . . . Those who listen to the Word and follow the best (meaning) in it, those are the ones whom God has guided, and those are the ones endued with understanding. (Q 39:22–3)

But also we are cautioned:

> He it is Who hath revealed unto thee (Muhammad) the Scripture wherein are clear revelations. They are the substance of the Book, and others (which are) allegorical

> (symbolic). But those in whose hearts is doubt pursue, forsooth, that which is allegorical seeking (to cause) dissension by seeking to explain it. None knoweth its explanation save God. (Q 3:7)

There is a well-known tradition that no unauthorized person should attempt the explanation of the Qur'án by his own personal opinion alone. This was intended to safeguard the purity of the Qur'án and to preserve the unity of the Muslim *ummah* (followers) but the Prophet himself foretold the division that would overtake his followers. My intention with this present work is not to pursue vague issues in order to misguide but rather to explore this subject of the Last Day because it is a very important one and we have arrived at a time when the signs are either already visible or imminent. The point of this exploration is not to fuel speculation or doubt but rather to establish with certainty a more cohesive and meaningful picture of the vast, fragmented and vague references and traditions pertaining to the Last Day. The early followers of Islam were cautioned not to indulge in interpretation because it can only result in waywardness. Ultimately the knowledge of such abstruse matters explained allegorically in the Qur'án is with God alone and the future events are far away in space and time and not accessible, so to pursue the meaning of them will not yield results. But if we do not connect those symbols and imagery with our modern lives, we will not be able to recognize the signs they foretell. We are now some 1400 years after the passing of the Prophet Muhammad. Ultimately it is for each person to judge and interpret the Qur'án for himself or herself.

Ḥadíth

The Qur'án is authentic and is none other than the revealed Word of God, so it is not to be doubted as a source of reliable information. However, in order to understand references to things unseen, as we have discussed earlier, we must be able to appreciate the imagery and language used to convey an appropriate meaning in the language of symbolism. Without this understanding everything appears very vague and fantastic and we cannot connect it with our reality, despite many people agreeing that we are very close to, or already in, the Last Day, the Day of Decision, of Resurrection, of Gathering, the Day of Judgement.

The *ḥadíth* are the reported sayings and discussions of the Prophet as remembered by his companions and their descendants and eventually compiled by respected authorities. The Sunnah, or the habits, ways and doings of the Prophet, are also a guide to right living and his authenticated sayings that were not directly a revelation also have great significance.

After the passing of the Prophet people recalled from memory his sayings and recorded or shared them with their friends and families. The compilers of *ḥadíth* had to establish the authenticity of the *ḥadíth* by checking the chain of reporters, and whether they were each reliable sources, and then, secondly, if the *ḥadíth* was confirmed by other reliable sources, and thirdly, if it did not contradict any other authenticated sayings or verses of the Qur'án. Thus we have a vast body of *ḥadíth* that fall into different categories. There are *ḥadíth* that have been authenticated and which are considered sound or reliable (*ṣaḥíḥ*) and some that are plausible but not completely reliable, and still others that are doubtful or even unreliable. Thus there are *ḥadíth* that are considered weak or unfamiliar and some that we categorized as invented and have therefore rejected.

The *Ṣaḥábah* were the faithful companions of the Prophet and so it was very important to them to record his sayings in their purity and entirety. They would not willingly or purposely distort anything that the Prophet said. However, there is always a possibility of distortion, as the method of transmission was word of mouth. It was not until quite some time after the passing of the Prophet that the compilers set about authenticating and recording the *ḥadí<u>th</u>* in written form and made them publicly available. So these traditions, no matter how sincere and devoted the narrators, are open to error owing to human imperfection. The Qur'án differs from *ḥadí<u>th</u>* in that it is the direct revelation as captured by the companions, whereas the *ḥadí<u>th</u>* are the inspired sayings of the Prophet as remembered by the companions. The Qur'án was immediately and deliberately written down or committed to memory by several *Ṣaḥábah*, and then shortly after the passing of the Prophet it was compiled after a stringent process of authentication and verification and acceptance by all the companions of the Prophet. In contrast, the *ḥadí<u>th</u>* were written down by some but largely passed on by verbal tradition over many generations until the work of authentication and compilation was taken up in earnest by much later scholars.

There is a clear dividing line between the Qur'án and *ḥadí<u>th</u>* and this is commonly accepted by all. The *ḥadí<u>th</u>* are never accorded the same potency and significance as verses of the Qur'án. The Messenger of God was a perfect source, free from error in revealing his message. His sayings and doings are also very important but not equivalent to the Qur'án. They can be used as explanation only insofar as they concur with the Qur'án. The Prophet, of course, would not utter anything at variance with the Qur'án and so this gives us a guide for evaluating and authenticating *ḥadí<u>th</u>*. However, there are many subjects mentioned in the Qur'án which are elaborated in the *ḥadí<u>th</u>* because the companions of the Prophet wanted clarity on some things that seemed vague or disturbing to them. Thus we cannot always compare *ḥadí<u>th</u>* against the verses of the Qur'án which they seek to explain.

Furthermore, as we humans can make mistakes, in the process of authenticating the *ḥadí<u>th</u>* it was very important to keep it free from human error, misinterpretations, and false witness. But as time went by and the Muslims were broken up into many opposing groups, different people desired to persuade others of their opinions and this has led to false narrators – people who have falsified the *ḥadíth* – for whatever reason.

Harun Yahya, in his work *Signs of the Last Day*, offers this note of caution:

> At this point, there may arise some doubt in the reader in regard to the truth and authenticity of these *ḥadíths* about the end. It is a recognized fact that, in the past, there had been a number of fabricated *ḥadíths* falsely attributed to the Prophet (SAWS), but the *ḥadíths* that form the subject of our inquiry will be easily recognized as issuing from the Prophet (SAWS). There is a method to distinguish those that are true from those that are false. As we know *ḥadíths* about the doomsday relate to events that are to take place in the future. For this reason, when a *ḥadíth* comes true in the course of time, all doubt as to the source of the words is removed.[17]

> How shall we know the word which the Lord hath not spoken? When a prophet speaketh in the name of the Lord, if the thing follow not, nor come to pass, that is the thing which the Lord hath not spoken, but the prophet hath spoken it presumptuously . . . (Deut. 18:21–2)

Besides this method, thankfully the task of authentication and compilation has, to a large extent, been accomplished by such renowned scholars and compilers as Bukhárí, Muslim and Tirmidhí. For the purposes of our exploration I will be making quite extensive use of a very complete compilation entitled *Before and After the Last Hour* by Ibn Kathír Ad-Damishqi (700–74 AH/14th century CE).

Read!

The Qur'án has layers of meaning with which to inspire each of us according to our capacity to understand spiritual truths clothed in words and symbols. The Qur'án opens with Iqrá, which enjoins not only Muhammad but also his people to read, proclaim or recite the verses of God:

> Proclaim! (Read) And thy Lord is Most Bountiful, He who taught (the use of) the pen, taught man that which he knew not. (Q 96:3–5)

How significant that these should be the first rays of divine light to illumine the darkened world of man. Muhammad was not given outer miracles and powers like other Prophets. He was given the miracle of the Qur'án, and it is a sign of the approaching maturity of humankind that we are drawn now to belief not by witnessing miracles but by identifying ourselves with the Word of God, by understanding it. Thus God explains to us by way of a written script, made possible by the pen, which enables us to record, preserve and share not only our ideas but, more importantly, the Revelation or Word of God. The pen is the gift of God to man and it is the means by which we progress towards true knowledge. It has made possible the advance of humankind through the ages both in material and spiritual terms. Muhammad repeatedly enjoined his followers to seek knowledge from the cradle to the grave, even unto China – or the furthermost reaches of the known world.

> The search for knowledge is incumbent upon all males and females amongst Muslims.[18]

Yusuf Ali, drawing on the inspiration of Imam al-Ghazali, also explains:

> If we take the physical light as ordinarily understood, it is a phenomenon or appearance, and is therefore liable to pass away. For its illuminative power it has to depend upon the perceiving faculty or the perceiving instrument, the Eye. But the Eye has many defects. It is only the perceiving faculty of intelligence which is properly entitled to the name of Light considered as a source of enlightenment.
>
> The verses in the Qur'án in relation to Intelligence have the value of sunlight in relation to eyesight. The Qur'án is therefore spoken of as the light: 'For we have sent unto you a light (that is) manifest'. (Q 4:174)
>
> Thus the physical eye sees by the sun; the spiritual eye sees by Revelation (the Qur'án).
>
> . . . From the material world, the world of Sense, we rise through the world of Intelligence to the spiritual world, or the world of the Realm Supernal (or Celestial).[19]

The Prophet of God also revealed a beautiful prayer (which has been a lighted candle for me in my own dark times):

> *Rabbí zidní 'ilman wa razuqní fahma* (My Lord, increase me in knowledge and grant me understanding).

Prayer is a light and a fountain of living waters. Knowledge is the foundation of faith and the means to spiritual progress. There is purpose, stability and order in this world only because of God's Revelations, which take shape as religion, giving rise to cultures which regulate the education and behaviour of people and teach them about God and the purpose of the physical reality.

We learn about God:

> No vision can grasp Him but His grasp is over all vision; He is subtle . . . well aware. (Q 6:103)

> To God belong the East and the West: whithersoever ye turn;

> there is God's face, for God is All Embracing, All-Knowing. (Q 2:115)

> The Lord doth encompass mankind roundabout . . . (Q 17:60)

> It was We Who created man, and We know what suggestions his soul makes to him: for We are nearer to him than (his) jugular vein. (Q 50:16)

> Verily to thy Lord is the return of all. (Q 96:8)

> . . . and to Us is the final Return. (Q 50:43)

Those who have attained unto the Light of God have embraced purity:

> In the name of God the Most Gracious the Most Merciful. Say: He God is One, God the Eternal and Absolute (on whom all depends). He does not beget nor is He begotten and there is none like him. (Q 112:1–4)

Those who have attained unto the Light of God obey His decree:

> Verily all things have We created in proportion and measure. And Our Decree [*Al-Amr*] is but a single Word – like the twinkling of an eye. (Q 54:49–50)

Those who have attained unto the Light of God have accepted His sovereignty and majesty as described in 'The Miracle of the Throne' (*Áyatu'l-Kursí*) or 'Verses of the Throne', the throne being a symbol of the dominion and lordship of God:

> God. There is none worthy of worship besides Him, the Ever-Living, the One Who sustains and protects all that

> exist. Neither slumber nor sleep overtakes Him. To Him belongs whatever is in the heavens and whatever is on the earth. Who is he that can intercede with Him except with His permission? He knows what happens to them (His creatures) in this world, and what will happen to them in the Hereafter. And they will never compass anything of His knowledge except that which He wills. His Throne extends over the heavens and the earth, and He feels no fatigue in guarding and preserving them and He is the Most High, the Greatest. (Q 2:255)

We learn that God is the All-Knowing, the Most Loving, the Most Wise, the Oft Forgiving, the Most Gracious and Merciful. He is also the Friend and the Helper, the Most Feared and the Destroyer of the wicked. The 99 names of God recount all these attributes yet He transcends all that we can perceive and understand, so far exalted is He above all names and attributes. The Qur'án is God's gift to us and we are supposed to read it and try to understand its teachings and fathom its mysteries.

Heaven and Hell

Another area of revealed knowledge that is difficult to understand are those verses pertaining to the *Á<u>kh</u>irah*, the hereafter or spiritual afterlife – the unseen realm, or the realities of heaven and hell. Such descriptions are given as analogy to things that we can perceive and imagine, in order to help us understand what is beyond our faculties:

> The parable (similitude) of the Garden, which the righteous are promised! Beneath it flow rivers: perpetual is the fruit thereof, and the shade therein: such is the end of the righteous; and the end of the unbelievers is fire. (Q 13:35)

and again:

> Then he, whose balance (of good deeds) will be (found) heavy, will be in a life of good pleasure and satisfaction. But he whose balance (of good deeds) will be (found) light-weight, will have his home in a (bottomless) pit. And what will explain to thee what this is? (It is) a Fire blazing fiercely. (Q 101:6–11)

> Woe to every scandal monger and backbiter, who pileth up wealth and layeth it by, thinking that his wealth would make him last forever! By no means! He will be sure to be thrown into 'That which Breaks to Pieces'. And what will explain to thee 'That which Breaks to Pieces'? (It is) the Fire of God kindled (to blaze) . . . (Q 104:1–6)

> And what will explain to thee what Hell-fire is? Naught doth it permit to endure, and naught doth it leave alone. (Q 74:27–8)

The Qur'án itself tells us that these are parables and metaphors to help us understand. An Arab living in the desert is given analogies suited to the conditions of his life so that he can connect something meaningful to the descriptions given. The most pleasant and desirable place on earth for people of the desert is a garden through which rivers flow, verdant with trees full of every type of fruit, the rivers of cool water or milk and honey. And the thing which they dislike the most and which is most displeasing is the heat of the desert. So hell is described to them as a blazing fire, in which the only drink they will be offered is foul boiling fluids. This symbolism helps us to appreciate the conditions of the afterlife and the consequences of our actions in this life. These things are meaningful to people from different backgrounds and so have a binding and powerful effect on human behaviour and thinking. These metaphors cause people to align themselves with the teachings of the Messenger, to avoid the things forbidden and to do the things that are compulsory and good. They provide a very clear, vivid and consistent description and so it's not difficult to understand why so many people imagine the afterlife to be literally as it is described. But the description is in fact symbolic and the actual conditions of heaven and hell are not physical realities.

The soul is mentioned several times in the Qur'án:

> (To the righteous soul will be said:) Oh (thou) soul, in complete rest and satisfaction! 'Come back thou to thy Lord well pleased (thyself) and well pleasing unto Him! Enter thou, then among my devotees! Yea enter thou My Heaven!' (Q 89:27–30)

Yusuf Ali explains that this stage of the soul is the final stage of bliss and that it is the soul which enters heaven and not the gross body, which perishes.[20] Furthermore:

> In the agonies of death! The angels stretch forth their hands, (saying) 'Yield up your souls' (get your souls to come out of your bodies) . . . and behold! ye come to Us bare and alone as We created you for the first time. (Q 6:93–4)

> When the soul of the dying man comes up to his throat, while you gaze on, we are nearer to him than you, though you do not see Us, why if you are not to be judged, do you not restore his soul to him, if what you say is true? If that dying person is one of those who will be brought near to God, he will have rest, ease and a garden of bliss . . . but if he is one of those who denied the truth and went astray he will have boiling water. He will burn in hell. (Q 56:83–94)

> We have decreed death to be your common lot, and We are not to be frustrated from changing your Forms, and creating you again, in forms that ye know not. (Q 56:60–1)

> Then shall the dust return to the earth as it was: and the spirit shall return unto God who gave it. (Eccles. 12:7)

After death the physical body is left behind and the soul ascends to God for its judgement, to balance our book of deeds and to determine if we go to heaven or hell, or rather, whether we have sufficiently developed ourselves during our life on earth and are capable of living in a heavenly reality or continue to suffer in a condition of insatiable desire. What the soul is and what are its origins and substance none but God knows, for it is His mystery, but it is not physical and material because the living cannot perceive it. Upon the death of a person his soul leaves his body but none of those who remain by the body's side can see it or witness its leaving, nor do they witness the angel of death or perceive God. This returning to God after death is our personal future as an individual soul but there is also the matter of our collective material and spiritual future on this earth, which is also something that is not easy to communicate to people.

Prophecy and the Future

The Prophets reveal to their people certain things about the future that are suitable for their progress and necessary for the unfolding of destiny. The Prophet is either gifted with the vision of the unseen or the future or such knowledge is given to him or revealed through him for the benefit of humankind. The Prophets Abraham, Joseph, Moses, Ezekiel, Elijah, Jesus and Muhammad, amongst others, all spoke about the future and warned humanity and apprised it of future events. They explained, in the language of symbolism, the future of the followers of the Prophet, the future of humankind, and the future of the world and creation. We can draw on them for reference and explanations, and so I will refer to the holy Scriptures of the world's great religions as background to our developing theme. There are numerous references in the Qur'án and *ḥadíth* to the people, personalities, cultures and events of the near and distant future and it is these that will form the main body of our exploration, for the intention here is to uncover the true meaning of the Last Day.

If it were God's intention to reveal exactly and clearly the events of the future then such a thing would be easy for Him. In fact, all things are easy for Him because He is the All-Knowing, the All-Powerful. However, the Prophets were inspired to reveal only such things that God has permitted, those that would be conducive to the development of mankind. Often the Prophets themselves were bewildered by the visions and prophecies. Thus the descriptions of the future and the Last Day appear to be somewhat vague and cryptic because they are meant to be that way.

> This is how it has always been revealed by every prophet as an apostle bringing 'books' of 'dark prophecies'. (Q 35:25)

> For every Prophecy is a limit of time, and soon shall ye know it. (Q 6:67)

The Prophet Muhammad explained many details to clarify the verses of the Qur'án. He was often asked about different subjects and one of the subjects that intrigued or frightened his companions was the Last Day. Sometimes he said that the knowledge of it is with God alone, and when Gabriel asked him about the Last Day he said that the one who is being asked knows no better than the one who is asking. God revealed the following to Muhammad:

> They ask: 'When will this promise be fulfilled?' Say: 'As to the knowledge of the time, it is with God alone: I am a plain warner.'(Q 67:25–6)

Sometimes a person, in front of a group of others, would ask Muhammad about the future and he would explain. At times he would speak of it himself, warning people; at other times he would rise, very agitated and with tears in his eyes and recount some of the signs. Thus many people heard different things about the future from the Prophet himself.

> Sayyidiná Abú Sa'íd narrated: The Prophet led us in the *'Aṣr Ṣalah* and then delivered a sermon till sunset, touching upon events till the Last Day. Those who could remembered, but some forgot . . .[21]

The description of future events is embellished with several authentic symbolic signs, which many people take literally, and which are then embroidered with much that is human fabrication. In order to separate the true believers from the worldly and wayward, the exact location and time of the coming of the Promised One could not be revealed by the Prophet. The people of the world have to come to his message themselves by recognizing its beauty and not by prior knowledge or by the fulfilment of signs.

> Surely the hour is coming – I will keep its time concealed, so that every soul may be recompensed for what it strives. (Q 20:15)

Those who recognize the Messenger and God's words are the ones who are ready to bear his Revelation. They must be distinguished from the wicked and perverse that would swallow and destroy its purity. Foreknowledge of the Messenger would remove the freedom of choice and the element of independent investigation of the truth from the people and would compromise the true religion of God. The ranks of the sincere followers of truth would be polluted with those looking for outer signs.

Thus a clear contrast is made which is the vehicle of

change. By opposition and struggle the new proceeds out of the old. Enkindled by their love of truth and ablaze with their sacrifice and persecutions, the believers emerge with the power to transform the old. It is the only way. It is the test and dividing line. The appearance of the Prophet is the promised judgement, resurrection and gathering of mankind. The future was not meant to be known in its entirety because this would affect man's spiritual development:

> Let there be no compulsion in religion: Truth stands out clear from error . . . (Q 2:256)

> If God so willed, He could make you all one people: but He leaves straying whom He pleases, and He guides whom He pleases: but ye shall certainly be called to account for all your actions. (Q 16:93)

The Jewish people were given vague prophecies regarding the return of the Prophet/herald Elijah and the coming of the messiah/saviour Jesus Christ. They believed that Elijah would descend in a chariot of fire, as he had ascended, and burn away all things before the appearance of the messiah, Christ. The Jewish priests, with the Roman leaders, persecuted and ridiculed the very Messenger of God for whom they had been waiting for a thousand years, calling for the death of the one who had come to give them life. But all this was necessary so that God could separate the true followers and the people of understanding from the pretenders and usurpers. The Revelation of the Prophets is a reckoning and a sorting of men. The pure ones are separated from the imitators and hypocrites and are given the task of renewing the true religion of God. If the coming of the new Messenger were given in clear and precise language, then everyone could easily identify him. But people are not saved by their mechanical following of a Prophet or their blind allegiance to him but rather by identifying with his teachings and understanding his Revelation, thus awakening faith and higher consciousness, and enabling them to change and grow spiritually.

Secondly, it is necessary for the protection of the promised Messenger that prophecies are not clear and explicit. When the powers that be, the Romans, discovered the prophecy of the anticipated messiah, such was their anxiety that they decided to kill all the young boys of the Jews to prevent the rise of their 'king' – just as the Egyptians had done before to the people of Moses, and the evil king in the time of Krishna. Had God made the preceding prophecies more clear, the enemies of faith would have more easily been able to find His Chosen Ones.

Finally, the future is not meant to be known clearly because this would affect the followers' natural spiritual development within the framework and limits described and institutionalized in each religious dispensation. Emphasizing a future unknown Prophet would compromise the progress of the presently emerging faith and the rules and laws which uphold it, thus diminishing the authority of the current Messenger who is in the process of revealing his religion. Every Messenger must establish that he is the way and light regardless of what has come before and what is to come in the future.

So the future is not meant to be known clearly, at least not until it comes to pass. There is a very delicate balance between revealing information about the future so that it becomes established among the people that a certain personage will appear at some distant time and place, and concealing the reality to protect the life of the personage, or Chosen One, while preserving people's freedom of thought and the purity of the faith that he will renew.

The priests and leaders of the Jewish people during the time of Christ were to outward seeming the religious leaders of their people and showed all the physical signs of piety and religious knowledge but they were utterly bereft of wisdom and higher knowledge, as shown by their response to the teachings of Christ. They were awaiting the 'return' of Elijah in a chariot of fire from the heavens and many other dramatic things, so they refused to listen to the beautiful teachings of John the Baptist and Jesus. The disciples of Christ, on the other hand, were simple folk, fishermen and shepherds, but pure of heart and of good character and they were chosen to be the vehicles of God's renewed faith. The most learned of men were revealed to be fools and the lowest and 'ignorant' were made into the lights of divine guidance. Those who claimed to be the authorities informing public opinion and who appeared to be very reliable in explaining the day-to-day aspects of religion and seemed knowledgeable in abstruse religious complexities were revealed to be worldly pretenders who knew very little.

In trying to make sense of these vague prophecies pertaining to the future I am certainly not challenging the authenticity or established meaning of the Qur'án and *ḥadíth*, nor am I claiming for myself greater wisdom or piety than the respected scholars who have commented on them. I am simply looking, from a modern perspective, at the unfolding signs of the Last Day and trying to explain them by what I see in our contemporary culture and un-civilization.

The traditions current among most people, learned or not in the Qur'án and *ḥadíth*, are based on a literal appreciation of the prophecies and sayings, and these were formed a long time ago and have been accumulating over the centuries. Unfortunately, dogma follows imitation and blindly rejects anything that does not agree with tradition. The seeker of truth must be able to separate the works and doings of God and His Messengers from the works and doings of men and their leaders and institutions. God is perfect and infallible but man is given to error and limited understanding. In fact, one of the major signs of the Last Day is that so-called religious leaders will be leading the people astray and will be issuing unjust decrees in the name of Islam. We shall explore the specific *ḥadíth* regarding this later but its implications are stupendous for it calls into question the current Islamic institutions and the interpretations of their apparently learned leaders, muftis and *mawlánás*.There are many examples from history and this is because it is a condition of our existence which God lovingly helps us to transcend. Through the process of revelation we change and so we can only truly appreciate the progress of man, the exalted Revelation of Muhammad, the true meaning of his religion and the Last Day by walking through history and the epic story of revelation through the ages, specifically the legends and traditions of all the world's great religions that pertain to the Last Day and its glorious promise that:

> . . . the Earth will shine with the Light of its Lord. (Q 39:69)

2

THE PASSAGE OF TIME

The history of humanity is more clouded and unclear the further back in time we go. History is that which we have recorded or remembered and only began to become clearer when we were instructed in the use of the 'pen'. For many civilizations this is the dividing line between clear history and vague pre-history. Prior to the written script all things were passed down from one generation to the next through oral traditions, legends, stories, myths and songs. We learn from the history and pre-history of the world that mankind has always had religion in some form and that people have always worshipped God. We are taught that God has sent something like 124,000 *nabís* or Prophets, of which some 315 were *rasúls* or Messengers entrusted with a 'Book', to show to all people that He is 'Lord of the East and the West: there is no God but Him . . .'(Q 73:9)

> And there never was a people, without a warner having lived among them (in the past). And if they reject thee, so did their predecessors, to whom came their apostles with clear Signs, Books of dark prophecies, and the Book of Enlightenment. In the end did I punish those who rejected Faith: and how (terrible) was my rejection (of them)! (Q 35:24–6)

> We did aforetime send Messengers before thee: of them there are some whose story we have related to thee, and some whose story we have not related to thee. It was not possible for any messenger to bring a Sign except by the

> leave of God, but when the Command of God [*Amru'lláh*] issued, the matter was decided in truth and justice. (Q 40:78)

And furthermore:

> To every people [*ummah*] there is a messenger . . . and to every people is a term appointed . . . (Q 10:47–9)

> We have never sent a messenger who did not use his own people's language to make things clear for them . . . (Q 14:4)

Looking back with our modern minds to the ancient past, we find it hard to understand those pre-historic religious forms and to discern anything positive and meaningful from them. But in truth those forms were the height of divine guidance for their time or day, and for the people; and more than this, they were the foundation for the superstructure of monotheistic religion that followed. It is not necessary to spend too much time exploring the mysteries of the ancients and immersing ourselves in the details of their cultures and ways but a brief exploration of the salient features of their civilizations and religions is highly instructional in what they teach us about the progress of humanity and the progressive nature of God's Revelation. While a deep and thorough exploration of human history and pre-history would certainly enhance our developing theme, it is simply not practical, within the scope of this work, to go into such great detail, so we will limit ourselves to a very brief religious history of the world.

The world is very big and diverse. Nowadays we have modern technology: transportation that enables us to travel easily to any place; telecommunications and the Internet to communicate with people around the world; TV, radio, print media and again the Internet to learn what is happening in faraway places and maintain a knowledge base. We have mapped the whole world and know most of its lands and peoples and we can interact either through translations or through a common language and share in a sort of global consciousness and culture. But not so long ago, before the realization of the tools and methods of modern technology, the world was vast and the peoples and nations of the world lived in exclusive, separate realities that, if at all, only briefly interacted through competitive trade or conflict.

The diversity of conditions in which people lived made their respective experience of reality very different. They lived in hot jungles, cold mountaintops, dry deserts, warm savannas, icy glaciers, temperate meadows and shaded valleys – places that were warm and hot or cool, cold or icy; humid or dry; low or high; fertile or lifeless; rainy or drought stricken; stable or volatile. They had different climates, shelters, foods, landscapes, temperatures, flora and fauna, and developed different activities, abilities, skills, physical characteristics, social structures, cultures, languages, needs and desires, fears and anxieties.

There is an inherent quality or active force in nature – some call it evolution, some call it God, some call it simply Nature – but whatever you call it, it is that adaptability which enables all organisms, plants and animals and human beings to change and adjust to their given conditions and environment, and to co-exist with all others who share it. In material and intellectual qualities they adapt to their environments and become suited to the challenges they face and better equipped to survive. This adaptability is a God-given gift and a quality inherent in all natural systems and organisms. We look at all the amazing diversity of nature and its forms and marvel at how perfectly each one is designed to fill some niche in the organic market, distributing the energy captured from the sun by photosynthesis – perfect links in the food chain. We look at all the various peoples of the world and marvel at how diverse are their physical attributes but what we do not realize is that this is a result of the perfect adaptability of the human form. The height, colour, size, hair, facial features, body fat distribution, etc. are all shaped through epigenetic responses adapting the human form to suit the living conditions in which people find themselves over prolonged periods. Just one example is how people whose ancestors lived in hot, sunny climates have darker skins than those whose ancestors lived in cool, cloudy conditions.

Human movement and settlement are largely determined by the water and nutrition supplying capacities of any chosen habitat. If people are hungry, thirsty and struggling to survive, then they will up and move, in search of better conditions. But where there are abundant and reliable food and water sources, people will stop roaming and they will settle, gather, hunt, farm, develop, trade and communicate; and this changes many things: their activities and interactions, their accommodations and facilities. Every social aspect of life changes.

Religion, which gives rise to culture, essentially describes a moral code, or how we should relate to one another. Religion and culture are sources of the peace, stability and order within any society. Religion gives people an understanding and awareness of God appropriate to their level of development, gives them suitable forms of worship and rituals to keep them connected to God, and gives them laws and rules, norms and structures that minimize conflict and maximize opportunities for loving interaction. People are often competitive and divisive, while religion has always tended to bring about unity and cooperation. You will notice that through human history, the forms of religion change as social conditions change. And this makes perfect sense because religion is ultimately designed and engineered by God to answer the questions 'How are we supposed to live together?', 'How do I conduct myself as an individual within a family within a given society?' Every Revelation and religion and culture give rise to a form of social hierarchy and power appropriate to the perpetuation of its principles and noble teachings. Religion is not static – it is progressive.

Ancient religions are not false or heathen or wicked – they are simply outdated and no longer relevant to new human aspirations and societies.

Traditional Tribal Religion

In Africa, and many other parts of the ancient world, the scattered nomadic tribes moved about as hunter-gatherers, and later as farmers and pastoralists, in search of water, fertile lands and security. In the conditions of Africa these were only to be found in rare instances and for brief periods and so the tribes of Africa were given to roaming and to an unsettled group or family existence. Often these were small family units but in other times they grew to become larger clans and tribes and in rare instances they became vast kingdoms or settled civilizations.

The family unit has become more highly developed in mammals than other animals owing to the birthing of live young. A mother who gives birth sees her child as an extension of her own self, while the helpless infant is completely dependent on its mother for survival, and this original relationship is the basis of the family. It is the primal love and source of practical unity which binds individuals together to face the struggles and challenges of life. The family is the first social structure, and the first main struggle facing the family is food and water. The more long-term struggle is 'How do we co-exist?' 'What is appropriate behaviour?' 'What is my purpose here?' and 'Who am I?'

Most of the tribes of Africa never produced a written script so what has reached us of their traditional/tribal religion has been passed down the ages by oral tradition and, recently, has been caricatured, corrupted and spoiled by the colonization of Africa by Europeans. It has been distorted in western literature, which attempts to describe it; it has been distorted in practice because the tribal setting which gave it meaning has mostly dispersed across a rapidly and traumatically urbanized Africa; and it has been distorted in the minds and hearts of most Africans who have been coerced into viewing their heritage with suspicion and shame. Despite these challenges we are still able to discern the original beauty of the tribal faith. The people of Africa believed in God and were essentially monotheistic. Here is a tradition from the Pygmy peoples of Central Africa:

> In the beginning was God, Today is God, Tomorrow will be God.
> Who can make an image of God? He has no body.
> He is as a word which comes out of your mouth.
> That word! It is no more, It is past, and still it lives! So is God.[1]

And the following is a medley of authenticated brief names and titles of God found in the traditions of many African tribes from all over the continent:

> Unkulunkulu, the Great Great One, the greatest of the great
> He who is of Himself, He who knows and sees all
> The marvel of marvels, only He is wise, the discerner of hearts
> Who sees both the inside and outside of man
> The watcher of everything, whose ears are long
> The Great Eye
> He of many names, the nameless One
> God was nowhere and nowhen, He is everywhere
> The Almighty, the All-Powerful, He who bends down
> He who roars so that all nations are struck with terror
> The everlasting one of the forest, the one who clears the forest
> His arms are long, He who makes the sun set
> Mvelincanti: the rain giver, the water giver
> He who is there now, as from ancient times, the Ancient of Days

The author of day and night
He is made by no other, and no one beyond Him is
The unexplainable, the unknown, the fathomless Spirit
The One who fills everything
The first, who had always been in existence, and would
never die
No father nor mother, nor wife, nor children hath he
He is all alone, He is neither a child nor an old man
He is the same today as he was yesterday
Father, Mother and Son, Giver of children, Giver of life
He does not hunger, He does not eat
The Eternal One, the mighty immovable rock that never
dies
He is kind, and he is merciful
He who supplies the needs of His creatures,
Protector of the poor, keeper of the poor
He who walks with you, and is always present
Biheko, He who carried everyone on His back,
The deliverer of those in trouble
Haragakiza, Our Saviour, Wele, the one who saves, helps
and guides
The Father Creator who creates and uncreates
The ever-ready shooter, the killer Mother
God evens things out, moulds and shapes, Borebore
Who created things in an ordered fashion
He never ceases to create things,
The pure King, who is without blemish
The ruler of all tribes
The ruler of the sky, the earth and the underworld
The master of all, the Lord of magic power, the Lord of
heaven
He is the supreme judge, and owner of the universe[2]

How simple and beautiful are these names and traditions, how profound and lofty, how much they remind us of names and descriptions given in the Qur'án. The African peoples did not have books or scriptures but lived very closely connected to nature and natural phenomena, and also to the spiritual world. Not only did they believe that the dead still lived in a spiritual afterlife but their moral system was based on the influence of the ancestors. That is not to say that they worshipped their ancestors. This is a common misperception but the truth is that worship was only ever directed to God. The ancestors were intercessors and enforcers of tribal law and morality and the spirits or angels were responsible for natural phenomena but were under the command and direction of God. The spirits or ancestors communicated with the tribal elders through *shamans* or *inyangas* (so-called 'witch-doctors') and oracles, through dreams, voices and frightening frenzied spirit possession, and the reading of bones and other esoteric tools.

The African peoples knew that the hereafter is a continuation in spirit form of this reality and is not distant or detached but essential to this reality and they experienced it as such. A respected elder who died would be hailed and remembered for many generations until eventually he would be forgotten and disappear into nobody-knows-where. Despite colonialists portraying the Africans as barbaric, they had an advanced social structure, culture and order. They had rituals for important transitions in life such as birth, marriage and death, and they had festivals and celebrations for tribal worship and thanksgiving, requesting protection and prosperity. They believed that there is punishment for wrongdoing and evil, that some will suffer and some will be happy. One African culture has a tradition that after a person dies he or she must cross a great river to get to the other side. The Yoruba of Nigeria have a tradition that says:

> All that we do on earth, we shall account for kneeling in heaven, we shall state our case at the feet of God.[3]

Interestingly, the Sonjo of Tanzania wear a mark that guarantees them recognition when their national hero/saviour returns to save them. However, John S. Mbiti explains in his book *African Religions and Philosophy* that, generally speaking, in the African tradition

> There is no resurrection for either the individual or mankind at large, nor can such a concept be accommodated where the process of dying sweeps the individual from the Sasa (living present) into the Zamani (past), from the period of intensive personal experience to the everlasting vanishing period where humanness is completely obliterated. The departed do not grow spiritually towards or like God, though some may act as intermediaries between men and God and may have more power and knowledge than human beings.[4]

The tribal form of religion was beautifully adapted to the conditions and circumstances of the time. I use Africa to describe this religious mode because it is the most recognizable, still existing form but a similar form of this traditional religion was practised by all the scattered people of the old world who shared similar material and social conditions, from the Africans and Native Americans to the Aborigines, Inuits and pre-modern Europeans and Asians. The original traces of it are to be found even in ancient India, China and Persia, in fact all mankind, since we all share a common ancestry. The traditional tribal religion, while it enabled its people to progress and prepared them for future developments and revelations, did not leave any prophecies or clues to our question of the Last Day. However, among the titles and epithets are these:

The Ancient of Days
The Author of Day and Night
God is the shining One, the Sun.[5]

The Ancient Religion and the Age of Empires

Leaving Africa and finding the reliable water sources of the temperate and fertile regions, wandering tribes settled to produce some of the earliest civilizations: the Egyptian, Mesopotamian, Persian, Indian, Chinese, Central American and Greek. In these places people gathered together and began establishing settled cities based on the farming and agricultural activities that were made possible by the physical conditions and climate. Most importantly, the presence of a great river allowed for reliable fresh water, fishing and fertile soil for farming. The nomadic wandering families and tribes were naturally attracted to such places and they settled and began a new mode of collective living, a new social order. This collective living changed everything.

In these comparatively vast ancient cities, human endeavour and thinking came to have a new face and ambition. In this collective condition there was less anxiety over security and survival because there was safety in numbers and an abundance of food. New challenges of collective living arose, such as the need for transport, communication and access, methods for supplying food and water, removal of waste, the need for control and governance, order and stability, the need to increase efficiency, maximize productivity and utilize cheaper and better forms of power and energy. Communal life caused people to differentiate and specialize their activities and skills, to devote more attention and focused, motivated minds to the immediate challenges they faced. These diverse, free and vibrant communities afforded many the opportunities to explore and observe, to contemplate and formulate. They needed ways to exchange and evaluate, they needed rules of interaction and laws. Their vocabulary and language expanded and they had practical need of a script and way to record things. They needed a currency to facilitate exchange of goods and services. This also resulted in power struggles internally (political) and externally (conquest and colonization).

These settled ancient cities were given a mode of religion which was grandiose. It was hierarchical, administered by a priestly caste of which the king, pharaoh or emperor was the high priest and supreme leader invested with temporal and spiritual authority as the manifestation of a god on earth. They too, naturally, believed in the ancestors and called upon the spirits for assistance, intercession, for wealth, health and abundance in all things. They associated the spirits and spiritual reality with the heavenly bodies – the sun, moon, stars, constellations and planets. They had dramatic rituals, the most significant of which were the pre- and post-harvest ritual sacrifices and offerings. They built enormous and elaborate structures: temples, pyramids and observatories on earth reflecting the heavens and the celestial phenomena they experienced. Despite the fantastic forms their religions appear to have had and the diversity of such expressions around the world, there was an essential similarity in the key features, which allows us to group them together. For some it was because they shared a common pre-culture but for all it was due to the fact that as settled ancient civilizations they shared the same living conditions.

It may appear to modern historians, looking at the ruins and remnants, listening to the distorted traditions and mythologies, that these people were pagans, polytheists and idol worshippers. But the real experience of their primitive religion is lost and we can only know in disjointed fragments what their beliefs were. It is a common feature of all revelation that the purity and unity of the teachings are lost in time and must always be renewed in order to foster greater growth, and so the original expression of these ancient religions is today only to be known through the crumbled ruins that hint at what once was.

What has clearly been preserved, albeit in much diminished form, is their belief in God, the Most Exalted, and the greatest of all. And while they revered many so-called 'gods', God was far exalted beyond all others, although this truth was not always preserved in practice. The human mind is materialistic and has difficulty comprehending God, who transcends matter. The primitive mind could only appreciate and engage those things which represent God in this world of form and function. The angels and spirits were part of the ancient peoples' religious awareness and worship. Angels have always been the spirit messengers of God. In the same way that Muhammad and other Prophets received revelation through Gabriel, and some through Michael, it is not inconceivable that prehistoric cultures were also visited by such spiritual Messengers.

We can only imagine what the ancient religion was like and how the angels and spirits featured in its rituals and ceremonies. The important things we should take away from this chapter are that the capacities and mind of man are growing all the time and becoming more able to know and worship God; that God is the grand architect of the whole process of human evolution, civilization and religion throughout time; and that human societies are ever growing in size and complexity.

Ancient Egypt

In the northeast of Africa, that gateway to the bigger world, is a mighty river which we call the Nile. It flowed from the heart of Africa, through the desert and out into the Mediterranean Sea. Its seasonal flood made the lands surrounding it very fertile and ideal for agriculture, which is the prerequisite for large-scale settled civilization. The civilization of the ancient Egyptians goes back very far, perhaps even ten or fifteen thousand years, and they have left many remarkable relics in stone monuments and pyramids, etched with carvings and hieroglyphics, and strewn with papyrus documents and stone tablets. Using a method of translation that is not merely linguistic but which also accounts for the ancient religious symbolism and spiritual hierarchy, E. A. Wallis Budge presents in his work *Egyptian Religion* a selectively classified compilation of epithets from ancient Egypt about God, or the Greatest Spirit:

> God is One and alone, and none other existeth with Him; God is the One, the One who hath made all things. God is a Spirit, a hidden Spirit, the Spirit of spirits, the Great Spirit of the Egyptians, the Divine Spirit. God is from the beginning, and He hath been from the beginning. He hath existed from of old and was when nothing else had being. God is the eternal One, He is eternal and infinite, and endureth forever and aye.
>
> God is life, and through Him only man liveth. He giveth life to man, and he breatheth the breath of life into his nostrils. He is the king of truth, he resteth upon truth, He fashioneth truth, and He executeth truth throughout all the world. He is the creator of what is in the world, of what was, of what is, and of what shall be . . . He is the creator of the heavens and the earth . . . What His heart conceived came to pass straightway, and when He had spoken His word came to pass, and it shall endure forever . . .[6]

Again we note how similar these are to the revelation of the Qur'án and the Bible. In fact, so remarkable are the similarities that we might be tempted to think that perhaps there was some influence from the purely monotheistic religion of the Jews. Yet this compilation has been drawn directly from ancient sources, reflecting the names and titles of God extant at the time of the building of the great pyramids, and so these beliefs are truly, indigenously Egyptian, predating Moses and Abraham. The ancient scrolls and carved hieroglyphic tablets say yet more about God and creation:

> God is the hidden being and no man hath known His

> form. No man hath been able to seek out His likeness; He is hidden from gods [spirits/angels] and men, and He is a mystery unto His creatures. No man knoweth how to know Him. His name remaineth hidden; His name is a mystery unto His children. His names are innumerable, they are manifold and none knoweth their number.
>
> He is the great Master, the primeval potter who turned men and gods out of His hands, and He formed men and gods upon a potter's table.[7]

The ancient Egyptians believed in God the Almighty; they believed in the existence of the soul and the spirit; they believed in a judgement and an afterlife, however crude, mechanical and material their ideas may have been. Their fantastic pyramids were the tombs of the Pharaohs and in it they were buried with food and drink, with stores and reserves, treasures, gifts and weapons, and even, sometimes, with servants and guards. One carving in an Egyptian tomb shows the death scene, which the Pharaoh and every person face after death. The dead stand before Osiris the overlord, a record of the person's life and deeds is read and his heart or soul balanced against the truth or the good. If he is found wanting then he becomes the food of the hound of hell but if he is successful then his soul is received by Osiris and ascends to heaven or the heavens, the stars. Many spirits are depicted as lesser divinities and performing functions under the supreme leadership of Osiris.

The following passage from the Hymn to Ra links up with our theme of revelation as a light and the Messenger of God as a shining spiritual sun.

> Homage to thee, O thou who risest in Nu [the sky personified], and who at thy manifestation dost make the world bright with light; the whole company of the gods [spirits] sing hymns of praise unto thee after thou hast come forth . . . O cast thou thy light upon me and let me see thy beauties,

> and when thou goest forth over the earth I will sing praises unto thy fair face. Thou risest in heaven's horizon, and thy disk is adored when it resteth upon the mountain to give life unto the world . . . Thou art the giver of laws, O thou Lord of the world and of all the inhabitants thereof; all the gods [spirits] adore thee.[8]

The ancient Egyptians believed in many spirits, or 'gods' or angels, and other cosmic personalities. These were all subordinate to God, although in later times, as their religion declined, the Egyptians focused on the more material aspects of it. Or to say it differently, they could not help but think in material terms and to focus their minds using symbols, idols and personalities. Thus the essential monotheism was obscured but not entirely lost. The great ancient cities became great ancient empires conquering each other and new territories. This further complicated the social structure and religion. It is a common feature of all nations that God establishes Himself amongst them but eventually His light fades or He loses the limelight, darkness and ignorance prevail and people conjure up their own religious expressions. These are the Days of God.

In his introduction to the fourth chapter of his book, 'The Judgement of the Dead', E. A. Wallis Budge summarizes:

> There seems to have been no idea of a general judgement when all those who had lived in the world should receive their reward for the deeds done in the body; on the contrary, all the evidence available goes to show that each soul was dealt with individually . . .[9]

Thus the ancient religions leave us no clues to the mystery of the Last Day. Although the followers of these ancient religions had developed ideas pertaining to the afterlife, they were still rooted in the material and unable to break the religious aristocracy, which made all people dependent on a priestly caste and the Pharaoh, who was often given divine status as the possessor of real knowledge. This was the only way their religion and civilization could function but what the common man experienced of it was a far diminished version of some of the high-minded ideals that we find transmitted through the ages. But a time was reached when their consciousness had come full circle: the seeds had developed and were harvested and the land was again ready. The people of the ancient world were being educated in the foundational grades of spiritual truth. Their language was being enhanced with a spiritual vocabulary. Their minds and hearts were being opened to the Word of God.

The reality of God is so far exalted above human imagination that it is difficult to describe the relationship of humans with Him. Using words like monotheism, pantheism, polytheism, monism, etc. to describe the mode of religion and worship of ancient (and modern) peoples is limiting, as they fail to take into account the reality of the oneness, completeness and allness of God. Fortunately, our spiritual progress does not depend on intellectual definitions and categorizations but on practice and personal transformation. So when we look back at religious history it should not be with distrust and confusion but with faith that God has a plan.

India

The early civilizations of the Indian subcontinent, based on the great Sindh and Ganges Rivers, initially had a similar kind of religion which had all the features of the grand ancient religion but also received some of the world's earliest known Messengers. Because India's method of religious renewal is cumulative rather than revolutionary, many struggle to discern the true beauty of Hinduism amidst the layers of religious forms simultaneously practised. There is much that is inspiring and enlightening in the Hindu scriptures but even with good translations they can still be quite a challenge for the uninitiated.

Hinduism is a collective name given to all the faiths of India but among them there is great diversity. The Hindus have many books from different ages which are all considered authoritative: the Vedas, the Upanishads, the great epics of the Ramayana (story of Rama) and the Mahabharata (story of Krishna) which contain the Bhagavad Gita, the Srimad Baghavatam, the Puranas, and so on. This religious system is not renewed in the way that the faith of the Middle Eastern Prophets is. Rather, it is overlain, one layer upon the next, and so the highest spiritual teachings co exist, side by side, with the ancient forms. The unique division of society through the caste system (which divided society into four groups: the priestly, the warrior, the trader and the worker; the Untouchables were classless) and the tolerant nature of the Indian culture has allowed for this – a unique religious form for a unique social order.

The Vedas are described by Hindus as being some of the oldest scriptures in the world, and as such give us a glimpse into the ancient religion and its sacrificial rites. They are not meant to be read as a book but rather they were originally spoken or chanted during ritual offerings. The Upanishads which followed are much more lucid and philosophical. In the Upanishads (ancient Hindu scriptures) the following is revealed:

> Everything animate or inanimate that is within the universe is controlled and owned by the Lord. One should therefore accept only those things necessary for himself, which set aside as his quota, and one should not accept other things, knowing well to whom they belong. (Isopanishad)

> The Supreme Lord walks and does not walk. He is far away, but He is very near as well. He is within everything, and yet He is outside of everything. (Isopanishad)

In the Bhagavad Gita (Divine or Celestial Song) God explains through His Messenger Krishna the essence of monotheism and the nature of His material creation:

> I am the origin of the whole universe and that into which it dissolves. There is naught whatsoever beyond Me. All this universe hangs together on Me, as pearls on a string . . . Reflect on this that as the mighty air everywhere moving is yet fixed in space, even so all beings are dependent on Me. (Gita)

> All this world is pervaded by Me in form unmanifest; all beings abide in Me, but I stand apart from them. And yet beings are not rooted in Me. Behold the scheme of My sovereignty; Myself the origin and the support of beings, yet standing apart from them! Using nature, which is Mine own, I create again and again all this multitude of beings dependent on and bound by nature. Under My over-seeing eye, Nature brings forth the moving, and the unmoving and keeps the world rolling on. (Gita)

> I am the radiant sun among the light-givers: This is my Infinite Being; shall the sun lend it any light – or the moon, or fire? For it shines self-luminous always. (Gita)

> Suppose a thousand suns should rise together into the sky: such is the glory of the Infinite God. (Gita)

What beautiful scriptures and majestic words. When we allow for language and style, we have to admit that these are very similar in content to the Qur'án and Bible. Of course, not everyone meditates on these scriptures and many people who call themselves Hindus are engaged in various forms of religion, worshipping idols and images, hailing many gods or spirits or divinities, and practising ritualized sacrifice and symbolic offering and sometimes performing animistic rites, even given to nature and animal worship (mainly the cow but also the elephant, monkey and rat). So although it is difficult for many to recognize the beauty of Hinduism, if we look to the authentic teachings of the Hindu scriptures we find that they do not contradict the teachings of Muhammad or Christ but actually complement them and reveal the same universal meaning.

The 'Avatars of Vishnu', the 'Messengers' or 'Manifestations of God', are divine luminaries who have illumined the subcontinent. Among the Avatars are Rama and Krishna (and Buddha). As the sons of kings and triumphant leaders, their epic, legendary, mythical life stories have inspired billions. In practice the majority of Hindus participate in ritual sacrificial offerings and prayers under the auspices of the priestly Brahmins, in a hopeful, wishful, mediated relationship with God. But there are also those who take the scripture to its deepest implication and, renouncing the world, they seek to advance spiritually through asceticism/detachment or finding a guru (someone who has advanced on the spiritual path of detachment and attained a certain degree of 'realization' or 'awakening' and has begun to teach selected students the path to Nirvana (Liberation or Enlightenment). The two methods are not mutually exclusive because many of the first type include their favourite gurus in their daily rites and offerings. And many ascetics continue to make ritual offerings.

Besides the Avatars there have been many gurus including Caitanya Mahaprabhu, Guru Nanak, Ramakrishna, Shirdi Sai and Sai Baba. Many Hindus also accept the Prophets of the Middle East as Avatars for another time and place, and recognize Christ and Muhammad as divinely inspired. Hinduism is thus an inclusive, vast conglomeration of religious systems and practices. The casual reader may be forgiven for feeling confused when even the most erudite scholars have failed to apprehend Hinduism as a religious entity.

Around the beginning of the 20th century many Indian

gurus and thinkers brought Indian religious ideas and practices to the West. Swami Vivekananda, the Hindu philosopher sage, was groomed by his guru, Ramakrishna, to travel and lecture throughout the western world. Speaking about the spiritual condition of India he said:

> . . . the present deep dismal night . . . no pall of darkness had ever before enveloped this holy land of ours. And compared with the depth of this fall, all previous falls appear like little hoof-marks.

The 'deep dismal night' refers to the age of darkness or ignorance that sets in long after a Revelation. The Hindus view the progress of man in great ages or epic cycles, much like the Qur'ánic and biblical Days of God. Here the purpose and time frame of Revelation are explained:

> Twelve thousand divine years . . . constitute the period of the four Yugas, or ages. They are thus distributed: the Sat age has four thousand divine years; the Tretá three thousand; the Dwápara two thousand; and the Kali age one thousand: so those acquainted with antiquity have declared. The Sat, Tretá, Dwápara, and Kali constitute a great age, or aggregate of four ages: a thousand such aggregates are a day of Brahmá.
>
> One set of duties (or rules) for men in the Sat Yuga, a different one in the Treta Yuga, and in the Dvapara, and yet another in the Kali. (Manu 1:85)

The condition of man defines the character of the 'age'. We are said to be now in the Kali Yuga, the 'Age of Ignorance'.

The Hindu scriptures explain that at the height of the Kali Yuga there will appear the Kalki Avatar, or 'Fulfilling Manifestation', whose advent will mark the end of the Kali and the beginning of the Sat Yuga, the 'Age of Enlightenment' or the 'Golden Age'. In the Bhagavad Gita the process of renewal is described:

> Whenever there is a decline in righteousness, O Bharat, and the rise of irreligion, it is then that I send forth My Spirit. For the salvation of the good, the destruction of the evil-doers, and for firmly establishing righteousness, I manifest Myself from age to age. (Gita 4:7–8)

> If I were not to act this world would perish. I would have been considered as a cause of confusion among people and accountable for their destruction. (Gita 3:24)

It is said of the Kalki Avatar that:

> He will then establish righteousness upon the earth and the minds of the people will be awakened and become pure as crystal, and these men, the remnant of mankind, will thus be transformed . . . (Vishnu Purana 4:24)

The following are signs describing the conditions at the height of the Kali Yuga, the 'Age of Ignorance':

- Wealth will be the deciding factor in establishing nobility or class.

- Mutual liking will be the basis for choosing marriage partners and not family arrangements.

- Cheating will be the order of the day in business relations.

- Satisfaction of sensual pleasure will be the main consideration of people's excellence and worth.

- Dharma, or religion, and teaching will decline, break down and be lost.

- People will be greedy and will take to wicked behaviour.

- The caste system will be undermined.
- There will be deceit, lethargy, violence, despondency, delusion, fear; and poverty will prevail.
- There will be a decline in chastity and people will think only of gratifying their sexual desires and other appetites.
- Countries will be laid waste by robbers and vagabonds.
- Kings will exploit their subjects.
- Men will abandon their parents and brothers, friends and relatives.
- People who are ignorant of religion will occupy high seats (and pulpits) and will (pretend to) preach religion.
- There will be drought, disasters and famines.
- People will be weighed down by doubt, anxiety and fear and heavy taxation.
- Men corrupted by unbelievers will refrain from adoring God.

Many of these signs are applicable to times gone by but the first three are modern phenomena. Thus we can conclude that we are living in the prophesied time of the Age of Ignorance or the Kali Yuga. We shall see later how well the prophecies of Hinduism correlate with prophecies from various other traditions and indeed with the Qur'án and *ḥadí<u>th</u>*.

With time the true teachings of religion are obscured and human misinterpretations occupy the minds and hearts of men and allow them to lapse into thoughts and actions that do not lead to liberation and the fulfilment of their purpose on this planet. In India, the social system, the ancient religion and the revelations of the Avatars and the guru disciple tradition were able to co-exist. But the maturity of humankind was approaching, and as we shall see in the next chapter, reformers began to appear in different places around the world, sparking spiritual revolutions that made a clear break with the outdated, ancient, religious remnants and dogmas. The limitations in primitive thinking and behaviour, and rituals had to give way as the time for higher consciousness had arrived.

> What is with you must vanish: what is with God will endure. (Q 16:96)

3

SPIRITUAL REVOLUTIONS

As human societies progressed and developed, so too did their religions give rise to appropriate cultures. Those given to scattered nomadic family existence had what we term 'tribal religion' and those who settled into large stable cities developed 'ancient religion'. Religion gave them some measure of internal stability and cohesion, common purpose and worship, as well as laws of interaction with suitable rewards and punishments, controlling the behaviour and thinking of people by natural social coercion and fear of the supernatural. In these periods people were not free thinkers and had not really exercised their moral imaginations. But the next level of human evolution, or the next wave of revelation, was one which would necessarily raise man to a higher mode of existence in which he became a thinker, contemplated truth for himself and independently came to identify with God's revealed Word, and thus entered into true communion and came into the presence of God. In the East the main religious theme was 'self-realization', in the Middle East it was 'God Consciousness' while in the West the main theme was 'scientific logical reasoning'.

The tribal religion was practised from time immemorial in diverse forms by all the scattered, unsettled peoples of the world including the Africans, Native Americans, Aborigines, Inuits, Arabs and Europeans. Remnants of these traditions persist even today but the original forms of the religious practices have been distorted and rendered meaningless by colonization, modernization and the subsequent cultural dissolution.

The classical religion of the settled, proto-civilizations of the era 10,000 BCE to around 800 CE was practised in varying forms by the ancient Babylonians, Egyptians, Indians, Persians, Chinese, Greeks, Romans and Central Americans. Each of these great cities or civilizations reached a peak then steadily declined and was overshadowed by a mightier one. One of the key features of the distortion of the classical religion is a preoccupation with idols and pagan rituals which still persists in our day.

The tribal religion and the classical religion both served to develop human intellectual and spiritual faculties, to regulate human behaviour and establish social structures and culture and an appropriate vocabulary for the expression and expansion of spiritual principles, forming the basis for moral teachings to come and developing our awareness of Reality. These so-called pagan beliefs were the foundations of our present religions, just as our current belief systems are the basic structure of some grand, as yet unfulfilled, design which we all begin to manifest and which is our destiny.

The foundational religious forms prevailed during a certain time and under certain conditions and we need not delve any deeper. What we have thus far surveyed will serve to illustrate the theme of the progress of humankind and religion. Having served their purpose, for their time, these religions became unable to accommodate ever-expanding social structures and unable to satisfy the changing needs of the people. They became limiting to the development and progress of humankind and so their edifices crumbled. The population of the nations and the earth in general was multiplying; social structures were expanding in scope and complexity; and the interaction between foreign cultures was ever increasing owing to trade, developments in transportation and 'technology', and warfare as vast, powerful empires emerged. Warfare has been a characterizing feature of human societies for as long we can remember but during the period 1000 BCE to the birth of Christ, the Age of Empires was in full swing, resulting in expansion never before seen. Just as previous religious forms had extended people's allegiances beyond themselves, their families and their tribes, so the need had arisen for new religious forms to open people up to embracing other races and nations. The negative remnants of ancient religious forms occupied the populations with empty rituals and superstition. The imagination and intelligence of a significant proportion of humanity were fertile and ready for the seeds of new revelation. A critical mass had been reached. The next wave of revelation would have to provide an extension of the boundaries of self and society, introducing the individual to the possibility of personal transformation in line with the qualities and virtues required for social harmony, and empowering each to embrace a broader sphere of unity. And as we have seen, revelation comes to mankind through Prophets and Messengers.

> O believers, say: 'We believe in all the prophets of the world and make no distinction between them by accepting some and rejecting others' . . . (Q 2:136)

God has sent to all peoples Prophets and Messengers, some of whom are mentioned in the Qur'án and a vast number who are not. They were reformers and restorers. They were the source of guidance and truth and they brought moral teachings and laws to live by. Many were sent at such an early time in human pre-history that they are remembered only through legends and myths while others are completely forgotten; but some left behind their messages in oral traditions that were later collated into scripture. From these ancient records we have come to recognize some of the great reformers of the past. Among them, as we have already mentioned, were Krishna and Buddha, sent to the ancient Indians. Among them too were Quetzalcoatl of the Aztecs of

Mexico; Zoroaster who was sent to the ancient Persians; Lao Tzu and Confucius who appeared in China; the great philosophers Socrates, Plato, Aristotle and Pythagoras of classical Greece; and, most significantly for our developing theme, Abraham who emerged among the ancient Chaldeans and Moses who arose among the ancient Egyptians. Although Abraham and Moses preceded most of the other reformers, who came roughly around 600 years before Christ, we will discuss them in chapter 4, where we consider the succession of the desert Prophets, the Prophets of the Middle East.

Buddha

Siddhartha Gautama, the Buddha, was born sometime between 563 and 400 BCE. The son of a Hindu king of the warrior caste, he was a prince who chose the life of a vagabond. As the heir to his father's throne, he lived all his young life in his palace, having his every pleasure fulfilled, sheltered from the real world. When Siddhartha was born the king invited many great men and sages to bless the young prince and they duly informed the king that his son was destined to be a great religious figure. The king had different plans for his son, however, and decided to keep him sheltered from every manifestation of suffering. Kept behind high palace walls, the prince was never to know the pain of birth, sickness, old age and death. However, one day he went out of the palace and discovered the suffering of his people. He could not comprehend such suffering nor could he accept his life of ease as a prince. He left the palace and his family and went out in search of himself, in search of truth. Disgusted with his life of indulgence, he went to the other extreme, becoming an ascetic, denying his body everything he had previously enjoyed, as this was considered to be the behaviour of holy men at the time. The profound teaching of the Hindu faith – that detachment is the only path to freedom and self-realization – had been reduced by human limitations into material concepts: people had taken literally the spiritual, symbolic teachings of their faith.

For years Siddhartha Gautama wandered the jungles with other ascetics, his body wasting away, his mind contemplating religious ideas and yearning for answers, until he came to the realization that the middle way is the path to success, in the balance or harmony between the extremes. It is the way of all things. He abandoned the hermit's life of seclusion and self-mortification, just as he had abandoned the prince's life of luxury and pleasure. Walking this balanced way, he recovered his strength and clarity and began teaching his *dharma*.

One day while sitting under a banyan tree he was divinely inspired. It was a personal, individual realization of divinity that Gautama experienced, something people imagine as a rapturous moment and which they call 'Enlightenment'. But it was more than a moment; it was more like an awakening to Reality. It then became Gautama's purpose to share the *dharma* and his journey towards self-knowledge, the inner process of transformation, which is the essence of Hinduism. This Enlightenment of the Buddha reminds me of the Prophet Muhammad meditating in the cave of Hira and the beginning of his Revelation, the baptism of Christ in the River Jordan when the Spirit descended upon him, and the epiphany of Abraham.

As prophesied, Buddha challenged the rigid caste system. He taught his message and practices to everyone he met, including people of lower castes and the 'untouchables', many of whom went on to distinguish themselves among his most respected disciples and students. He taught that:

> Not by birth is one an outcast, not by birth is one a Brahmin [superior or holy]. By deeds one becomes an outcast, by deeds one becomes a Brahmin.

Buddha did not like philosophizing about things with

no practical value to spiritual growth. Once a student demanded to know whether or not the universe was infinite and whether or not there is a soul, otherwise he would not continue with the practices. Buddha replied that his student's behaviour was like that of a man who had been shot with a poisoned arrow but was refusing to have the arrow removed until he knew the name of the person who had shot it and the size of his bow. The focus of Buddha's teaching was on that which was practically beneficial to the awakening of others and the cessation of suffering. But when pressed he commented on the all-pervading divine Reality:

> In all the visible and invisible worlds there exists one single, equal Power, without beginning or end, without any laws but its own, without preference or aversion. It kills and saves without any other aim than to carry out its destiny. Death and suffering are the shuttles of its loom; love and life are its children. But do not try to measure the Incommensurable with the rope of thought . . .

He described the nature of his own Revelation, or awakening, as 'a lamp that is carried into a dark room which allows us to see what is already in there . . .' One day while walking in the forest he questioned his students, 'Which are more numerous, the leaves in my hand or those in the trees overhead?' to which the monks replied, 'There are far more in the trees.' 'Such is the comparison between the truths I have realized and revealed to you and those which I have not revealed.'[1]

Among the later Buddhist writings we have the following description of the light of Revelation and awakening:

> The light of his wisdom is measureless, all conditional forms without exception are enveloped in the dawning Light; therefore take refuge in the True Light. Buddha declared

> that all things embraced by his light are freed from all forms of being and non-being. Take refuge in the one who is universally enlightened. Nothing can be compared to his pure light, the result of encountering this Light destroys all causative bondage, so take refuge in him who is the ultimate haven. The radiance of his light of Truth surpasses all, so he is called Buddha of pure light; those who are embraced in the light are cleansed from the dirt of causative bondage and attain emancipation. However far his light illumines, love penetrates, the joy of faith is attained, so we are told . . . he is known as the Buddha of the light of transcendental wisdom because he dispels the darkness of ignorance . . . As there is a constant flow of Light, he is known as the Buddha of Constancy; because of perceiving the power of light with uninterrupted faith, we are born in the Pure Land . . . as his wondrous light transcends form and description, he is known as the Buddha of Inexpressible Light; his light has the power to enlighten all being . . . (Buddhist scripture)

> The wisdom of the perfect One is the sun of the mind . . . (Buddhist scripture)

Buddhism is the development and fulfilment of Hindu teachings, detached from its rich mythology and colourful rituals. I saw on a travel documentary on TV a very interesting festival played out in a remote, far-northern Indian town up in the mountains, where every year people of the town dress up in fantastic costumes representing the gods of the Hindu faith and then, in a show of song and dance, these figures are chased out of the town by the teaching of the awakened one. Buddha represented a clear challenge to all Hindu tradition preceding him, and his teaching represents not a mere development of Hindu thought but a revolution making a clear break with tradition, refocusing the minds and hearts on what is essential and discarding what was added as human innovation and the decaying remnants of the ancient religious forms. (However in the East, golden statues of the Buddha's likeness are worshipped by many, in seclusion, with very elaborate rituals and a mythology of their own. Some would say this is ironic but I would say it is simply natural, as the persisting ancient mind set absorbs other dimensions of the Revelation).

Buddhism is a practical 'religious' system, which received some opposition initially but was then warmly welcomed by many in northeastern India to whom Buddha was seen to be a Manifestation, an Avatar or Messenger. During his lifetime the Buddha's fame spread far and wide and his *sangha* or community grew to number many hundreds of students and thousands of lay followers. His main disciples were very instrumental in the progress and expansion of Buddhism. It was some time later that Buddhism became a threat to the political powers and the king eradicated it from India, restoring the traditional forms of Hinduism and preventing Buddhism's spread within India. Peoples of the surrounding areas, however, such as China, Japan, Nepal, Tibet and Burma, were primed and ready for this teaching of transcendence. Buddhism travelled in some places as an organized system of beliefs, rituals and religion but in other places it was more as a diffusion of ideas, stories and parables of wisdom, spiritual principles and practical guidelines and systems for experimentation and implementation. Its influence was very widely felt and in modern times it has gained widespread popularity among people in the developed, western nations, who find in it a means of detachment from the rampant materialism and commercialism of the rat race, and a meaningful spiritual path.

Buddha, the bringer of this message, lived and taught it. He brought to each person the possibility of attaining liberation and the practical psychology of self-realization, which codified the spiritual principles and practices into a logical framework. His primary teaching is the Four Noble Truths: 1) Life is suffering; 2) The origin of suffering is attachment, which gives rise to desire, passion and insatiable craving; 3) Ending suffering is possible; and 4) There is a path to end suffering. Buddha taught that the way to end suffering was through gradual self-improvement, by practising the Noble Eightfold Path of right mindfulness, right understanding, right speech, right action, right living, right effort, right concentration and right consciousness. This is achieved through the cultivation of higher consciousness in meditation combined with the practice of mindfulness during normal, everyday activities. Above all else, what is required is real detachment by recognizing that all things in the material reality are transient and ephemeral except for the underlying law or source.

> The things of the world and its inhabitants are subject to change . . . but in the changing things there is constancy of law, and when the law is seen there is truth. The Truth lies hidden in material reality as the permanent in its changes. (Old Buddhist canon)

The Buddha also discussed the conditions of the future:

> Goods not being bestowed on the destitute, poverty grows great, stealing, violence, murder, lying, evil-speaking, adultery, abusive and idle talk, covetousness and ill-will, false opinions, incest, wanton greed and perverted lust . . . till finally lack of filial and religious piety and lack of regard for the head of the clan grows great. From these things growing, the life-span of those beings and the comeliness of them wasted . . . among such humans, the dharma (teaching) will disappear and there will be no respect. The world will fall into promiscuity, like goats and sheep, fowls and swine, dogs and jackals . . . among such humans, keen mutual enmity will become the rule, keen ill-will, keen animosity, passionate thoughts, even of killing between close family members.

He also commented on the future, prophesying his own return or the arrival of another Buddha, Meteyya or Maitreya Buddha:

> At that period, brethren, there will arise in the world an exalted one named 'Meteyya Arahat', fully awakened, abounding in wisdom and goodness, happy with knowledge of the world, unsurpassed as a guide to mortals willing to be led, a teacher for spirits and men, an exalted one, a Buddha, even as I am now. He by himself will thoroughly know and see, as it were, face to face, this universe with its world of the spirits, its Brahma and its Maras and its world of recluses and Brahmins, of princes and peoples even as I, now, by myself, thoroughly know and see them.
>
> The Truth, lovely in its origin, lovely in its progress, lovely in its consummation will Meteyya Buddha proclaim both in the spirit and letter, the higher life will he make known in all its fullness and in all its purity even as I do now. He will be accompanied by a congregation of some thousands of brethren even as I am now accompanied by some hundred brethren.

It is said that he will come from a land to the west of India and that:

> . . . in the heavens there is the future Buddha, to whom I have already preached the Dharma . . . A Buddha named Meteyya, the Buddha of Universal Fellowship . . .

> . . . but after me 'Meteyya' comes, before this auspicious aeon (Kali Yuga) runs to the end of its years . . .

> . . . those who accept him shall rejoice and those who deny him shall tremble . . . and the warriors shall march under the banner of Meteyya.

It is also mentioned that he will travel over the oceans with ease. Interestingly, Meteyya, or Maitreya, means 'loving kindness' or 'friend' and he will be a Bodhisattva (one who foregoes his own enlightenment realizing that he is inseparable from all of life and serves mankind to uplift each and all). While the Buddha is usually depicted sitting in deep meditation (or sometimes sitting and laughing heartily), the Meteyya Buddha is usually pictured standing or in motion.

Zoroaster

The Zoroastrian Faith is said to be very ancient but many historians place the most recent and illustrious Prophet of this faith, Zoroaster (or Zarathustra), at about 10th or 11th century BCE while others date his appearance to around 600 BCE, or close to the time of the other reformers. God in Zoroastrianism is known as 'Ahura Mazda'. 'Ahura' means 'the Lord' or 'the Master' and 'Mazda' means 'the Wise'; hence 'Ahura Mazda' means 'the Wise Lord' or 'the Wise God'. Listed below are some qualities of God as gleaned from the scripture of the Zoroastrians, the Dasatir:

> He is one.
> Nothing resembles him.
> He is without an origin or end.
> He has no father or mother, wife or son.
> He is without body or form.
> Neither the eye can behold him, nor the power of thinking conceive him.
> He is above all that you can imagine.
> He is nearer to you than your own self.

Some Zoroastrian teachings and sayings refer to the appearance of a revolutionary religious figure of the distant future. Some speak of two figures: the herald, Ushidar Mah, and the fulfilling Messenger, Shah Bahram.

Mayest thou blaze in this house, mayest thou increase in this house even for a long time till the powerful restoration of the world, till the time of good, powerful restoration of the world.

Whose name will be the Victorious, 'Soeshyant' and whose name will be 'Astvat Ereta'. He will be Soeshyant the 'Beneficent One' because he will benefit the whole bodily world. He will be Astvat Ereta or 'he who makes the world rise up' because as a bodily creature and as a living being he will stand against the destruction of the bodily being to withstand the idolaters and the like and the errors of the Mazdaynians (Zoroastrians).[2]

And there shall his friends come forward, the friends of Astvat Ereta, who are fiend-smiting, well-thinking, well-speaking, well-doing, following the good law and whose tongues have never uttered a word of falsehood.[3]

The wise men of Iran and others will join them.[4]

Tai-Chi – Lao Tzu and Confucius

The Chinese were sent the two Prophet-Sages, Confucius and Lao Tzu, as complementary reformers at around the same time, 600–500 BCE. Confucius taught virtuous and ethical service to the community and state, thus concentrating on the practical and earthly, while Lao Tzu focused on the Tao, the 'Integral Subtle Way', the mystical path to harmonizing with the Way. Confucius taught his students and made them into virtuous and ethical civil servants, thus transforming Chinese modes of education and governance. Lao Tzu, legend has it, retired from serving as the interpreter of the I Ching oracle. While in the mountains, he was asked by someone to write down his wisdom teachings and in two days he composed the Tao Te Ching, or the Subtle Way of the Universe or Reality. It is difficult to describe such a unique classic of spiritual revelation: remarkable, profoundly simple, paradoxical, intangible and elusive, it flows as naturally and rhythmically as a river to the sea and expands in the mind like ripples in a clear lake.

It is believed by some that the two great minds of ancient China met, or that Confucius was the disciple of Lao Tzu, but whatever the truth, it is marvellously reminiscent of the powerful Chinese symbol and philosophy of the Tai-Chi or interweaving of the opposite but complementary natures. One focuses on the inner and mystical, and the other on the outer and practical. The Tai-Chi symbol places light and dark (or white and black) in a flowing embrace, where one follows the other in a cyclical manner, much like our theme of day and night. All things display this dynamic equilibrium – positive and negative in vibrant oscillating embrace; the love attraction of male and female; or the forms of masculinity and femininity; the light and darkness giving us day and night; wisdom and ignorance; waking and sleeping; life and death. From the *Tao Te Ching and Hua Hu Ching* by Lao Tzu:

> Those who want to conquer the world and make it conform to their own desires will never have success, for the sovereignty of the world is a subtle thing. He who tries to shape it spoils it. He who tries to hold it loses it. The things of the world are constantly changing. There is a time for things to move ahead, and a following time for things to retreat; a time to withdraw internally, and a following time to expand externally; a time to grow luxuriantly and a following time to decay; a time to rise up, and a following time to sink down low. Therefore one who does not separate his being from the deep nature of the universe avoids all extremes, extravagance and excess.[5]

Here are some of the teachings and prophecies of these two famous masters of old China about paganism and the ancient religion:

> Those who turn to deities as intermediaries between themselves and the divine (subtle truth) are like beggars who look outside themselves for the very treasure contained within their own nature. It is only when one discovers one's own divine nature that prayer or any form of worshipping the one universal life (God) can be a true and effective spiritual cultivation of the wholeness of eternal life. (*Hua Hu Ching* 17)

And regarding leadership and virtue:

> How does the sea become the queen of all rivers and streams? By lying lower than they do! Hence it is the queen of all rivers and streams. One who humbles himself, therefore, can serve all people. By putting himself last, he comes to be their leader.[6]

> High Beings of deep universal virtue work unassertively; they help all people, yet people are barely aware of their existence. Leaders of great achievement earn the friendship and praise of people . . .[7]

> When great people of the highest awareness hear the subtle Way (teaching) of the universe (God) they cultivate themselves diligently in order to live in accord with it. When mediocre (dull) people hear the subtle Way of the universe, they are unimpressed . . .[8]

> The great perfection seems imperfect, yet its usefulness is unfailing. The great fullness appears to be void, yet its usefulness is boundless. The great accomplishment seems unfinished. The ultimate straightness appears crooked. Profound skilfulness appears clumsy. Fluent eloquence seems mute. Movement overcomes cold. Stillness overcomes heat. Maintain clarity and purity, and be a model of deep virtue for all people.[9]

> What is well planted cannot be pulled up. What is closely embraced cannot slip away. The wise establish virtue firmly within themselves, and are honoured for generations ever after . . .[10]

And on the subject of the future times and the Last Day:

> In the future, in the Age of Confusion, people will create many obstacles to knowing the simple truth and hold fast to their own blindness and falsehoods. They will persuade others to follow them and persecute unbelievers and even start wars against them . . . the muchness and suchness of truth is included in this very moment, a thousand galloping horses cannot catch up with it.[11]

> In the future, humanity will over-emphasize the intellectual element of the mind. Instead of recognizing the wholeness of life, people will perceive life as having a worldly aspect and a spiritual aspect that are separate and unrelated to each other. People will lose themselves in isolated fragments of conceptual information and become the victims rather than the masters of their knowledge . . .
>
> The people of the future should not blindly accept the new nor blindly reject the old. Things that were developed long ago may still have great value if they have been proven safe and effective by the test of time. The new inventions that will appear may seem to be shortcuts, but things of temporal convenience will bring hidden troubles later. Future generations will need to re-evaluate all old and new discoveries and inventions to ensure that they are useful and healthy, according to the standards of a holistic way of life . . . never be so childish as to think that one may concentrate on spiritual cultivation and moral discipline without making oneself virtuously useful by serving others. This kind of attitude is either a psychological illness or a childish game that trades religious devotion for psychological

protection and transient emotional blessings.[12]

In future generations, because people procreate prolifically as the silkworm produces eggs, with little moral control or heavenly guidance, there will inevitably be many disabled and sick individuals. This blind and ignorant multiplication of the population will degrade the quality of humanity. In the future there will also be collective murder, slaughter, plagues, and finally a big war with the crisis of total destruction . . . What is needed is the total awakening of all so that the majority of people will know to eliminate negative influences . . . each individual becomes responsible for his own evolution, but true achievement comes mostly from one's virtuous fulfilment in helping and serving his fellow human . . .

A teacher of Universal Life is an angel or spirit who resides in the world to help people. He radiates his virtue to nourish his surroundings and, if he is misunderstood by people, he does not stop extending his virtue to them. Also with his integral awareness, he cannot be enslaved by the world. In future generations the world may not become a slaughterhouse, if teachers of Universal Life are respected and their precious teaching seen as the safeguard of each generation of life . . .

A time of world destruction will not come, in the future, in which many lives are lost, if those who are able to save themselves and the world practise selfless virtuous fulfilment and follow the Universal Way of life. Only ones of immortal virtue will be able to support the world and start a better one.[13]

People of the future will be more intelligent but they will have more troubles. Their life will be more abundant but they will be more unhappy . . . it will be from the misuse and partial development of intelligence that a time of confusion will arise and grow progressively worse. People will lose their appreciation for a healthy natural life of plainness after being attracted to and entrapped by all kinds of accumulated bad habits. Slavery will pervade human life and all human relationships under different names and reasons. If one is not the slave of social undevelopment, he will be the slave of all kinds of emotional entrapment; if not the slave of his desires, then the slave of his ego. The forms of slavery are many. Most people become slaves to natural demands, fashionable luxuries, social power, artificial religion or ideology, destiny, and most of all psychological excuses. All kinds of unnecessary conflict will be brought about, aggravating turmoil and creating unprecedented calamity on a large scale . . .

About great leaders of the future:

> There will be great people who awaken during the Era of Great Confusion and Darkness. Through a vast social renaissance, the awakening of the universal divine nature within people will be reached. Its true foundation rests on the people who will achieve themselves through individual emancipation and self-cultivation . . . in general; people create a variety of complicated situations and become stuck in their concepts and false images. They remain unaware of the situation on the large scale by being stuck and trying to convince others to follow what they think is right. Thus, confusion is added to confusion and slaves follow slaves in terrible darkness.[14]

> Those who study and practise the scripture will acquire the subtle light that illuminates all time and space . . . the human world is like a big ship in need of someone to steer it. If there is no one at the helm, it could drift aimlessly into dangerous waters and imperil the lives of all its passengers. There must be someone who is willing to shoulder the responsibility of navigating the vessel of the world . . .

a person of universal subtle truth is not ambitious as a leader unless the responsibility falls to him; he will make no scheme to take it. He fulfils the task that is appointed to him and then takes no credit and holds no attachment to it. He merely offers himself to serve others. He knows that individuals are the foundation of human society, thus the way to guide the world is to correctly guide each person who comes to him. The work does not merely skim the surface of the social problem, but goes deeply into the source.

Whoever undertakes such an endeavour must prepare himself to meet the following qualifications: One must deeply plant and firmly root one's spirit in the universal subtle truth. One must be truly virtuous and sincere. At a practical level one must be willing to improve himself by eliminating all negative attitudes and habits. In this way one is able to build a stable, broad, receptive and creative personality. Only then may one plunge into the ocean of bountiful spiritual knowledge and training to become a Mentor of the Universal Way. True Mentors are the embodiment of the Universal Way. They are the direct expression of the universal subtle truth. They must have attained spiritual maturity through true-life experience before they can become the spiritual light to those in darkness. To be with them is to experience the living truth. Their minds are as deep and all encompassing as the universal truth. By breaking through the mystery of life and death and the dream-like quality of their own mental faculty they have fully developed and integrated all aspects of their being, and their personal nature is one with the Universal Truth. Their speech and behaviour are the manifestation of their own spiritual attainment, responding to the different personalities and environments they encounter. Their lives are an expression of wisdom and pure law. They are the revelation of the mystery of the great universal triad: Heaven, Earth and Man. Their smiles radiate light, wisdom and bliss. They teach others selflessly, not out of any desire for

> self-aggrandizement. They are the true father and mother, true brother and sister, and true friend of their followers. Their grace always illumines the dark corners of their followers' minds. They share their divine energy with their followers and are always aware of their problems. They dissolve the pain of their followers in the ocean of their compassion. The sadness, imperfection and false personalities of the followers vanish before their eyes and they see only their true nature. Because they know the traps and obstacles of life, they can guide their followers out of troubled waters. They can direct the stream of their peoples' lives toward the infinite ocean of Universal Truth.[15]

Confucius was a brilliant man who travelled widely, making many friends and some enemies in old China, and also gathering a following of students. He hoped that he would find some noble king or leader, like those famous sage-kings of old, who would embrace his philosophy or wisdom-teaching of ethical and moral service to mankind. He was disappointed in this but he lived on through his students, his teaching academy and his writings, and in time his school became renowned for the quality of people it produced and eventually his wisdom-teaching spread to all of China and Confucius was given a divine station in the temples and also in the minds and hearts of the Chinese.

> What the Great Learning teaches is to illustrate illustrious virtue; to renovate the people; and to rest in the highest excellence. The point where to rest being known, the object of pursuit is then determined; and, that being determined, a calm unperturbedness may be attained to. To that calmness there will succeed a tranquil repose. In that repose there may be careful deliberation, and that deliberation will be followed by the attainment of the desired end.
>
> Things have their root and their branches. Affairs have their end and their beginning. To know what is first and

what is last will lead near to what is taught in the Great Learning. The ancients, who wished to illustrate illustrious virtue throughout the kingdom, first ordered well their own states. Wishing to order well their states, they first regulated their families. Wishing to regulate their families, they first cultivated their persons. Wishing to cultivate their persons, they first rectified their hearts. Wishing to rectify their hearts, they first sought to be sincere in their thoughts. Wishing to be sincere in their thoughts, they first extended to the utmost their knowledge. Such extension of knowledge lay in the investigation of things.

Things being investigated, knowledge became complete. Their knowledge being complete, their thoughts were sincere. Their thoughts being sincere, their hearts were then rectified. Their hearts being rectified, their persons were cultivated. Their persons being cultivated, their families were regulated. Their families being regulated, their states were rightly governed. Their states being rightly governed, the whole kingdom was made tranquil and happy. From the Son of Heaven down to the mass of the people, all must consider the cultivation of the person the root of everything besides. It cannot be, when the root is neglected, that what should spring from it will be well ordered. It never has been the case that what was of great importance has been slightly cared for, and, at the same time, that what was of slight importance has been greatly cared for . . .[16]

By three methods we may learn wisdom: First, by reflection, which is noblest; second, by imitation, which is easiest; and third by experience, which is the bitterest . . . He who learns but does not think, is lost! He who thinks but does not learn is in great danger . . . The essence of knowledge is, having it, to apply it; not having it, to confess your ignorance . . . To see what is right and not to do it, is want of courage.[17]

The Greek Philosophers

To the Greeks, at the height of their civilization around 500 to 400 BCE, was sent the great philosopher sage Socrates and his disciples Plato and Aristotle, as well as Pythagoras, who wrote: 'Every man has been made by God in order to acquire knowledge and contemplate. Truth is so great a perfection, that if God would manifest himself to men, he would choose light for his body and truth for his soul.' These, together with others, were widely considered the fathers of modern science, philosophy and democracy. These were not Prophets in the ordinary sense of the term but Pythagoras and his followers were persecuted and Socrates was brought to trial for his beliefs and teachings, for corrupting the youth of Athens. Socrates was called the wisest man of his times but he was not convinced that he was and so he went in search of someone wiser than he.

> I am called wise, for my hearers always imagine that I myself possess the wisdom which I find wanting in others: but the truth is, O men of Athens, that God only is wise; and by his answer he intends to show that the wisdom of men is worth little or nothing . . . I know I am intelligent, because I know that I know nothing
>
> . . . Wisdom begins in wonder.

The city of Athens was a great bustling metropolis of the ancient world, with a representative government and courts of justice, great works of architecture and construction, and agriculture. It was the centre of a vast confederacy, more like an empire of Greek lands extending even further. So Socrates went about town and interrogated various people on their beliefs, people who were held in high regard – poets, politicians, thinkers and talkers – and he got them talking about the things they professed to be experts about. And all he did was show them the flaw in their thinking and ways.

He showed that they were not really thinkers grounded in knowledge and understanding but were imitators trying to sway public opinion and hiding from the consequences of reason. He dismantled these illogical, worldly pretenders and found none to be wiser than himself, even though he thought that he did not know much. Needless to say he aroused suspicion and made many enemies, but also he inspired the youth with his clear, intelligent reasoning. So many young people were beginning to question things in the style of Socrates and this obviously was a big problem for the authorities. He was brought to trial under the charge of impiety and corrupting the youth (but really for political reasons). During this lengthy court case he represented himself and was given a platform on which to promote the freedom of thought albeit, ironically, in defence of his life. He defended himself saying:

> Men of Athens, I honour and love you; but I shall obey God rather than you, and while I have life and strength I shall never cease from the practice and teaching of philosophy, exhorting any one whom I meet and saying to him after my manner: 'You, my friend, a citizen of the great and mighty and wise city of Athens, are you not ashamed of heaping up the greatest amount of money and honour and reputation, and caring so little about wisdom and truth and the greatest improvement of the soul, which you never regard or heed at all?' And if the person with whom I am arguing, says: 'Yes, but I do care'; then I do not leave him or let him go at once; but I proceed to interrogate and examine and cross-examine him, and if I think that he has no virtue in him, but only says that he has, I reproach him with undervaluing the greater, and overvaluing the less. And I shall repeat the same words to every one whom I meet, young and old, citizen and alien, but especially to the citizens, inasmuch as they are my brethren. For know that this is the command necessity of God; and I believe that no greater good has ever happened in the

> state than my service to God. For I do nothing but go about persuading you all, old and young alike, not to take thought for your persons or your properties, but first and chiefly to care about the greatest improvement of the soul. I tell you that virtue is not given by money, but that from virtue comes money and every other good of man, public as well as private. This is my teaching, and if this is the doctrine which corrupts the youth, I am a mischievous person . . .[18]

> Clear knowledge of the truth is essential for the correct conduct of life. Action is informed by knowledge, thus virtue can be taught because correct action involves thought. (Socrates)

The Greek jury found him guilty and sentenced him to death by poisoning. This was a terrible tragedy for his friends, students and disciples, who considered him the wisest and most virtuous person around. Socrates was not a writer and so it is to his famous disciple, Plato, and his student Aristotle that we must look for the brilliance of these ideas. (This is something he shares in common with the Prophets: inspiration, his martyrdom and the spread of his ideas.) Plato in his works reports the dialogues of Socrates. But it is no mere reproduction for it also represents a development and application of the ideas. In his definitive work entitled *The Republic*, or better translated as *Constitution*, he discusses the nature of the good as the ultimate object of knowledge. Here an inquirer, Glaucon, is pressing Socrates to explain what is 'the Good' and Socrates declines, saying that it is beyond him to explain, but offers his persistent interrogator an extended analogy of the sun:

> 'Whose light would you say it is that makes our eyes and makes objects be seen most perfectly?'
>
> 'I should say the same as you or anyone else; you mean the sun of course.'

'Then is sight related to its divine source as follows?'

'How?'

'The sun is not identical with sight, nor with what we call the eye in which sight resides.'

'No.'

'Yet of all sense organs the eye is the most sun-like.'

'Much the most.'

'So the eye's power of sight is a kind of infusion dispensed to it by the sun.'

'Yes.'

'Then, moreover, though the sun is not itself sight, it is the cause of sight and is seen by the sight it causes.'

'That is so.'

'Well, that is what I called the child of the good . . . the good has begotten it in its own likeness, and it bears the same relation to sight and visible objects in the visible realm that the good bears to intelligence and intelligible objects in the thinking realm.'

'Will you explain a bit further?'

'You know that when we turn our eyes to objects whose colours are no longer illuminated by daylight, but only by moonlight or starlight, they see dimly and appear to be almost blind, as if they had no clear vision.'

'Yes.'

'But when we turn them on things on which the sun is shining, then they see clearly, and obviously have vision.'

'Certainly.'

'Apply the analogy to the mind. When the mind's eye is fixed on objects illuminated by truth and reality, it understands and knows them, and its possession of intelligence is evident; but when it is fixed on the twilight world of change and decay, it can only form opinions, its vision is confused and its opinions shifting, and it seems to lack intelligence.'

'That is true.'

'Then what gives the objects of knowledge their truth and the knower's mind the power of knowing is the form

> of the good. It is the cause of knowledge and truth, and you will be right to think of it as being itself known, and yet as being something other than, and even more splendid than, knowledge and truth, splendid as they are. And just as it was right to think of light and sight as being like the sun, but wrong to think of them as being the sun itself, so here again it is right to think of knowledge and truth as being like the good, but wrong to think of either of them as being the good, whose position must be ranked still higher . . . The sun, I think you will agree, not only makes the things we see visible, but causes the process of generation, growth and nourishment, without itself being such a process.'
>
> 'True.'
>
> 'The good therefore may be said to be the source not only of the intelligibility of the objects of knowledge, but also of their being and reality; yet it is not itself that reality, but is beyond it, and superior to it in dignity and power . . . And you won't go wrong if you connect the ascent into the upper world and the sight of the objects there with the upward progress of the mind into the intelligible region. That at any rate is my interpretation, which is what you are anxious to hear; the truth of the matter is, after all, known only to God. But in my opinion, for what it is worth, the final thing to be perceived in the intelligible region, and perceived only with difficulty, is the form of the good; once seen, it is inferred to be responsible for whatever is right and valuable in anything, producing in the visible region light and the source of light, and being in the intelligible region itself controlling source of truth and intelligence.'

Plato and his student Aristotle taught about the relationship between knowledge, virtue and morality. Plato also taught about the immortality of the soul, that although the body dies and disintegrates, the soul continues to live forever. After the body dies the soul migrates to the realm of the pure forms. He also introduced the study of psychology and politics by delving into the nature of the human individual and social existence, and elevated the intellect and rational thought to the height of human endeavour.

The Greeks developed the rational mind and the world of ideas and explored the nature of things and the possibilities of mathematics such as geometry. Plato founded the Academy as a college for educating philosophical, or enquiring, ethical leaders and thinkers. The power and vitality that free thinking and independence awakened won for his school renown and eminence. Aristotle, despite being a disciple of Socrates' 'heathen' school of thought, was made the tutor and mentor to Alexander the Great, Macedonian conqueror and would-be emperor of a vast Greek domain. The combination of an enlightened teacher and a dynamic leader led to the great flourishing of Greek thought and culture. They opened a great library and took the Academy to new heights. It laid the foundations from which modern universities and education have developed. There was freedom of thought and the exchange of ideas and cultures, debate and the critical examination of beliefs, traditions, ideas and theories. Fritjof Capra explains in his *Tao of Physics*:

> As the idea of a division between spirit and matter took hold, the philosophers turned their attention to the spiritual world, rather than the material, to the human soul and the problem of ethics. These questions were to occupy Western thought for more than two thousand years after the culmination of Greek science and culture in the fifth and fourth centuries BC. The scientific knowledge of antiquity was systematized and organized by Aristotle, who created the scheme, which was to be the basis of the Western view of the universe for two thousand years. But Aristotle himself believed that questions concerning the human soul and the contemplation of God's perfection were much more valuable than investigations of the material world.[19]

Altogether the Greek philosopher-sages worked a revolution in human thinking and social organization and governance, and introduced the scientific method, philosophical and thoughtful contemplation, and democracy, nurturing the seeds of representative governance and enhancing the sense of individual independent investigation of the truth. Alexander, the young rebellious leader of Greece and student of Aristotle, conquered many lands, travelled far and wide, and envisioned a great empire in which there was learning and freedom. All the spoils of war and the cultures and peoples, ideas and beliefs of these places flowed into Athens, and there was a wonderful crystallization of the wisdom of the ancients of diverse countries, the sharing and debate of different social structures and philosophies, and different beliefs and religions, moral and ethical codes and ways of doing things, technologies and crafts. Conversely, the crystallized diffusion of these teachings and systems spread to these lands.

The humble and poor man Socrates came to have a dynamic and far-reaching impact on all of Greece and the lands beyond it as well. Education was entirely reformed and the seeds of higher thinking and learning were scattered far and wide. In time they would come to have a global impact and to usher in the age of reason and logic. The exploits of Alexander paved the way for later Roman conquests and Rome was securely built on the firm foundations of Greek culture and ideas. The Romans would carry their ideals to most of Europe and, by extension, via the British to what became the United States. The source of the strength of the West is its embracing the modern mind – independent, free-thinking, logical and inquiring – and its innovativeness and vibrancy are directly linked to this philosophy of freedom. The West's ideas and expressions of democracy have their roots in the ideas of these ancient philosophers.

Over time many of the characteristics of the classical

scientific and philosophical methods were diluted or lost. As Socrates warned the Athenians and Aristotle taught his students, the improvement of the soul is the most important thing. But this is something that every culture seems to forget. Mainstream modern science cannot verify the existence of the soul or God by its sense-orientated instrumentation and so what our youth are taught in school is coldly materialistic and devoid of spiritual content. Disconnected from this loving impulse, the intelligence of our scientists can be misdirected to the creation of things like weapons of mass destruction. Anxiety over a nuclear holocaust of planetary proportions has plagued the past two generations. Numerous movies have depicted a near future in which the doomsday prophecies are fulfilled as global superpowers wreak mass destruction on the cities of the world. Regarding the future, the Greek philosophers, being rational and scientific, left us no prophecies or clues to the Last Day but science is clearly also in need of a 'saviour' to guide mankind's emerging intellectual powers.

Having surveyed the spiritual revolutions in the millennium preceding Christ we can summarize as follows: In the West the main theme was 'scientific logical reasoning' and the process was 'looking outward' into the material reality. In the East the main theme was 'self-realization or awakening' and the process was 'looking within'. In the Middle East the main religious theme was 'God Consciousness' and the process was 'looking beyond' or 'looking to God'. Originally in all of these inspired revelations, as we have already seen, the focus was on the development of virtue. As we explore the revelations of the desert Prophets, this will stand out again as the most pervasive fundamental objective underlying all principles, teachings, laws, rituals and forms of worship.

4

THE PROPHETS OF THE DESERT

We have surveyed the traditional, ancient and reformist religions of virtually every part of the earth. All those who have not been specifically mentioned will now be drawn into the unfolding drama because something was stirring that was destined to illumine the whole world. A global movement was developing, from very humble beginnings, in the desert, where the lonely earth was the companion of the searching wanderer who knew the precious value of water. Because the desert is one of the harshest conditions known to man, its inhabitants resign themselves to the Will and Providence of God. The story of the desert Prophets is a story that has no beginning, no parallel in human experience. No scriptwriter could have written a plot so majestic and gripping. Fantastic and unbelievable, yet most of the world's inhabitants are believers – such is the power of the miraculous and awesome Word of God.

Through a series of prophetic revelations linking many apostles of God – from Adam, the first, through Noah and Abraham – the seed of a pure monotheistic faith was planted in the harsh dry desert sands. It took root, pierced the earth, grew and turned its leaves to the sun of truth. It grew bigger and stronger, flowered from time to time and brought forth fruits from season to season, eventually growing into a great tree, albeit with fiercely divided branches. These Prophets and Messengers are mentioned by their Arabic names and confirmed in the Qur'án: Adam, Núḥ, Ibráhím, Ismá'il, Isháq, Ya'qúb, Yúsuf, Hárún and Músá, Ilyás, <u>Dh</u>u'l-Kifl,

Húd, Ṣáliḥ, Shu'ayb, 'Ísá and Muhammad – the Prophets of the desert. Their books include the Torah, Injíl, the Zabúr and the Qur'án.

> Say: 'We believe in God, and in what He has revealed to us and what was revealed to Abraham, Ismail, Isaac, Jacob, and the tribes and in the Books given to Moses, Jesus, and the Prophets, from their Lord; we make no distinction between one and another among them and we are Muslims (bowed in submission) unto Him (God).' (Q 3:84)

This tree of revelation could take root in no other land, could grow in the hearts of no other people. God is the All-Knowing, the All-Wise and the perfect planner. His religion and revelation is not for any one nation or people alone; it is for all humanity but only the future would reveal this truth. All things on earth must have a beginning and a way to progress. The humble beginning of a new phase in human evolution was this faith which was unique in the world – unique not just because of its pure monotheism but also because it put man in direct communion with his Creator, revealed to him a fuller picture of reality, both earthly and spiritual, established the law of God among men, and successively, by degrees, explained and developed the station of man and his relationship to God.

Abraham

This progressive revelation of God's faith has its origins in unknown antiquity. It builds sequentially, revelation upon revelation, developing each time the message and the human consciousness receiving it. But it is to the teaching of Abraham, the descendant of Adam, that we can trace the seed of the religious movements which in our day have encompassed almost the whole world. Abraham or Ibráhím, as he is known in the Qur'án, lived among the Chaldeans where the ancient classical religion was still practised, including the worship of idols and spirits, natural phenomena and heavenly bodies. But he had an inquiring soul and an independent spirit and would not accept the ways of his people, so God guided him towards truth:

> So also did We show Abraham the kingdom of the heavens and the earth, that he might have certitude. When the night covered him over, he saw a star, he said: 'This is my lord.' But when it set, he said: 'I love not those that set.' When he saw the moon rising in her splendour, He said: 'This is my lord.' But when the moon set, he said: 'Unless my Lord guide me I shall surely be among those who go astray.' When he saw the sun rising (in splendour) he said: 'This is my lord; this is the greatest (of all).' But when the sun set, he said: 'O my people! I am indeed free from your (guilt) of giving partners to God. For me I have set my face, firmly and truly, towards Him Who created the heavens and the earth, and never shall I give partners to God.' (Q 6:75–9)

Abraham taught his epiphany/revelation to the pagan idol- and nature-worshippers of his time, to his family and his people. But being rigidly attached to their ancient beliefs and practices, they could not understand the truths that Abraham was revealing, and they rejected him as a madman and a troublemaker. One day he entered their shrine and destroyed all their stone and clay idols except the biggest one. When they questioned him, he told them to ask the big one if it would answer. In their shame, they were forced to admit that the idols did not speak. Abraham's people decided to kill him and prepared a fire in which to burn him. The fire was kindled to such a fierce heat that the makers of the fire perished in it. Into this inferno Abraham and his companions were thrown. But God made them immune to the heat. The wicked king watched as Abraham and his companions moved around within the flames unhurt and he marvelled at this miracle, humbled himself before the God of Abraham and released them. God said to Abraham:

> Now the Lord had said unto Abram, Get thee out of thy country, and from thy kindred, and from thy father's house, unto a land that I will shew thee: And I will make of thee a great nation, and I will bless thee, and make thy name great; and thou shalt be a blessing: And I will bless them that bless thee, and curse him that curseth thee: and in thee shall all families of the earth be blessed. (Gen. 12:1–3)

> 'I will make thee an Imam [leader in religion, leader in prayer, and example, a guidance and an evidence] to the people.' He pleaded: 'And also (Imams) from my offspring!'(Q 2:124)

This was God's covenant with Abraham. If Abraham believed the promise of God to be true then he had to leave all that he knew and go out into the wild unknown with nothing but his faith. He had no family – his wife could not bear children – but God promised to make him the father of many nations.

Abraham and his followers trekked into the semi-desert of Canaan from Mesopotamia. They became nomadic herdsmen adjusting to a new country and wandering the lands, moving around and through the Middle Eastern desert regions. Few believed in him but that was not a problem because the two most valuable believers were yet to be conceived.

Abraham's wife Sarah could not bear him any children so they agreed that he would marry her servant Hagar (Hájar) to have a child. This he did and the child was named Ishmael (Ismá'il). God tested Abraham's faith by asking him to sacrifice his son and heir. Abraham was commanded by God in a dream to offer up his son by his own hand, in the same way that ritual animal sacrifices were offered up in those times. Abraham explained his dream to his son, who showed extraordinary devotion and resolve by encouraging his father to do as God had commanded saying: 'God willing, you will find me steadfast.' (Q 37:102) Poised with knife in hand, atop one of the mountains of Moriah, his young son lying on his side like a lamb, Abraham was ready to sacrifice that which was most precious to him. This amazing event in history, miraculous and awe-inspiring, brings the past of the world's unbelief into sharp focus and places on the shoulders of Abraham the weight of the ancient mind set: 'Do you believe?' Abraham proved his faith, not just to God and his young son, but to all the future peoples and nations. This remarkable act has reverberated through the ages, celebrated in the holy days of the Jews, Christians and Muslims. It has captured the imagination of billions with its powerful response: 'I believe.' Abraham was the man who would sacrifice everything, even what was most dear to him, for the good pleasure of God, and for this God saved Abraham's son, provided a ram instead for the sacrifice and commended Abraham and Ishmael for their faith.

Bruce Feiler went in search of Abraham, the Father of civilization, in his sincere and soul-searching work *Abraham*:

> The great patriarch of the Hebrew Bible is also the spiritual forefather of the New Testament and the grand holy architect of the Koran. Abraham is the shared ancestor of Judaism, Christianity and Islam . . . Abraham occupies such sacred space because he is the first person to understand that there is only one God. This is his greatest contribution to civilization and the shared endowment of the Abrahamic faiths. It gives him power but is also a flash point, as everyone wants dominion over that moment. Muhammad may be more important for Muslims, Jesus for Christians and Moses for Jews; yet all three traditions go out of their way to link themselves to their common patriarch. It's as if Abraham were the rock, tugging everyone to a common

> hearth, the highest place, the earliest place. The place closest to God.[1]

After some time God gave to Abraham and Sarah another miracle: a son born in their old age. This son was Isaac (Isháq). This created a situation in the household because the firstborn son, Ishmael, and the child of Abraham's wife, Isaac, were innocent little brothers but also equally potential heirs to the legacy of Abraham. Abraham resolved to relocate Hagar and Ishmael and to name Isaac his heir. The great significance of this act would only be known thousands of years later with the rise of Muhammad but at the time Isaac became the son of the father of the multitudes. Isaac became the father of Israel. He begat Jacob and Jacob begat twelve sons, one of whom was Joseph, the beautiful and pious youth.

Abraham's life is a pivotal point in human history and his legacy goes forth like a mighty river split into two streams destined to converge. Though he leaves us no clues to the mystery of the Last Day, he foretells the rising sun of another Day:

> As Abraham and Ishmael built up the foundations of the House [Ka'bah in Mecca] they prayed: 'Our Lord, accept [this] from us. You are the All-Hearing, the All-Knowing. Our Lord, make us devoted to you, make our descendants into a community devoted to you. Show us how to worship and accept our repentance, for you are the Ever-Forgiving, the Most-Merciful. Our Lord, make a messenger of their own rise up from among them, to recite your revelations to them, teach them the scripture and wisdom and purify them. You are the mighty, the wise.' (Q 2:127–9)

Joseph

Egypt, around this time, was ruled by the Hyksos, a Syro-Canaanite alliance that conquered ancient Egypt. The glory and splendour of Egypt and its ancient religion, the age of the pharaohs, had passed its peak and was on its way down a one way street.

Joseph was the second youngest of twelve sons born to Jacob, also known as Israel, but he was the most beloved of his father. His brothers were jealous and plotted a devilish scheme to be rid of the youngster. They took Joseph out hunting with them one day and then threw him into a deep pit. They took his shirt and smeared it with the blood of an animal. They returned to their father and reported that Joseph had been killed by a wild animal. But travelling Egyptian slave traders happened upon the old well and found the young lad inside. They saved him but only so that they could sell him as a slave in Egypt. And so the young Joseph was sold into slavery. The story goes that Joseph was a very handsome young man and that the lady of the household that he served made sexual advances towards him. Being chaste, he rejected her and so she made claims that he had assaulted her. He thus fell even further, from slave to prisoner, after being falsely accused of indecency. But this sorely mistreated youth was destined for things far greater than his oppressors could fathom. Their wickedness was the very means of him fulfilling his destiny.

The interpretation of dreams, magical skills and fortune-telling were highly prized abilities in ancient Egypt. The pharaoh was plagued by a recurring dream which none could explain. He would see seven fat cows come up out of the Nile and after these would come seven thin cows. The thin cows would devour the fat cows but still remain just as thin. Joseph, wise beyond his tender years, explained the dream: the seven fat cows represented seven years of plenty and the seven thin cows represented seven years of drought.

Joseph thus won the favour of the pharaoh and was given a high position in service to him. He was tasked with the responsibility of preparing Egypt for the impending disaster and so rose to the highest ministerial position in all the land.

The drought that followed affected not only Egypt but surrounding lands as well and Joseph helped to prepare Egypt and all the other people for a very difficult time ahead. The drought brought his own wicked brothers to Egypt and to his door to beg for help. He forgave them and gave them all they needed. But many others faced similar hardships in the surrounding deserts and so also came to Egypt for help. Joseph was able to secure food for them and a place to stay and he taught the religion of Abraham to his people, who had been gathered under his protection. But as time passed and Joseph passed away, his people were enslaved into the service of the mighty Egyptian empire. The Egyptians were harsh in their dominance and used them in their construction and agricultural industries to do hard labour and treating them very poorly. The believers and descendants of Abraham, the Jews, held firmly to their faith, even under the cruelty and imposing might and grandeur of the Egyptian religion. They cherished in their hearts their ancient inheritance and the idea of their deliverance, as promised by the Prophets of old and by Joseph, that God would send them a messiah who would lead them to freedom and their own promised land:

> I am about to die, but God will visit you, and bring you up out of this land to the land that he swore to Abraham, to Isaac, and to Jacob. (Gen. 50:24 ESV)

Moses

There was, at a certain point after centuries of enslavement, a great deal of excitement and expectation among the Jews that their promised one would be born soon. The pagan

Egyptian priests and doctors also perceived some impending calamity, and when they caught wind of the rumour amongst the slaves, they informed the pharaoh. Out of fear and uncertainty, ignorance and arrogance, the pharaoh barbarically decided that all the young males of the Jewish slaves would be put to death. But God's plan would not be frustrated. No empire, no matter how mighty, could resist His Will, yet how subtle and gentle are his fingers of might. Moses was born and his mother, inspired by her love and faith, placed the little baby in a basket and cast him upon the Nile River. The basket floated past the pharaoh's palace and the pharaoh's daughter spotted it and ordered it brought in. When she saw the baby Moses she fell in love with him.

Pharaoh's daughter brought Moses up as a prince in the Egyptian court but she needed a wet-nurse to breastfeed the child, and so it came to pass, through the grace of God, that Moses was delivered back to his natural mother to be nursed. As a prince Moses learned the Egyptian sciences, literacy and religion. He developed the qualities and leadership powers of independent thinking and free living, while imbibing from his mother not only milk but her love, influence and prayers; thus enabling him to grow up to be a bold and strong young man. But one day his life changed dramatically. He intervened when he saw an Egyptian beating a slave: he struck and killed the Egyptian. Afraid of the reaction to his deed, he fled to the East and started a new life as a herdsman, shepherd and husbandman in the desert near the foot of Mount Sinai. One day while Moses was atop the mountain, God spoke to him through a blazing light, the legendary burning bush, and gave him the weighty mission of leading the Jews out of Egypt on an exodus to the promised land. God renewed His covenant with mankind through Moses, a direct descendant of Abraham through Isaac's line.

Moses returned to Egypt and declared his mission openly. Many believed in him, and many were astonished by the miracles he performed, but the Pharaoh, too attached to the concept of his own greatness, resisted the Will of God, the Most Powerful. God gave Moses a miracle to enable him to capture the imagination of his people: when he threw down his staff, it turned into a serpent. The magicians of the Pharaoh, thinking this to be a mere illusion conjured up by clever trickery, also threw down sticks which turned to snakes. But when the serpent of Moses devoured all the other snakes and then returned to him as his staff, they were all dumbfounded but still they would not believe. Even when he turned a portion of the great River Nile blood red they persisted in unbelief. For their disobedience God sent plague upon plague to the Pharaoh and his people, until eventually the Pharaoh released the Jews to Moses and they departed on their long and hard journey. The Pharaoh, seeking vengeance and knowing that they were blocked by the sea and had no means of escape, gave chase. On the command of Moses the sea split and made a narrow strip for Moses and his followers to cross. When the Pharaoh and his army pursued them the sea gave way, drowning them. The glory of ancient Egypt was no more.

God worked many miracles through Moses to deliver the believers but also to sustain them, develop a community and strengthen in them a faith that would endure for all time. The sea was made to part on his command and food snowed down from heaven. Eventually, after a trying trek through harsh deserts, with many people facing constant hunger and pain, they reached Mount Sinai where Moses received revelation and the commandments for moral living. Moses established the believers as a people, developed their religion and led them to the very threshold, the gateway to their ancient promise and hope. It is no coincidence that Moses heralded the collapse of ancient Egypt and the birth of a religious community destined to generate the first ever monotheistic civilization. Moses did not speak of the Last Day but prophesied the coming of a Messenger after him, the 'next day', in a manner of speaking:

> The Lord thy God will raise up unto thee a Prophet from the midst of thee, of thy brethren, like unto me; unto him ye shall hearken; According to all that thou desiredst of the Lord thy God in Horeb in the day of the assembly, saying, Let me not hear again the voice of the Lord My God, neither let me see this great fire any more, that I die not. And the LORD said unto me, They have well spoken that which they have spoken. I will raise them up a Prophet from among their brethren, like unto thee, and will put my words in his mouth; and he shall speak unto them all that I shall command him. (Deut. 18:15–18)

Judges, Kings and Prophets

After Moses passed beyond the veil his followers entered the promised land, a strong-willed and vigorous people, with a new faith, heart and mind. After great struggles and battles they came to prosper and subdue many lands and establish themselves and their ascendancy in the promised land. They were ruled first by the judges and then, in time, as they grew in might, by great Jewish sage-kings such as Saul, David and Solomon. They consolidated the Jewish peoples in the area and developed an enlightened kingdom of great strength and wealth, which was respected across the ancient world. This was the height of their civilization, around 1000 BCE. However, after some time the spiritual power turned to material power and the kings were corrupted and allowed pagan beliefs to gain the ascendancy.

To revitalize His people and return them to monotheism, God sent Elijah, and other Prophets to succeed him, who rebuked these wayward kings who caused divisions and allowed pagan practices and beliefs to supersede monotheism. Other Prophets such as Isaiah and Jeremiah were among the succession of lesser Prophets sent to guide the Jews and prepare them for a future coming. But the kingdom declined further and was overrun by an expanding empire that came to conquer its people. The Jews were captured and enslaved in the ancient imperial centre of Babylon.

In Babylon the Jews imbibed some of the positive aspects of Babylonian living and culture. They marvelled at the fertile fields, the impressive city and its fortifications. They learned about the wider world and became literate, developing the skills of reading, writing and recording. They began documenting and compiling their beliefs and traditions. The Prophets Ezekiel and Daniel prophesied during this time. They were followed by others and eventually an enlightened conquering Persian Empire under Cyrus returned the Jews to the Holy Land, where they brought their new learning and skills. Prophets such as Ezra, Nehemiah and Micah were given the tasks of rebuilding the city, restoring the people and their traditions and compiling their works. Eventually John the Baptist was entrusted with a unique task in the history of mankind.

There is a great wealth of information concerning the Last Day in the prophecies of the Prophets mentioned in the Qur'án by their Arabic names: Ilyás, Lúṭ, Idrís, Dhu'l-Kifl, Ayyúb, Dáwud, Sulaymán, Yúnus, Zakariyá, and Yaḥyá. Some of these prophecies are found in accounts of vague dream-like visions, which require imaginative explanations, but others are in simple language and easily apprehended. Many Prophets were literate and themselves wrote parts of the Old Testament, and through it can be gleaned their sincerity and devotion. Some parts of the Old Testament are not easily understood and remain inaccessible to people, not because it is false or fabricated but rather because it is so old and much of its symbolism is not appreciated. These were Prophets of God and the Torah and Zabúr are His Books; and the followers of Abraham, Moses and the Prophets are all considered 'people of the Book'. To doubt their authenticity and sincerity is to doubt the wisdom of God, who chose these men as beacons of His light and as guides to His servants. All the Prophets are to be respected and admired even as Moses, Jesus or Muhammad, though their rank in terms of the potency and fullness of the message is not equal. With so many Prophets, you can imagine that the volume of prophecy is quite substantial and that when we talk prophecy, we're talking of the Last Day or the coming of the Saviour and the renewal and resurrection of mankind.

> The Mighty God, even the Lord, hath spoken, and called the earth from the rising of the sun unto the going down thereof. Out of Zion, the perfection of beauty, God hath shined. Our God shall come, and shall not keep silence: A fire shall devour before him, and it shall be very tempestuous round about him. He shall call to the heavens from above, and to the earth, that he may judge his people. Gather my saints together unto me; those that have made a covenant with me by sacrifice, and the heavens shall declare his righteousness: for God is judge himself. (Ps./Zabúr 50:1–7)

> The people that walked in darkness have seen a great light: they that dwell in the land of the shadow of death, upon them hath the light shined . . . For unto us a child is born, unto us a son is given: and the government shall be upon his shoulder: and his name shall be called Wonderful, Counsellor . . . The Prince of Peace. Of the increase of his government and peace there shall be no end, upon the throne of David, and upon his kingdom, to order it, and to establish it with judgement and with justice from henceforth, even for ever. (Isa. 9:2–7)

It is possible that in a certain way these verses can refer either to the first coming of Christ or to the dispensation of the return of Christ. While Daniel prayed he was visited by the Angel Gabriel in the manner that Muhammad was, and Gabriel gave to Daniel some cryptic clues to the future:

> Seventy weeks are determined upon thy people and upon

> thy holy city, to finish the transgression, and to make an end of sins, and to make reconciliation for iniquity, and to bring in everlasting righteousness, and to seal up the vision and prophecy, and to anoint the most Holy. Know therefore and understand, that from the going forth of the commandment to restore and to build Jerusalem unto the Messiah the Prince shall be seven weeks, and threescore and two weeks: the street shall be built again, and the wall, even in troublous times. And after threescore and two weeks shall Messiah be cut off, but not for himself: and the people of the prince that shall come shall destroy the city and the sanctuary; and the end thereof shall be with a flood, and unto the end of the war desolations are determined. And he shall confirm the covenant with many for one week: and in the midst of the week he shall cause the sacrifice and the oblation to cease, and for the overspreading of abominations he shall make it desolate, even until the consummation, and that determined shall be poured upon the desolate. (Dan. 9:24–7)

Some Christian scholars interpret the Bible 'day' to be a 'year' – the 'year-for-a-day' principle. If this is accepted, we are presented here with a sequence of events and rough periods between the events. After 490 years the Most Holy is anointed: that is to say the period between Daniel's prophecy and Christ's mission would be roughly five hundred years. This has come to pass. It is then stated that after his revelation, or the going forth of his commandment, 50 years will lapse and then after another four hundred years the street will be rebuilt. After another four hundred years the Messiah will be cut off but not in opposition to himself. Micah talks about the degeneration and then restoration of Zion and Jerusalem.

> Hear this, I pray you, ye heads of the house of Jacob, and princes of the house of Israel, that abhor judgement, and pervert all equity. They build up Zion with blood, and

Jerusalem with iniquity. The heads thereof judge for reward, and the priests thereof teach for hire, and the prophets thereof divine for money: yet will they lean upon the Lord, and say, Is not the Lord among us? none evil can come upon us. (Micah 3:9–11)

But in the last days it shall come to pass, that the mountain of the house of the Lord shall be established in the top of the mountains, and it shall be exalted above the hills; and people shall flow unto it. And many nations shall come, and say, Come, and let us go up to the mountain of the Lord, and to the house of the God of Jacob; and he will teach us of his ways, and we will walk in his paths: for the law shall go forth of Zion, and the word of the Lord from Jerusalem. And he shall judge among many people, and rebuke strong nations afar off; and they shall beat their swords into plowshares, and their spears into pruninghooks: nation shall not lift up a sword against nation, neither shall they learn war any more. But they shall sit every man under his vine and under his fig tree; and none shall make them afraid: for the mouth of the Lord of hosts hath spoken it. For all people will walk every one in the name of his god, and we will walk in the name of the Lord our God for ever and ever. (Micah 4:1–5)

I saw in the night visions, and, behold, one like the Son of man came with the clouds of heaven, and came to the Ancient of days, and they brought him near before him. And there was given him dominion, and glory, and a kingdom, that all people, nations, and languages, should serve him: his dominion is an everlasting dominion, which shall not pass away, and his kingdom that which shall not be destroyed. (Dan. 7:13–14)

The wilderness and the solitary place shall be glad for them; and the desert shall rejoice, and blossom as the rose. It shall

> blossom abundantly, and rejoice even with joy and singing: the glory of Lebanon shall be given unto it, the excellency of Carmel and Sharon, they shall see the glory of the Lord, and the excellency of our God. (Isa. 35:1–2)

> Afterward he brought me to the gate, even the gate that looketh toward the east: and behold, the glory of the God of Israel came from the way of the east: and his voice was like a noise of many waters: and the earth shined with his glory . . . and I heard him speaking . . . and he said unto me, Son of man, the place of my throne, and the place of the soles of my feet, where I will dwell in the midst of the chil dren of Israel for ever, and my holy name, shall the house of Israel no more defile, neither they, nor their kings, by their whoredom, nor by the carcases of their kings in their high places . . . This is the law of the house; upon the top of the mountain the whole limit thereof round about shall be most holy. (Ezek. 43:1–12)

> The sun shall be no more thy light by day; neither for brightness shall the moon give light unto thee: but the Lord shall be unto thee an everlasting light, and thy God thy glory. Thy sun shall no more go down; neither shall thy moon withdraw itself: for the Lord shall be thine everlasting light, and the days of thy mourning shall be ended. (Isa. 60:19–20)

> Rejoice greatly, O daughter of Zion; shout, O daughter of Jerusalem: behold, thy King cometh unto thee: he is just, and having salvation; lowly, and riding upon an ass, and upon a colt the foal of an ass. (Zech. 9:9)

There are many more references that are relevant to our theme but the above will suffice to convey the central idea. Many of these prophecies pertain to the distant future of peace that is destined for man but the fulfilment of many of the prophecies was at hand. Over the years irreligion had taken hold and the leaders of the people had become impious usurpers of the authority invested in them. They had all the outward trappings and appearances of piety but none of the inner light that illumines the dark world of man and serves as a guiding light like dim stars in the night sky before dawn.

The Jews, in the last centuries before Christ, were expecting the 'return' of Elijah, one of the early Jewish Prophets who lived around 850 BCE. He is a very mysterious Prophet of the wilderness who, legend holds, brought down fire from the sky and ascended to heaven on a chariot of fire. Elijah came at a time when true religion had been darkened and the King had allowed the ancient religion to supplant monotheism. The cult of Baal and other gods and goddesses of the pagans were being hailed and worshipped by many in King Ahab's land. Elijah rebuked him and warned of drought and troubles. He took to the wilderness where he roamed until he had a confrontation with the King and the false prophets on Mount Carmel. A miracle of God confirmed him and he was able to win back the spiritual kingdom for God. Much later, while walking with his successor, Elisha, he entered the waters of the River Jordan. The waters parted and a fire came down from heaven and bore Elijah upwards.

> And it came to pass . . . there appeared a chariot of fire, and horses of fire, and parted them both asunder; and Elijah went up by a whirlwind into heaven. (II Kings 2:11)

Malachi, a later Prophet, around 450 BCE, prophesied the return of Elijah:

> Behold, I will send my messenger, and he shall prepare the way before me: and the Lord, whom ye seek, shall suddenly come to his temple, even the messenger of the covenant, whom ye delight in: behold, he shall come, saith the Lord of hosts. (Mal. 3:1)

> For, behold, the day cometh, that shall burn as an oven; and . . . all that do wickedly, shall be stubble: and the day that cometh shall burn them up, saith the Lord of hosts, that it shall leave them neither root nor branch . . . And ye shall tread down the wicked; for they shall be ashes under the soles of your feet in the day that I shall do this, saith the Lord of hosts . . . Behold, I will send you Elijah [Elia] the prophet before the coming of the great and dreadful day of the Lord . . . (Mal. 4:1–5)

Thus the Jews of two thousand years ago were, as they are today, awaiting the dramatic descent of Elijah in a chariot of fire, from heaven, to burn away all things and make way for the King of the Jews, the Saviour, who would lead them to freedom and salvation. Despite the preparation and descriptions, they failed to recognize him because they held fast to literal descriptions of vague prophecies and clung to the ways and traditions of their forefathers. Part of their rejection of Jesus was that Elijah had not descended as they had expected.

John the Baptist (Yaḥyá) was a Prophet who took to the wilderness of the desert and travelled and preached the new message of the coming of the Messiah. He baptized people in the rivers, particularly in the great River Jordan. In Peter Lemesurier's *The Armageddon Script* we learn:

> The details of John's mission had, we may be sure, already been spelt out for the Teacher of Righteousness. At the appropriate time John must identify himself as Elijah by adopting Elijah's outlandish garb (Elijah wore a camel hair robe as did John). Long-haired and unshaven, he must proceed to the spot on the east bank of the Jordan . . . where the river emptied into the Dead Sea (to perform baptisms). This, after all, had been the site of Elijah's dramatic and legendary disappearance in a 'chariot of fire' some eight centuries before. Thus doubly identified as 'Elijah returned', he must then proclaim the imminent appearance of the Messiah himself.

John the Baptist preached that the Day of Judgement was at hand. He prophesied, in imagery similar to that of Malachi, that the Messiah was coming. He bore many similarities to Elijah: he wore a coat of camel hair secured with a leather belt; he also frequently preached in wilderness areas, near the Jordan River and in the area of Samaria/Galilee. He was not afraid of the wicked forces which prevailed over his people, and he spoke boldly of the restoration that was about to begin. Many people began to think John was the promised one but he took little interest in such things and replied saying:

> I indeed baptize you with water unto repentance: but he that cometh after me is mightier than I, whose shoes I am not worthy to bear: he shall baptize you with the Holy Ghost, and with fire: Whose fan is in his hand, and he will throughly purge his floor, and gather his wheat into the garner; but he will burn up the chaff with unquenchable fire. (Matt. 3:11–12)

The leaders and clergy of the Jews and Romans could not see in this dishevelled, 'crazy', 'locust-eating prophet of the wilderness' the signs of divine inspiration. Not only did they fail to recognize him but they also persecuted him and eventually killed him. Later, the disciples of Jesus were also perturbed by the fact that Elijah had not appeared out of heaven and so Jesus explained:

> But I say unto you, that Elias [Elijah] is come already, and they knew him not, but have done unto him whatsoever they listed. Likewise shall also the Son of man suffer of them. Then the disciples understood that he spake unto them of John the Baptist. (Matt. 17:12–13)

The question of the 'return' is very important for our exploration. It is a sensitive one and one that is difficult to comprehend, for it transcends our materially oriented intellect and reaches up into the spiritual and the unseen. Half the people of the world are awaiting the 'return' of Christ, and the majority of the remaining half are awaiting the return of some similar messianic figure. We have explored what this return means to different peoples of the world but a significant saying of Jesus explains that John the Baptist came (returned):

> . . . in the spirit and power of Elias [Elijah]. . . (Luke 1:17)

Jesus

Soon the Israelites were overrun again by an expanding empire and if earlier empires had been mighty beasts, then this one was the mightiest of all, the Roman Empire. In the land of Israel, when Roman imperial might was realizing its ascendancy and reaching its climax, great expectation and excitement was brewing among the Jews. They were awaiting the imminent appearance of their herald Elijah and Messiah, the King of the Jews promised by the Prophets of old, who would gather all of them together and lead them to freedom. The Romans perceived all other religious traditions under their protectorate as pagan and primitive in comparison to the grandiose expression of their own civilized and impressive ancient religion and so were more inclined to be concerned with the political implications of religions and cults within their dominion. Herod, who was a client king of the Roman provinces of Judea, Galilee and Samaria, ordered that all the male children of the Jews in Bethlehem and the immediate vicinity be put to death to prevent the rise of their king, or the rise of Jewish ambitions, but God's Will cannot be frustrated.

Mary, a chaste and pious woman, miraculously conceived a child while still a virgin.

> And (remember) her who guarded her chastity: we breathed into her from Our Spirit, and We made her and her son a sign for all peoples. (Q 21:91)

And so the child Yashua (Jesus) was born to a miraculous and tragic life. His earthly lineage, on the one hand, could be traced to the great King David, himself a descendant of Abraham; while on the other hand, the virgin birth rendered the other half of his lineage truly supernatural.

After his humble birth in Bethlehem, Jesus was taken away by Mary and Joseph to Egypt to avoid the cruelty of Herod. They returned after some years and settled in Nazareth. As a youth Jesus displayed remarkable knowledge and intelligence, and often explained difficult religious concepts to groups of much older men, who were astonished by his wisdom. Jesus grew to be a wise and loving young man, pious and truthful. He became a carpenter, patiently shaping wooden pieces to fit together to form useful and sturdy structures.

John the Baptist began his mission of preparing the people for the coming of the promised one, the Messiah, the coming of the King of the Jews. He showed great wisdom and spiritual understanding and travelled widely in the land spreading this message. Jesus heard about this religious figure prophesying in the wilderness like the Prophets of old, saying that the time was at hand. Jesus went out to him and found him preaching in the shallows of the River Jordan. He went forward and was baptized by John. As Jesus came up out of the water he saw the heavens open up before him – a glorious vision – and he experienced the 'Spirit' descend upon him like a dove. Jesus was confirmed a Messenger of God and was strengthened with *Rúḥ* or the Holy Spirit.

> To Jesus the son of Mary We gave clear Signs and strengthened him with the Holy Spirit. (Q 2:87, 253)

John the Baptist, or Yaḥyá as he is named in the Qur'án, was later seized by the authorities and executed but his mission was fulfilled. Jesus began teaching his revelation, first to a few selected disciples who were simple honest men, and then openly as he travelled from town to town.

> (I have come to you) to attest the Torah which was before me. And to make lawful to you part of what was (before) forbidden to you. I have come to you with a sign from your Lord, so fear God and obey me. (Q 3:50)

Jesus was given the authority to confirm all that had gone before but also to abrogate laws. His disciples learned from him the gospel as they journeyed together and witnessed his beauty and his miracles. He healed the sick, gave sight to the blind, materialized food and drink to feed many people and even gave life to the dead. He gathered many followers and believers who loved him dearly, and word of his doings spread far and wide. He would often seek solitude and peace to clear his mind, to meditate and to pray and draw strength. He was Jewish and built upon his existing faith a new revelation emphasizing the love of God, the eternal fatherhood of God, the brotherhood of man, and the gift of knowing the mercy and grace of God through His Manifestation, or Messenger.

> Thou shalt love the Lord thy God with all thy heart, and with all thy soul, and with all thy mind. This is the first and great commandment. And the second is like unto it, thou shalt love thy neighbour as thyself. (Matt. 22:37–9)

Jesus unravelled mysteries of spiritual knowledge with remarkable parables and taught about the beautiful qualities that please God, thereby bringing the true believers closer to him, enabling them to enter into direct, personal communion with him and to awaken in them the desire to emulate his example and manifest his qualities. When the time was right he entered the holy city of Jerusalem as described in the prophecies but the authorities rejected him as a liar and an impostor. Based on their traditions and their literal interpretation of prophecy and signs, they expected a great king with power to lead the Jews and conquer their enemies. They therefore failed to recognize the Christ, despite the beauty of his being and the truth of his teaching, as a king whose dominion was spiritual and whose kingdom was heavenly.

Jesus challenged the ways of the people and their ignorant leaders. He changed the Sabbath, chased the moneylenders out of the temples and established pure worship. Because they were attached to the ways of their fathers and to their ignorance, the people sought to destroy what from their limited perspective did not accord with their beliefs. Thus they committed the most horrid acts of torture and the crucifixion of Jesus Christ, the essence of mercy. Jesus was made to bear his own cross through the streets of the holiest city; he was dressed in the robes of a king and, to complete the perverse mockery, a crown of thorns was placed upon his head, which dug into his skin, causing blood to stream down his blessed face. And the mindless crowds hated him and cursed him and threw dirt in his face, all at the instigation of their leaders, while the hearts of the faithful cried out and broke, and the heart of the earth and the heavens trembled and wept. They drove nails through his body, impaled it upon the cross, lifted it to stand among the worst of criminals and marked it with the title 'King of the Jews'.

Many Muslims believe that Jesus was not killed on the cross. Some hold that Judas Iscariot was made to look exactly like Jesus and it was he who was killed on the cross while Jesus was lifted in bodily form into the heavens. However, heaven is not a place of physical form – it is spiritual. Further, there is no authentic source for this belief: the tradition that the treacherous Judas Iscariot was made to look like Christ and crucified in his stead has no basis in the Qur'án or the *ḥadí<u>th</u>*. It is based on a misinterpretation of the verses:

And because of their saying, 'We slew the Messiah Jesus son

> of Mary, God's messenger' They slew him not nor crucified, but it appeared so unto them; and lo those who disagree concerning it are in doubt thereof; they have no knowledge thereof save pursuit of a conjecture; They slew him not for certain, but God took him up unto Himself. God was ever Mighty, Wise. There is not one of the people of the scripture but will believe in him before his death and on the Day of Resurrection he will be a witness against them. (Q 4:157–9)

This is a very significant verse for our discussion because it is one of the rare Qur'ánic verses that specifically links Ḥaḍrat 'Ísá, or Jesus Christ, and his second coming with the Last Day, or the Day of Resurrection. This verse tells us that he was lifted up to God, something that is beyond our comprehension and vocabulary to describe. But it is very important that we appreciate this because it affects the way we understand the return of Christ. It is not easy to understand this verse and the truth of this matter is known to God alone. The majority of Christians agree that Christ miraculously survived (or was resurrected) and ascended to heaven (as Elijah had, centuries earlier). And it is in this sense that this verse is to be understood. Christ's ascension to heaven was spiritual and not physical because heaven is a realm of non-material spirit. While the persecutors of Christ imagined that they had crucified and killed him and quenched his light, they had not.

The cross became a powerful symbol of the absolute certainty of the cause of Jesus Christ the Saviour, the truth of his Revelation and the purity of his unconditional love. His disciples spread far and wide to teach his message. Eventually, they compiled from their memory his teachings and, over the centuries, the New Testament slowly took shape.

To Jesus was given the Injíl, a divine inspiration or message. The first books are biographies and the remainder are letters and epistles written or inspired by disciples and later followers or visionaries, all interspersed with the direct words of Jesus and the direct Word of God. While Jesus was not instructed and inspired by Gabriel as was Muhammad, nevertheless he is called Rúḥ Alláh ('Spirit of God') as he was strengthened with the Holy Spirit, as confirmed in the Qur'án.

> Then will God say: 'O Jesus the son of Mary! Recount My favour to thee and to thy mother. Behold! I strengthened thee with the Holy Spirit, so that thou didst speak to the people in childhood and in old age. Behold I taught thee the Book and Wisdom, the Torah and the Ingeel (Gospel). And behold! Thou makest out of clay, as it were, the figure of a bird, by My leave, and thou breathest into it, and it becometh a bird by My leave, and thou healest those born blind, and the lepers, by My leave. And behold thou bringest forth the dead by My leave . . . (Q 5:110)

Some people do not accept the modern form of the Bible as authoritative and reliable. Even though it is filled with great beauty and wisdom, they deny that it is a true guide. The truth is that God is the director of all the affairs of mankind and the universe and all things unfold according to his Will. The Bible that is so well loved by more than a quarter of the world's population, that is a source of spiritual growth and morality and that has brought the light of God to so many souls who were still slumbering in the ancient mind and culture, is a reliable source when we account for its origins and content. The Bible was considered by Muhammad to be a 'Book of God' and its followers are considered among the 'people of the Book'. In later times people would develop some strange doctrines in the name of Christianity but to deny the authenticity of the Holy Bible is to deny the power and love of God, who gave to His sincere followers revelation captured in the form of a Book.

God is the all-powerful yet His methods are subtle to preserve the freedom of human thought. Everything unfolds according to His plan. The Bible should not be compared to the Qur'án for they are very different in many respects. Besides language and style and the method of authenticating and compiling, there is also the difference in the mode of revelation received by Christ and Muhammad, and a difference in the chosen method of propagation of their teaching and the spread of the religions. Thus it is not uncommon to find Muslims who completely discredit the entire Old and New Testaments and will not even read them. A person who simply wants to be critical can pick out inconsistencies in the Bible or even, for that matter, in the Qur'án (or any holy scripture). But the point of the Bible is not to engender criticism but to inspire. Through the Bible Jesus teaches us about many things, including the good conduct and behaviour that is conducive to spiritual development and peace, as well as prophecies about the future of the world and the continuity of revelation.

> Let not your heart be troubled: ye believe in God, believe also in me. In my Father's house are many mansions: if it were not so, I would have told you. I go to prepare a place for you. And if I go and prepare a place for you, I will come again, and receive you unto myself; that where I am, there ye may be also . . . If ye love me, keep my commandments. And I will pray the Father, and he shall give you another Comforter, that he may abide with you for ever; Even the Spirit of truth; whom the world cannot receive, because it seeth him not, neither knoweth him: but ye know him; for he dwelleth with you, and shall be in you . . . the word which ye hear is not mine, but the Father's which sent me. These things have I spoken unto you, being yet present with you. But the Comforter, which is the Holy Ghost, whom the Father will send in my name, he shall teach you all things, and bring all things to your remembrance, whatsoever I have said unto you. Peace I leave with you, my peace I give unto you: not as the world giveth, give I unto you. Let

> not your heart be troubled, neither let it be afraid. Ye have heard how I said unto you, I go away, and come again unto you. If ye loved me, ye would rejoice, because I said, I go unto the Father: for my Father is greater than I. And now I have told you before it come to pass, that, when it is come to pass, ye might believe. (John 14:1–29)

Jesus himself spoke about the signs at the time of his return:

> And as he sat upon the mount of Olives, the disciples came unto him privately, saying, Tell us, when shall these things be? and what shall be the sign of thy coming, and of the end of the world?
>
> And Jesus answered and said unto them, Take heed that no man deceive you. For many shall come in my name, saying, I am Christ; and shall deceive many. And ye shall hear of wars and rumours of wars: see that ye be not troubled: for all these things must come to pass, but the end is not yet. For nation shall rise against nation, and kingdom against kingdom: and there shall be famines, and pestilences, and earthquakes, in divers places. All these are the beginning of sorrows. Then shall they deliver you up to be afflicted, and shall kill you: and ye shall be hated of all nations for my name's sake. And then shall many be offended, and shall betray one another, and shall hate one another. And many false prophets shall rise, and shall deceive many. And because iniquity shall abound, the love of many shall wax cold. But he that shall endure unto the end, the same shall be saved. And this gospel of the kingdom shall be preached in all the world for a witness unto all nations; and then shall the end come.
>
> When ye therefore shall see the abomination of desolation, spoken of by Daniel the prophet, stand in the holy place, (whoso readeth, let him understand:) Then let them which be in Judaea flee into the mountains: Let him which is on the housetop not come down to take any thing out of

his house: Neither let him which is in the field return back to take his clothes. And woe unto them that are with child, and to them that give suck in those days! But pray ye that your flight be not in the winter, neither on the sabbath day: For then shall be great tribulation, such as was not since the beginning of the world to this time, no, nor ever shall be. And except those days should be shortened, there should no flesh be saved: but for the elect's sake those days shall be shortened.

Then if any man shall say unto you, Lo, here is Christ, or there; believe it not. For there shall arise false Christs, and false prophets, and shall shew great signs and wonders; insomuch that, if it were possible, they shall deceive the very elect. Behold, I have told you before. Wherefore if they shall say unto you, Behold, he is in the desert; go not forth: behold, he is in the secret chambers; believe it not. For as the lightning cometh out of the east, and shineth even unto the west; so shall also the coming of the Son of man be. (Matt. 24:3–27)

But take ye heed, behold I have foretold you all things. But in those days, after that tribulation, the sun shall be darkened, and the moon shall not give her light, and the stars of heaven shall fall, and the powers that are in heaven shall be shaken. And then shall they see the Son of man coming in the clouds with great power and glory. And then shall he send his angels, and shall gather together his elect from the four winds, from the uttermost part of the earth to the uttermost part of heaven.

Now learn a parable of the fig tree; when her branch is yet tender, and putteth forth leaves, ye know that summer is near: So ye in like manner, when ye shall see these things come to pass, know that it is nigh, even at the doors . . .

Take ye heed, watch and pray: for ye know not when the time is. For the Son of man is as a man taking a far journey, who left his house, and gave authority to his servants, and

> to every man his work, and commanded the porter to watch. Watch ye therefore: for ye know not when the master of the house cometh, at even, or at midnight, or at the cockcrowing, or in the morning: Lest coming suddenly he find you sleeping. And what I say unto you I say unto all, Watch. (Mark 14:23–37)

Jesus spoke to the people in parables. On one occasion the disciples asked him why he did this and he replied:

> Therefore speak I to them in parables: because they seeing see not; and hearing they hear not, neither do they understand. And in them is fulfilled the prophecy of Esaias, which saith, By hearing ye shall hear, and shall not understand; and seeing ye shall see, and shall not perceive: For this people's heart is waxed gross, and their ears are dull of hearing, and their eyes they have closed; lest at any time they should see with their eyes and hear with their ears, and should understand with their heart, and should be converted, and I should heal them. But blessed are your eyes, for they see: and your ears, for they hear. For verily I say unto you, That many prophets and righteous men have desired to see those things which ye see, and have not seen them; and to hear those things which ye hear, and have not heard them. (Matt. 13:13–17)

Many believed in Jesus, and his message of salvation and love spread like wildfire among the many people suffering under the oppression of the Romans and hungering under the spiritual poverty of the times. They recognized in his teachings a pure, heavenly, spiritual impulse and many embraced his faith and entered the sanctity of his revelation. St Paul writes in his epistle: 'For they that are after the flesh do mind the things of the flesh; but they that are after the Spirit the things of the Spirit. For to be carnally minded is death; but to be spiritually minded is life and peace' (Rom.

8:5–6). Thus this revelation of spiritual truth is an awakening and a resurrection that quickens the spiritually dead to new life.

The Romans were alarmed by this growing revolution and the more they tried to suppress it, the greater it grew. There was a terrible persecution of the followers of Christ, perpetrated by both the Jewish leaders and the Romans, who even offered them as food for wild beasts. Rome was sunk in moral and spiritual degradation. There was corruption and perpetual warfare, exploitation of the masses and jealously guarded wealth of the ruling elite minority. Over the centuries following Christ's Revelation, its beauty and purity were becoming apparent and the vitality of spirit that it released was awakening many slumbering souls to the truth of its spiritual message. Many Romans themselves accepted that system of beliefs that came to be known as Christianity and found much wisdom in the Bible.

A Jew named Saul of Tarsus, who had acquired Roman citizenship, was persecuting the early Christians until he had a life transforming vision in which he was chastised by the voice of Christ. This naturally changed everything and he devoted himself to promoting the Word of God and protecting the emerging Christian community. His great contribution will forever be recognized by his posthumous title 'Saint Paul of Tarsus'. He championed the cause and wrote numerous letters and epistles to the early believers and churches which are included among the earliest Christian 'scripture'. Being a Roman citizen he was able to latinize the emerging Bible and Christian teachings. This introduced Romans to the charismatic personality of Christ and his essential teachings, which contained the pure and personal spiritual food that the grand externalized Roman religion lacked. It made true spiritual growth possible by lifting people above the arena of the capricious whimsical 'gods' and into the presence of the all-loving God. The world and its difficulties and problems, and the individual and his struggles and suffering acquired a new meaning and purpose. A new and higher sense of awareness of reality was dawning on their minds and it spread like sunlight at dawn. As a result, eventually the mighty Roman Empire was conquered from deep within. In one small, obscure town, among a tiny, weak people, one man, strengthened with the Holy Spirit, inspired by the Word of God, subdued and conquered an empire. Constantine the Great legalized and later accepted Christianity and made it the official religion of the Roman Empire, paving the way for its further institutionalization in the form of the Roman Catholic Church.

God links, in His own irresistible and subtle way, the ancient Egyptians with the ancient Greeks with the Romans and makes their might the vehicle of His revelation through Christ. The legendary personality of the Christ, his remarkable life, and his elevated teaching and wisdom, his miracles and powers of healing and reviving, and his description of God as his heavenly 'Father', led the Roman–Christian world to appreciate Christ as being far more than an ordinary mortal human being – to them he became the Son of God.

The literal meaning of the term 'Son of God' does not fully explain the reality of Christ's being because such spiritual truths transcend human conception and explanation. Christ was the manifestation of God's grace and eternal love, a revelation of His truth and perfect wisdom. Words and human concepts should not deflect us from this truth. Christ says that he is the one who sits at the right hand of God. Christ never referred to himself as the 'son of God'. In the Bible he refers to himself as the 'Son of man'. Christ never claimed to be God nor did he claim to be physically the son of God. Rather 'Father' signifies a relationship of dependence and guidance. The term is used symbolically to describe God as the universal Father of all creation and this makes all of us His children. Christ usually spoke of 'the Father' or 'our Father', thus making both a personal and a universal statement about the overarching power and love of God. God is not physically the father of anyone but is the origin and source of all things. In the spiritual sense, we are all the 'children of God'.

The Qur'án explains the miracle of Jesus' birth:

> The similitude of Jesus before God is as that of Adam; He created him from dust, then said to him 'Be': and he was. (Q 3:59)

Over time the Romans were awakened to a new spirit and a new faith and they took its message and its teachings to all the corners of their empire. They spread Christianity to all their territories where it took firm root, most notably in Europe where the scattered clans and peoples were ready to receive its unifying force and spirit. The power of Roman culture and learning, scientific method, colonization, system of government, law and order, combined with the immense transforming and unifying potential of Christianity to revive and awaken the spirit and to extend the allegiances of people over centuries, reworked a divided European tribalism into groups of united peoples and nations with both a common purpose and reality, a new mind and a completely new mode of existence.

These combined forces began to awaken a slumbering potential within the separate ancient European clans, bringing together peoples and realizing new qualities and powers within them. Over time these clans grouped together in larger settlements, which eventually developed national identities. When the Roman Empire began to weary and decay, it was forced to withdraw from protecting its borders relatively suddenly to prevent internal collapse. This opened the floodgates, as Germanic tribes under pressure of population growth began to migrate and intrude on the lands of others. Antagonisms which had for a long time been held at bay under the Roman Empire, broke through, and territories were conquered and controlled by emerging dominant tribal leaders. These Germanic tribes were not centrally organized, as the Romans had been, but rather inherited societies styled on Roman power. Eventually they established a unique system of governance, while merging and becoming absorbed into the people whose lands they took over. Over time, the monarchies of Europe were established and society separated into classes: the nobility – an aristocratic elite of people born into privilege, owning land and being overlords of people; and the peasantry. The king was the leader of the nobles, and of the Church, and had supreme power in the land.

The wave of Christian consciousness reached most of Europe and would, in time, also come to the shores of the Americas, Australia and sub-Saharan Africa. But more immediately Christianity expanded south into Egypt and northern Africa, where it was well received and became highly developed, particularly in Egypt, Abyssinia (Ethiopia) and Nubia. The Coptic and Ethiopian Orthodox Churches are original expressions of African Christianity. This African Christianity was not a foreign, imposed religion but an indigenous reception of the original revelation of Jesus Christ and so came to be an African representation of the gospel. These regions of Africa were closer to, and thus more involved in, the happenings of the wider world than the rest of the continent. Most of Africa was excluded by geographical and temporal features but the northern and northeastern Africans were very much part of the age of the empires and the revelation of the desert Prophets.

The disciples, or apostles, of Christ were sincere teachers of their faith who were charged with the sacred mission to inform the world of Christ's teaching. This was a natural development of the Revelation of Christ and his chosen method of propagating his ideas within the technological limitations of the day and the context of oppressive Roman control. Missionaries went out to many parts to teach and spread the gospel. This made them very different from the

Jews of the time, who were not actively proselytizing or teaching monotheism.

The New Testament was compiled over the centuries following Christ's mission. It is a collection of biographies and letters, the Gospels and Epistles, as reported by his disciples, and narratives of their ministry. These contained the teachings, parables and wisdom of Jesus; and appended to them were other letters and epistles written later, inspired directly or indirectly by the Revelation of Christ. Many of these 'books' of the Bible were written during the first century after Christ, and some later. It was only four hundred years after Christ that the work of authentication and verification was taken up in earnest and the modern form of the Bible began to take shape. But this does not mean that it is not reliable. Those who compiled the Bible wanted to include whatever they thought had a pure connection with Christ, and since the disciples and early teachers were so important in putting his message across, their work was accorded almost divine significance and taken as scripture.

Early Christian scholars undertook the compilation of the biographies, utterances, letters and epistles into the Holy Bible we know today, and this is what is referred to as the Injíl in the Qur'án. There is no such thing as a 'Book' that comes directly out of heaven. God is not an author or a publisher. He sends His angels and His Spirit, His inspiration, and therefore His message is a 'revelation' – that is, it is revealed – but it is only when these revelations, sayings and teachings are written, collected and compiled and finally published that we can call it a 'Book'. It is in this sense that we receive the 'Books' of God and understand what is meant by the 'people of the Book' – the followers of that which God establishes among His servants as His decree and Word. The Bible and Christianity would, in due course, reach and illumine most of the globe. Billions of people, who were languishing in the primitive mind set and religion, were led into the light of truth, higher consciousness and a more mature relationship with God. So remarkable was Christ's life that the whole world is counting the years since his death. Our calendar every day tells us how many times the earth has gone around the sun since the birth of Christ – two thousand years or two 'days'.

The Old Testament informs us that there is a time for everything:

> To every thing there is a season, and a time to every purpose under the heaven: A time to be born, and a time to die; a time to plant, and a time to pluck up that which is planted; A time to kill, and a time to heal; a time to break down, and a time to build up; A time to weep, and a time to laugh; a time to mourn, and a time to dance; A time to cast away stones, and a time to gather stones together; a time to embrace, and a time to refrain from embracing; A time to get, and a time to lose; a time to keep, and a time to cast away; A time to rend, and a time to sew; a time to keep silence, and a time to speak; A time to love, and a time to hate; a time of war, and a time of peace. (Eccles. 3:1–8)

There are many sublime quotations and concepts from the Bible which we will refer to in later chapters as this exploration develops. We will see how the Bible foretells the coming of Muhammad and the return of Christ, as confirmed by the Qur'án, in which God tells us that Jesus clearly prophesied the coming of Muhammad:

> I (Jesus) am the messenger of God (sent) to you confirming the Taurat (which came) before me, and giving glad tidings of a messenger to come after me, whose name shall be Ahmad. (Q 61:6)

5

MUHAMMAD

Ishmael, Abraham's firstborn son by the servant Hagar, had to leave his father's homestead with his mother because Abraham's first wife, Sarah, had miraculously conceived a son and now there was the question of who would succeed Abraham. Abraham was obviously torn between his two sons but God guided him, saying that he should not fear, that God would raise from his son Ishmael a great people. And so Hagar and her young son Ishmael journeyed deep into the heart of the Arabian desert. The legend goes that as they travelled they became desperate for water. Hagar left the young Ishmael on the ground and went running back and forth between two hills in the heat and dryness of the desert, looking for water. Ishmael kicked his heels into the ground and the wellspring of Zam-Zam opened, cool water flowing at his feet. A spring or oasis is a very important thing in the desert and a town would grow around this one, a town that would become in time one of the most famous cities in history. Abraham and Ishmael built the Ka'bah here, a stone monument dedicated to the worship of the One God.

Not much is known about the life of Ishmael and his descendants but they did become prominent people in Arabia and leaders of the various provinces. They established their ascendancy over the land just as Isaac's descendants did in Canaan. Ishmael's descendants became absorbed into Arab traditional life and the pure monotheism of Abraham faded into the pre-existing prevailing culture and tribal religion characterized by idol worship and ritual sacrifice.

Ishmael's descendants, however, came to be a prominent and respected family in the Arab holy city of Mecca. They were the natural custodians of Abraham's monument, the Ka'bah, which became, over time, a house of the gods, filled with idols, images and relics. It was a religious centre to which pagan Arabs journeyed for pilgrimage to perform their worship and rituals. A large stone displayed in a glass and metal encasement in the vicinity of the Ka'bah bears the imprint of Abraham's feet as he built the Ka'bah. Also placed in one corner of the Ka'bah is the Black Stone which, legend holds, fell to Adam from the heavens. It is believed to be a meteorite. Abraham found the Black Stone and rebuilt the Ka'bah on that spot with his son Ishmael.

The glowing embers of the original religion of Abraham were kept alive by some of his direct descendants but mostly they were buried under the pagan cult and the political and economic interests of the leaders and priests. The Arabs were scattered warring tribes that fought senseless and never-ending battles and practised many barbaric acts like burying their unwanted daughters alive because they were seen as a burden. They treated their women like possessions, giving them no rights, using them as they needed and discarding them when no longer useful. They seized the possessions of helpless orphans, and indulged in promiscuous behaviour, sensuality and indecency. Moneylenders unfairly extorted large sums for interest on loans and exploited people. Although they were famous for their hospitality and poetic nature, they had no law and order and no moral code to live by. Those were truly times of ignorance and barbarism.

Mecca, however, was respected by all the tribes as a religious sanctuary. It was a major trading town on the route between Syria and Yemen, and close to the port of Jeddah. More importantly, it had the Ka'bah, which was the 'House of God' built by Abraham but which had degenerated into a house of idols at which the pagan Arabs gathered every year for a pilgrimage. Inside the Ka'bah were many idols of wood and stone, and images and statues and objects of worship, which people called the sons and daughters of Allah. Their belief in Allah, God the Creator, had been relegated to an imaginary myth compared with their physical idols, which were the objects of their devotion. The teaching of Abraham still lived on with some but for most it was just some strange ancient tale. They were far from God and far from truth.

Six hundred years after the Revelation of Christ, there were still large portions of the old world which had not yet been reached by the Messenger. There remained many peoples, such as the Africans, Native Americans, Arabs and Aborigines, who lived a tribal existence and practised the traditional tribal religion. There were also vast nations that would remain outside the expanding sphere of Christian influence. India and China were destined to develop in their own ways and thus remained largely secluded by geographic and social factors. But there still remained the old world empires, still languishing in the ancient religion: Egypt and Phoenicia, Persia, Syria, Yemen – all the old world settled civilizations/empires whose cultures had degenerated and who fought ongoing senseless wars.

Most significantly, in the old world was the vast Arabian Peninsula, which owing to geographical, climatic and economic factors was largely excluded from the expansion of Christianity (and Buddhism). The Persian and the Byzantine, or Eastern Roman, Empires were weakening but were, even at the height of their powers, unable and unwilling to civilize the harsh desert regions, which held no interest or economic potential for them. Tiny pockets of Jewish and Christian believers had settled in these Arabian deserts but, being largely outnumbered, they tended to remain within small, conservative minority communities. The Arabs still lived an ancient life style and pagan culture. They were wandering nomads of the desert living a harsh and trying life and they practised a kind of tribal religion, which took shape in idol worship and ritualistic sacrifice. They were also traders and sailors and so the Near East as well as the African north and east coasts were familiar to them and they had long been established in the trade of goods, spices and slaves. They also traded to the north with the more established cities such as Damascus in Syria and in the south with neighbouring Arab nations such as Yemen. Throughout this time Persia and Rome/Byzantium fought almost continuously. This was the beginning of the decline of the Age of Empires. A turning point in the history of mankind was approaching, a turning point in the ambition and aspiration of the nations and the individuals who make up those nations. It was into this changing world that Muhammad was born.

Muhammad was gentle, honest and gracious and came to be known as al-Amín, the Trustworthy, because of his pure character. He was a virtuous and wise young man. Later in his life, after marriage, he would often withdraw from his community and seek solitude in the heights of the hills and mountains that surrounded Mecca. His people were decadent and indulged in wild, self-gratifying life styles. They were devoid of peace, purpose and true love.

Muhammad would climb the rocky desert hills, like the great Prophets of old, to visit his favourite place, the cave of Ḥirá', on Jabal Núr, the Mountain of Light. Here he would gaze on the harsh haunting beauty of the desert and contemplate truth and the religion of Abraham, his ancestor. He would pray and meditate, and beg for guidance and meaning. Later it became his practice to withdraw for the entire month of Ramadan.

One night, when he was 40 years old, Muhammad sat alone in the cave and a presence came to him, a being. He did not know what was happening or who it was who was before him. He did not realize that it was Rúḥ, the Angel Gabriel, who appeared to him. This bearer of the Word of God commanded him: 'Read!'

Muhammad was shaken and confused. He may have been thinking: 'What in the world is going on? I am not literate. I am no poet or speaker. I have nothing to say, nothing to read.'

'I cannot,' he replied. He felt as though he was being squeezed tightly.

And again the angel bade him 'Read!' and again he replied, 'I cannot read.'

Once again he felt he was being squeezed to the point of loss of consciousness, and so this time he replied, 'What shall I read?'

Finally the angel let flow the first stream of divine utterance from the ocean of truth through the heart and mind and soul of Muhammad:

> Proclaim! (Read) In the name of thy Lord and Cherisher, who created; Created man, out of a leech-like clot. Proclaim! (Read) And thy Lord is Most Bountiful, He who taught (the use of) the pen, taught man that which he knew not. (Q 96:1–5)

Muhammad was bewildered: he could not understand what had happened. It was unlike anything he had ever seen or known. He was in awe, he was afraid. He remained for a time and then left to go home. As he made his way down the hillside he saw again the Angel Gabriel in the sky in glorious majestic form that filled his vision whichever way he looked.

Muhammad returned to his home and to his loving wife Khadíjah and related the amazing story to her. She comforted him, saying that he was the best of men and that God would not allow to be misguided one as honest, kind, loving and trustworthy as he. And so Muhammad fell asleep, reassured. In his dream he received further reassurance, and when he rose the next day he had been transformed from an ordinary mortal into the Messenger of God.

> So verily I call to witness . . . the Night as it dissipates, and the Dawn as it breathes away the darkness, verily this is the word of a most honourable Messenger. (Q 81:15–19)

Thus began the revelation of the Qur'án on the 'Night of Power', and so began a new lesson to the world and a new chapter in the 'Book' of God. The followers of Muhammad were able to read and write and preserve the exalted words of God in their pristine purity and were becoming capable of understanding and evaluating them independently, and thereby to enter into a new mode of religious awareness . . . a higher consciousness, an individual and personal identification with Truth.

This verse – 'Read . . . in the name of thy Lord . . . Who taught the use of the Pen . . .' – is the beginning of the revelation of the Qur'án and the start of Muhammad's mission. Muhammad's wife, Khadíjah, believed in him as did his best friend Abu Bakr, his young cousin 'Alí, an African slave named Bilal and a few others. God commanded Muhammad to declare his mission to his people. So he called a meeting of the people one day, and standing atop a hill, addressed them, asking: 'Oh people! If I were to tell you that there was an army on the other side of this hill, would you believe me?' They replied that surely they would, because he was al-Amín, the Trustworthy. Upon which he announced, 'Know then that I am a messenger from God bearing His Word', and he proclaimed to them verses of revelation.

Too attached to the ways and practices of their fathers, and being the custodians of the holiest pagan shrine, the people rejected Muhammad as a lunatic and a poet. The Word of God did not impress them and so they simply ridiculed him. But when Muhammad persisted in teaching his message they began to persecute him and his followers, with emotional and physical abuse, brutal torture, banishment and murder. They threw dirt at him when he prayed, cast thorns in his path and tortured his first followers. They placed a big, hot boulder on Bilal's chest but even under this torture he kept repeating 'One, one', meaning 'There is only one God!' Bilal was freed by Abu Bakr and he had a wonderful destiny in store for him but others were not so lucky. Many were killed with terrible and devilish methods of torture. Some were torn apart by the force of camels, others were bound and left to starve and die in the desert, while others were executed. Muhammad, his family and supporters were starved and denied contact and trade. Some of Muhammad's friends and followers brought them food and water but when the situation became intolerable they went to the Ka'bah to challenge the edict that proclaimed the banishment of Muhammad and his family. When they sought the proclamation, which was pinned up inside the Ka'bah, they found something very remarkable indeed. White ants had eaten it, all except for the words 'In thy name O God!' The two years of banishment ended on that note.

One night while Muhammad was still in Mecca and enduring these hardships, God took him on a very special journey. This night journey is called the Miraj or the 'Ascension' and is recounted in the Surah al-Isrá' or the 'Night Journey', and the 'Star'.

> Glory to God Who did take His servant for a journey by Night, from the Sacred Mosque to the farthest Mosque whose precincts We did bless – in order that We might show him some of Our signs. (Q 17:1)

The 'Night Journey' was no mere dream or vision, nor was it a literal physical journey, as we understand it. It was a spiritual experience. It was a very special and unique gift from God to Muhammad and his followers that they might know the power of God, begin to ponder the unseen and learn more about the spiritual realm. Muhammad was taken from the Sacred Mosque (Ka'bah) to the Farthest Mosque (Al-Aqsá – Jerusalem, the first Qiblah). Here he led the prayer in front of all the Prophets and then he ascended into the heavens, where he met with the Messengers, saw the glory of Joseph, spoke with Moses and received from God the gift of *ṣaláh*, obligatory prayer. During his journey Muhammad learned the history of man and was shown secrets and mysteries, past and future, and heaven and hell. Then he returned to his body as if mere moments had passed. The Muslims marvelled while the non-believers saw it as further evidence of his madness. Muhammad taught his followers the rules and procedures for cleansing themselves and performing the prayer five times a day facing the Al-Aqsá in Jerusalem.

As conditions grew worse for Muhammad and his followers, a group of men from the not too distant town of Yathrib came to meet Muhammad and invited him to their town, promising him a safe home there if he would come and mediate between the feuding tribes. Yathrib, or Medina, was a town where a form of Abraham's religion was still preserved. It had such a strong Jewish influence that it was almost an island of monotheism in the pagan Arab milieu. It was also where Muhammad's mother was born and where her family lived.

Muhammad decided to leave Mecca for Medina. On the night he planned to make his departure, a group of assassins was sent to his home. But God clouded their vision and allowed Muhammad to escape to Medina. Here he built the first mosque and established Islam and regular prayer. Throughout the remaining years of his life he revealed the verses of Qur'ánic scripture. He and his small group of followers faced many struggles, not the least of which was the opposition of the pagan Arab armies of the Quraysh and their allies, who were intent upon his demise and the destruction of his teaching. He fought and won many battles and sieges in which he and his men were heavily outnumbered and lacking in weapons but not in courage, holy fervour and, of course, the help of God.

Eventually Muhammad overcame his own tribe and

entered peacefully, triumphantly the town of Mecca, forgiving his oppressors and cleansing the Ka'bah of all their idols and symbols. He established it as the centre of the Islamic world, the focal point of his Revelation. He presented the Arab world with a pure monotheistic faith, with rules and clear guidance for a wayward people. He gave them fasting and obligatory prayer as a means of spiritual purification, and the message of Islam, which means submission to the Will of God, as the means of achieving heaven as a spiritual afterlife of peace and joy. He established the means for the protection of the weak and needy and raised women to a significantly higher status than they had previously had.

Muhammad confirmed the missions of the Prophets who had gone before him. Many chapters of the Qur'án are devoted to the Prophets of old, especially Adam, Noah, Abraham, Joseph, Moses and Jesus (as well as Mary, the mother of Jesus), and show great love and respect for them and their teachings which inherently demonstrate the progressive nature of revelation. Muhammad always protected the rights and freedom of the Jews and Christians who lived under his rule, treated all fairly and enjoined his companions and successors to do the same.

After Muhammad's passing at the age of 63, those who had committed to memory the entire revelation, or parts of it, set to work to compile and agree upon his exalted and beautiful utterances. With great care and love, they set out the Qur'án and offered it to all people.

The passion and zeal of Muhammad's followers, their militarized attitude and new-found power, and the instruction of the Prophet led them to advance upon and conquer new territories. In a short time they subdued and unified the entire pagan Arab world into a vigorous and determined empire, which then spread to the south to include Yemen, to the west into Egypt, and into parts of eastern and north Africa. They captured Syria and advanced into Israel, seizing the holy city of Jerusalem, then continued north and west where they met the forces of organized and settled Christianity. They entered the Byzantine, or Eastern Roman, world and eventually captured the heavily fortified and splendid ancient city of Constantinople. They continued east and captured Persia and made incursions into India and central Asia. The conquering Arabs were under the direct guidance of the caliphs, or righteous leaders, who were companions of Muhammad, and they followed his teachings strictly. They ensured that conquered peoples were not oppressed and that the Christians and Jews enjoyed full religious freedom. Soon internal divisions would split the Islamic empire and time would weaken the potency of the Prophet's influence but Muhammad's Revelation would be carried in its pure form, if not its practice and application, to all parts of what is now the Islamic world. They simply continued expanding until the forces of other established peoples and religions were strong enough to resist this incredible wave set in motion by one humble man inspired with the Word of God.

The aftermath of that encounter is still felt today, an unfortunate side-effect of the competitive primitive culture of war. But the expansion of Islam advanced the triumph of monotheism over paganism and the ancient religions. Monotheism, or faith in one divine power, is a rich, living mosaic, like pieces of a puzzle strewn across a fragmented globe. All around the world muezzins (those who call others to prayer) proclaim the sovereignty of God and invite people to be immersed in His presence. As the earth turns, it is always the time for prayer in some part of the world. At any given time, somewhere in the world the call to prayer, or *adhán*, is being chanted in beautiful melody, ringing out from lofty towers, balconies and windows, rooftops and open fields, shacks and colleges, offices and airports, homes and mosques:

> God is the Greatest, I bear witness that there is none worthy of worship beside God and that Muhammad is the

> Messenger of God. Come towards prayer, come towards fulfilment. God is the Greatest. There is none worthy of worship besides God.

It is significant also that the first person to sound this glorious call to prayer was an African slave, Bilal, whom Abu Bakr and Muhammad had freed and made equal, nay rather made to surpass his wicked masters who had tortured him to induce him to renounce his faith. In it is a marvellous symbol of the purpose of revelation and of prayer: Freedom! The Revelation of Muhammad called man towards brotherhood and established firm rules and guidance. Islam means 'submission to the Will of God' and the Muslim greeting '*Salám*' means 'Peace'. The Prophet Muhammad only ever fought in self-defence and was never the aggressor. After his passing the Islamic army advanced as this was their destiny but the religion and the teachings do not condone or advocate violence and warfare. A prayer Muhammad made before the very first battle is 'My Lord if this small band of men should perish what will become of your Faith?' A single man empowered with the Word of God subdued and unified a vast, sprawling collection of primitive barbarous tribes into a civilization of surpassing wealth, dignity and skill in religion, arts and sciences. When the message blossomed and began to bear fruit within this civilization, the popularity of the enlightened Islamic culture ensured the diffusion of the message, directly and indirectly, in its inner essence and outer expressions, into the world, sharing and shaping collective knowledge and ideas.

> O Prophet! Truly we have sent thee as a witness, a bearer of glad tidings, and a warner, and as one who invites to God's Grace, by His leave, and as a lamp spreading Light. (Q 33:45–6)

Islam was spread first by teaching and later by conquest.

The unified Arabs became the mightiest force the world had yet seen and they swept across the land with great speed. They conquered armies far greater than themselves and then established peace for these war-torn nations, bringing advances in science, law and order, spirituality and religious freedom and growth. The Arab army conquered nations by the sword but religious freedom ensured that most of those who embraced Islam did so out of their own free will. None were to be coerced – it was not the way of Muhammad, nor the way of his trusted *Ṣaḥábah* (companions) and caliphs.

> Let there be no compulsion in religion . . . (Q 2:256)

After the Light

Islam released a new mode of religious and community life. With the mosque and its *madrasah* (school) at the centre of community life, every Muslim community had a firm spiritual foundation and fell into a pattern and way of life intimately linked with prayer and the recitation of the Word of God. Alcohol and sexual deviance were eradicated, and fairness and justice prevailed. Pagan superstitions, idols and distractions were removed and a clear, pure, simple, sombre environment was cultivated for worship and prayer. Legal systems were based on the Qur'án and *ḥadí<u>th</u>*. The Islamic culture which took shape under these influences was bright, vibrant and inspired. Reverence and communion with God are sources of infinite inspiration and creativity. The wave of conquest generated a disjointed yet unified Islamic world, transcending race and even nationality. Despite falling into distinctly different religio-political nations, in time the Muslims considered themselves brothers and sisters in Islam. The Arab world absorbed, to a large extent, the Greek, Jewish, Egyptian and Persian worlds, revitalized their ancient wisdom, reworked their concepts and sciences, and introduced to the world new standards of literature, learning, mathematics and exploration, new laws and justice systems, ideas on governance and equality. They diffused this awakened consciousness into the world continuum as Arab culture, language, poetry, navigational technologies, medicine, knowledge and sciences became recognized as a dominant force in the world of learning.

The Muslims were enlightened by the Revelation of Muhammad but it was not really Arab culture that was awakened because the Arabs were a collection of scattered tribes without purpose (and civilization and its consequent accomplishments) which the Revelation of Muhammad unified and to which it gave meaning and purpose. And so their real contribution was brute force and vigorous endurance, a poetic and strong nature and language, and a vitality of awakened consciousness which was to revitalize all the treasuries of old world learning and knowledge of the ancient settled empires. Such was the superior culture and resurgence caused by the Islamic wave and teachings that even nations not directly conquered into the Islamic world were influenced by this revitalized consciousness.

The Muslims' sudden expansion and conquests and thirst for knowledge and new, enlightened standards of equality, freedom and truth led to the sharing of ideas and a melting pot of wisdom ancient and modern. They had quite suddenly unified under their rule the most lucrative trade route in the world, poised between the abundant supply of the East and the insatiable demand of the West. They took the numeral system of the Indians and, realizing its great potential and simple form, extended the range of mathematical expressions and relationships and took it from the sphere of practical mechanical usage to the realm of abstract and applied thought. They took the healing knowledge and medicines of the Chinese, the Indians and the Greeks and developed the beginnings of the modern science of healing. They studied the body and began detailing the anatomy. They were fascinated with the stars and began a rigorous exploration of celestial phenomena. They had an interest in alchemy and from this obscure esoteric science came the beginnings of chemistry. The Arabs valued poetic expression and their language, and its use of lofty and poetic imagery, its romantic and respectful prose, and its yearning detached heart, made its literary works famous and influential. They learned from the ancient Greek philosophers and thinkers, made numerous translations and commentaries, began to apply some of their philosophies and ideas, and began to diffuse these ideas to others. The spiritual forces released had a dramatic influence on the whole world, not just the Arabs. It was a leap forward in human development and civilization.

The Crusades saw a great deal of interaction and exchange between the Christian and Muslim civilizations. Though mostly hostile and violent, there was also an indirect diffusion of knowledge, manuscripts and technologies.

The Prophet did not leave clear instructions as to his successor but his companions knew his wishes. One of the only times that the Prophet performed his obligatory prayer, or *ṣaláh*, behind someone was towards the end of his days when he prayed behind his best friend Abu Bakr. Some took this as a sign that Abu Bakr should succeed him. Abu Bakr was appointed caliph and he began the process of compiling and authenticating the surahs of the Qur'án. He also made military advances in the name of Islam, as directed by the Prophet before his death. After Abu Bakr passed away Ḥaḍrat Omar was appointed caliph and he continued the expansion with great vigour, also taking up the task of overseeing the compilation of the Qur'án. Omar captured Jerusalem and signed the following agreement with the Christians of the fallen city:

> This is the assurance given by a servant of God, the leader of the faithful, Omar ibn Al-Khaṭṭáb, to the people of Ilia [Jerusalem]. This assurance is for their life, property,

> church and cross, for the healthy and the sick and for all their co-religionists. Their churches shall neither be used as residences nor shall they be demolished. No harm shall be done to their churches or their boundaries. There shall be no decrease in their crosses or riches. There shall neither be any compulsion in religion nor shall they be harmed.

Omar was assassinated and 'Uthmán was appointed caliph. With such rapid expansion there were obviously many different powers and forces that came suddenly into the Muslim community or under the banner of their expanding empire. There was external conflict with the forces of Egypt, Rome/Byzantium and Persia and internal conflict among Arab tribes and contending parties. 'Uthmán was assassinated in his home, and in the confusion there was great urgency to elect a successor. 'Alí, the Prophet's cousin, was the natural choice. Despite his reluctance, he took up the position of caliph in a sincere attempt to restore order and peace.

Although 'Alí enjoyed the love and respect of all the *Ṣaḥábah*, his appointment confused many people who were far from Mecca and not informed of things taking place there. Covert forces tried to subvert the unity of the movement. These were, however, political intrigues and had nothing to do with religion. A division arose between those who felt that 'Alí was the rightful caliph and those who believed that other forces were at work behind the scenes. Mu'áwiyah, the nephew of 'Uthmán, challenged 'Alí's caliphate and an internal war broke out that eventually led to the major division in the *ummah* between the Sunni and the Shi'a. Eventually Ḥaḍrat 'Alí was assassinated as well as his son Husayn. His son Hasan yielded to arbitration on the matter of the caliphate and when it was decided that Mu'áwiyah should be made caliph, Hasan submitted to the decision of the arbitrators as the Prophet had foretold. And so the fledgling empire was united very briefly. But there were so many competing powers that it broke up into many groups. Two separate streams of leadership continued, the Sunni and the Shi'a each completely disowning the other in a rift fuelled by so much hatred and bloodshed, and inflamed over the years, that it still persists and flares up even today. The Shi'a are the 'followers' or the 'party' of 'Alí. They believe that the line of Muhammad through his daughter Fatima and cousin 'Alí, and their sons Hasan and Husayn, is the true source of leadership. The Sunni are the Ahl al-Sunnah, the 'People of the Tradition'. The Sunni recognize, in hindsight, the rightful caliphate of 'Alí but they belong to the stream of leadership which broke away from the line of 'Alí because of the struggles and disputes described above. Numerous sub-divisions of the Muslim *ummah* have resulted from competing powers seeking, at times, to establish leadership but at other times seeking to control and usurp the wealth and energy of their people.

Sayyidiná Jábir ibn Samurah narrates that Rasúl Alláh (Muhammad) said: 'This religion will remain steadfast until twelve caliphs have ruled over you.' After that the Prophet spoke softly and the narrator did not hear what he said, so he asked his father, who said, 'All of them will be Quraysh.' People then asked what would happen after this and he said: 'There will be turmoil after that, tribulation and killing.'[1]

This is not a very clear and convincing report and similarly the succession is clouded in uncertainty. But apart from these divisions over power and leadership, many schools of thought and interpretations arose after the Prophet. Some focused on certain aspects of revelation and some on others but none really deviated from the essence of the revelation. Those mystics who were given to pondering deeper meaning and spiritual truth became known as the Sufis. Others followed the teaching of great Imams like the Shafi'ís and the Ḥanifís, and yet others were the followers of the many missionaries, teachers and saints, or 'Awliyá', who taught and travelled to foreign lands to teach the light of Islam and so also gathered a following based on their teaching that seemed to define them as yet another branch of Islam. Some who wanted power corrupted the traditions and produced their own interpretations, creating sects and false beliefs. Some claimed to be Prophets of God but they were liars and frauds, and they misled the people who followed them. And the *ummah* had to cling very firmly to the 'Seal of Prophethood'.

> The Hour will not arrive until almost thirty Dajjál (liars) are sent; each one of them will claim that he is the messenger of God.[2]

The Muslim *ummah* was divided upon itself geographically, politically, socially, and in terms of practice and interpretation. Power had very gradually fallen from being pure and spiritually based in the hands of the companions of Muhammad to being a symbol of temporal power, and leaders became the opposite of what they were meant to be. The *Ṣaḥábah* as caliphs were characterized by remarkable purity of character and simplicity. They took nothing for themselves and served their people, giving all that they had, and remained simple people. They lived and walked and prayed with their people, they had simple names and no titles, they gave more than they took, and they dressed, ate and lived simply and without extravagance. But the later leaders and self-styled caliphs, sultans, kings and shahs were usurpers, using their positions of authority to extract enormous treasures and wealth for themselves. They built fantastic palaces on the taxes they charged their subjects and allowed Islam to be compromised by political and economic needs, just as the Arabs had done with the Revelation of Abraham, just as the Jews had done with the Revelation of Moses. It is the same process each time.

The Jews divided into many different sects and sub-sects. The Christians also divided themselves into numerous sects often in opposition to one another, some locked in perpetual conflict. There have been so many political forces, religious reformers, saints and missionaries that there has never really been a common Christian brotherhood since Christ or perhaps the early Holy Roman Empire. Division is human nature but unity is divine nature. This dismantling into factions and sects is something that has been common to all faiths and overtakes the followers of every Messenger. It is also foretold of the followers of Muhammad:

> Sayyidiná 'Awf ibn Málik reported that God's messenger said: ' . . . By Him in whose hand is my life, my *ummah* will surely divide into seventy-three sects, one of which will go to Paradise and the rest to hell.'[3]

> Sayyidiná 'Abd Alláh ibn Amr reported that God's messenger said: 'God will not take away knowledge just like that, all of a sudden and remove it from people, but He will take away knowledge through death till there is no scholar left. People will make the ignorant their leaders who will issue edicts without learning. They will go astray and lead others on the wrong path.'[4]

> Islam will withdraw from different people as water from the wells.[5]

We have reached that time spoken of by the Prophet Muhammad when he said that division and irreligion will overtake his *ummah* (followers) and the leaders will be those who lead men astray, and that this is a sign of the coming of the Last Day. We are warned against this:

> As for those who divide their religion and break up into sects, thou hast no part in them in the least . . . (Q 6:159)

The following is a list of Islamic sects, schools, groups

and related faiths throughout the world. It is by no means exhaustive or entirely representative of all the sects, faiths and sub-sects that fall under the broad banner of, or are associated with, Islam. Which one is that true community that the Prophet Muhammad foretold?

Sunni Madhabs
Hanafi
Hanbali
Maliki
Shafi'i

Shi'a Sects
Ja'fariyyah
Isma'iliyyah
Zaydiyyah
'Alawiyyah
Dawudi Bohra
Sulaymani Bohra
Aga Khanis (Nizaris)
'Alavi Bohra
Ithna 'Ashari
Qarmatians

Kharijite Sects
'Ibadi
Sufri

Sufi Orders
Bektashiyyah
Qadiriyyah
Naqshbandiyyah
Suhrawardiyyah
Chishtiyyah
Shadhiliyyah
Rifa'iyyah

Other Sects
Ahmadiyyah-Qadiani
Ahmadiyyah-Lahori
Moorish Science
Nation of Islam
Submitters

Kalam Schools
Ash'ari
Maturidi
Murjite
Mu'tazili

Movements/sub-sects
Barelwi
Deobandi
Salafi
Wahhabi
Liberals
Islamism
Tabligh Jamaat
Najadat

Militant Groups
Taliban
Al-Qaeda
Hezbollah

Rejected Sects
Mu'ammariyyah
Khatabiyyah
Mughiriyyah
Janahiyyah
Bayaniyyah
Muqanniyyah
Nusayriyyah
Baqiriyyah
Muhammadiyyah
Musawiyyah
Azraqiyyah

Related Faiths
Yazidi
Druze
Bábí
Bahá'í

This list may be incomplete and may contain inaccuracies but it is not the detail that is relevant here. Rather it is the realization that prophecy has been fulfilled that is important. Numerous sects abound and many false prophets have appeared and been rejected. Many of these sects are in opposition to one another and many believe that theirs is the only true faith. Which one is that true community that the Prophet Muhammad foretold? How are they all connected? Are the differences and dividing lines stronger than the source and that which unites them? What will unite them fully and ultimately as one people? Many questions come to mind but ultimately what unites them are Muhammad and the Qur'án. These two essential dimensions of revelation, the Messenger and the book, had to be preserved and kept pure.

Seal of the Prophets

Muslims believe that Muhammad was the *khátam al-nabíyyín*, the 'Seal of Prophethood' and that no new Prophet shall arise after him. In the *ḥadíth* he is variously referred to as the 'last' of the Prophets or Messengers; however, in the Qur'án there is no such reference. The following Qur'ánic verse is unique in its purport and import:

> Muhammad is not the father of any of your men, but (he is) the Messenger of God, and the Seal (*khátam*) of the Prophets (*nabíyyín*) and God has full knowledge of all things. (Q 33:40)

Just as destiny had ensured that the events preceding the Prophet Muhammad's birth and the way his youth and life played out were all part of the unfolding plan of God, so his later life and progeny were also moved by the hand of the Almighty. It is no coincidence that Muhammad had many daughters but not a single son lived to maturity. This was undoubtedly a sad thing for him but it was necessary to safeguard the purity of the religion he had revealed. It is reported that Muhammad himself testified: 'Had Ibráhím [the Prophet's son who died in infancy] lived he would surely have been a nabí [Prophet].'

> We did send messengers before thee and appointed for them wives and children . . . (Q 13:38)

The revelation and the sanctity of the Qur'án would be affected if someone who was not a *nabí* (Prophet) or a *rasúl* (Messenger) were to be given the same status and eminence as Muhammad. This would lead to unauthorized additions and interpretations and create not just division among the followers but actual distortion of the religion. A clear proof of this is the way that some have raised 'Alí, the cousin of the Prophet Muhammad, to a station equal to or even higher than Muhammad, despite 'Alí never having advanced such claims or shown any sign of divine inspiration.

So it is not a coincidence that immediately after mentioning the name of the person who was the closest Muhammad had to a son – the orphaned boy Zayd, whom Muhammad had adopted – the Qur'án immediately gives a clear indication that Muhammad is the 'Seal of Prophethood' and the father of none. This was done to preserve the purity of the religion because the zeal of the followers and their thirst for guidance and leadership would cause them to raise any man of close connection or spiritual insight to a level that is reserved only for the true Messenger of God. The Qur'án is truth and contains no inconsistencies. So while preventing the rise of false prophets it was also necessary to make known the return of Jesus. Through the 'Seal of Prophethood' the Qur'án accomplishes this simultaneously – but what does it actually mean?

> Anas reported that when Allah's Apostle (may peace be upon him) decided to write to Kisera [the King of Persia], Caesar [Emperor of Rome] and the Negus [the Emperor of Abyssinia], it was said to him that they would not accept

> the letter without a seal over it; so Allah's Messenger (may peace be upon him) got a seal made, the ring of which was made of silver, and there was engraved on it (Muhammad, the Messenger of God).[6]

The Arabic word '*khátam*' literally refers to a ring or signet used, in the old days, to seal a letter. After writing a letter or scroll, the author would pour hot, molten wax onto the envelope or scroll into which he would impress his signet ring as the wax cooled and hardened, leaving a personalized seal. *Khátam* refers to the ring but also to the seal, which is a stamp or emblem, and it also refers to the action or quality of sealing or safely enclosing. Any letter sent is considered pure, valid and authorized only if it is sealed in this way.

This analogy is full of meaning because while it seems to connote finality, it also tells of purpose and purity. It tells us that Muhammad is the ring or ornament upon the hand of prophethood: he is its pride and glory. Muhammad is the emblem and sign of prophethood: he is the Muslims' confirmation and they are his, he bears the universal hallmark, he is the guarantee and assurance. Finally, Muhammad is the seal and encloser: he is the one who preserves and keeps fresh the revelation, pure and free from subtraction and addition and all distortion. These meanings also have the connotation of finality and completeness. A word close to it in written form and spoken sound is '*khatim*', meaning end, final or last of. While this works to enhance the intended allusion to finality, it has been confirmed by the Qur'án and *ḥadíth* that it is to be taken as 'Seal of Prophethood' and not as 'last of the prophets'. This is how Yusuf Ali and Marmaduke Pickthall, among others, translate this very important verse. Those who heard Muhammad use the phrase would naturally understand it as 'last of the prophets' rather than the more complex 'Seal of Prophethood'. And this is how it has been transmitted in some *ḥadíth*. However in the Qur'án the word *khátam* (seal) is used as revealed by God through Muhammad.

The word 'last' is used 29 times in the Qur'án in connection with the Last Day but never in connection with Muhammad, whereas the word 'seal' is used eleven times in connection with 'the hearts' and once referring to Muhammad as in the quotation above.

> God hath set a seal on their hearts and on their hearing . . . (Q 2:7)

> So of the people who did wrong the last remnant was cut off. Praise be to God, Lord of the Worlds!
>
> Say: Have ye imagined, if God should take away your hearing and your sight and SEAL your hearts, Who is the God Who could restore it to you save God? See how We display the revelations unto them! Yet still they turn away. (Q 6:45–6)

These verses contrast 'last' and 'seal' and also aptly explain, both through imagery and the obvious meaning, that if the heart is sealed only God can restore it. The same word *khátam* is used as in the above verse 'Khatamun Nabiyyeen' (Q 33:40). The word seal simply means to enclose or contain or preserve. Only God can open the hearts of the disbelievers, just as when a sealed letter is delivered to its intended recipient, the seal is opened and the contents of the document read and its meaning made known. All the Prophets of the past foretold a future coming. They warned their people to prepare for the next revelation and also for the Last Day. The lesser Prophets (*nabís*) did not share the same station as the Messengers (*rasúls*) but they came to guide and prepare. With Muhammad the whole prophetic cycle that preceded him is wrapped up and sealed. Muhammad made it clear in this way that no Prophet shall arise until the reappearance of Jesus.

A similar meaning is implied when the Prophet Daniel, to whom was given signs of the Last Day, is told:

> But thou, O Daniel, shut up the words, and seal the book, even to the time of the end: many shall run to and fro, and knowledge shall be increased [multiplied]. (Dan. 12:4)

Muhammad can indeed be thought of as the Seal or even the Last of the Prophets in this sense because the process of preparation is completed with him, after which the world awaits the fulfilment of the vision that is the Day of Judgement, associated with the return of Christ. Who is Jesus Christ, Rúḥ Alláh? He is the servant and Messenger of God. In his youth he proclaimed his knowledge. He is the 'Spirit' of God and he is a rightly guided leader. The title of the Prophet Muhammad as 'Seal of the Prophets' – or even if you choose to read it as 'Last of the Prophets' – does not contradict the second coming of Jesus, nor does it place any limitations on him as to how he will guide mankind and bring peace, justice and true religion to the whole world. Surely these things can only be attained through the mercy and guidance of God.

The word 'seal' is used again in the Qur'án:

> Woe on that Day to the deniers, those who deny the Day of Judgement! Only the evil aggressor denies it: when Our revelations are recited to him, he says: 'Ancient Fables!' . . . they will burn in hell . . . The truly good will live in bliss . . . they will be served a sealed [wine]. Its seal perfumed with musk. (Q 83:10–26)

To drink this pure drink it must first be unsealed. Sayyidiná Anas reports a *ḥadíth* in which the Prophet Muhammad describes a parable from the Day of Resurrection. People will go to the Messengers seeking help. They will go to Adam, the father of mankind, and he will say that he is unable to help. Then they will go to Abraham, Khalíl Alláh (Friend of God), to ask him to intercede on their behalf but again they will be disappointed. Next they will go to Músá, Kalím

Alláh (Pen of God), and he will also be unable to assist them. Eventually they will go to Jesus, Rúḥ Alláh (the Spirit of God) and he will instruct them as follows:

> . . . Tell me, if a vessel is sealed can its contents be used without breaking the seal? Muhammad is the Seal of the Prophets . . .

6

THE PERFECTION OF HIS LIGHT

A Drop in the Limitless Ocean

> Does man think that he will be left uncontrolled (without purpose)? (Q 75:36)

Anyone who claims that the light of God's revelation has been permanently extinguished has not fully appreciated the deficiencies of mankind and our complete inability to solve our problems without divine intervention. It is only God who can purify mankind. The stream of His mercy is unfailing and what we have been able to bear thus far is less than a drop in the limitless ocean of His utterance.

> Say: If the ocean were ink (wherewith to write out) the words of my Lord, sooner would the ocean be exhausted than would the words of my Lord, even if we added another ocean like it, for its aid. (Q 18:109)

> And if all the trees on earth were (made into) pens and the ocean were ink, with seven oceans behind it to add to its (supply) yet would not the Words of God be exhausted (in the writing): for God is exalted in power, full of wisdom. (Q 31:27)

'The Spirit is of the Command of my Lord of knowledge it is only a little that is communicated to you, O men!' If it were Our will we could take away that which We have sent thee by inspiration . . . (Q 17:85–6)

In his Qur'án commentary Yusuf Ali explores this theme:

What is the nature of inspiration? Who brings it? . . . Inspiration is one of those high spiritual mysteries which cannot be explained in the terms of our every-day human experience. It is spiritual. The Spirit (Gabriel) does not come of his own will. He comes by the command of God, and reveals what God commands him to reveal. Of the sum-total of true spiritual knowledge what a small part it is that ordinary mortals can understand! They can be only given that which they understand, however dimly. We are not in a position to ask anything that we wish. If we did so, it would only make us look foolish, for the guidance comes from God's Wisdom, not from our worldly knowledge.[1]

Christ, speaking of his return, told his followers:

I have yet many things to say unto you, but ye cannot bear them now. Howbeit when he, the Spirit of truth, is come, he will guide you into all truth: for he shall not speak of himself; but whatsoever he shall hear, that shall he speak: and he will show you things to come. He shall glorify me: for he shall receive of mine, and shall show it unto you. (John 16:12–14)

And the Buddha's words also graphically explain this:

I have revealed to you, as many things as there are leaves on a great tree. But as many things have been revealed to me as there are leaves in a great forest.[2]

Mahatma Gandhi, one of the most distinguished and well-loved humanitarians of our time, stated in his autobiography, *The Story of My Experiments with Truth*:

> The little fleeting glimpses that I have been able to have of Truth can hardly convey an idea of the indescribable lustre of Truth, a million times more intense than that of the sun we daily see with our eyes. In fact what I have caught is only the faintest glimmer of that mighty effulgence.[3]

Johannes Kepler, a key figure in the revolution of astronomy, which placed the sun at the centre of our solar system, wrote in *Mysterium Cosmographicum*:

> We do not ask for what useful purpose the birds do sing, for song is their pleasure since they were created for singing. Similarly, we ought not to ask why the human mind troubles to fathom the secrets of the heavens . . . The diversity of the phenomena of Nature is so great, and the treasures hidden in the heavens so rich, precisely in order that the human mind shall never be lacking in fresh nourishment.[4]

Sir Isaac Newton, perhaps the finest scientific and mathematical mind in history, given his many accomplishments and his laying of the foundations of modern science, astronomy and mathematics, had this to say:

> I do not know what I may appear to the world; but to myself I seem to have been only like a boy playing on the seashore, and diverting myself in now and then finding a smoother pebble or a prettier shell than ordinary, whilst the great ocean of truth lay all undiscovered before me.[5]

Albert Einstein, the most celebrated logical mind of our time, reiterated this sentiment in a number of statements:

> My religion consists of a humble admiration of the illimitable

superior spirit who reveals himself in the slight details we are able to perceive with our frail and feeble mind.

The important thing is not to stop questioning. Curiosity has its own reason for existing. One cannot help but be in awe when he contemplates the mysteries of eternity, of life, of the marvellous structure of reality. It is enough if one tries merely to comprehend a little of this mystery every day. Never lose a holy curiosity.

The most beautiful thing we can experience is the mysterious; It is the source of all true art and science.[6]

This humility seems to be the hallmark and defining quality of the truly great mind and genius. How is it that the greatest of scientific minds were so very humble before the great ocean of truth yet the mainstream modern scientific community, so fixated on sensory empirical data that they have difficulty even deducing the presence of God, can imagine they have solved the mystery of creation? From Socrates, Plato, Aristotle and Pythagoras to Galileo, Kepler, Newton and Einstein, they were one and all enchanted by the wonder of God's creation and humbled themselves before their inability to fathom even the very simplest of His mysteries. But we are changing and growing, we progress together upon this great earth, we progress materially, socially and spiritually, through the love and inspiration of our sustainer. We have the lesser lights or stars who are the great minds, geniuses, luminous souls, and then, far above and exalted beyond all, are the bright rising suns of divine guidance, the Prophets and Messengers of God, whose purpose is as described in the Qur'án:

A similar (favour have ye already received) in that We have sent among you a Messenger of your own, rehearsing to you Our signs, and sanctifying you, and instructing you in

> Scripture and wisdom, and in new Knowledge. (Q 2:151)

These beautiful Qur'ánic verses describe the efforts of the enemies of truth and the education of mankind as the perfection or completion of God's Light:

> Their intention is to extinguish God's Light (by blowing) with their mouths: But God will complete (perfect) His light even though the unbelievers detest it . . . (Q 9:32)

> The Day that God will not permit to be humiliated the Prophet and those who believe with him. Their light will run forward before them and by their right hands, while they say, 'Our Lord! Perfect our light for us, and grant us forgiveness: for Thou hast power over all things.' (Q 66:8)

If we rightly judge the so-called civilization of modern man, we have to acknowledge that we fall far short of our great potential to manifest beauty, love and tranquillity. The barbarism that prevails worldwide makes me hesitate to use the word civilization. We are very far from the perfected Light of God. We are only emerging into our maturity now and becoming more conscious of ourselves as humanity. We have only just attained the revelation of God with clear thinking and so are only beginning to purify our souls. Buddha, Jesus and Muhammad taught us about the brotherhood of all mankind and the oneness of creation but we have not understood these teachings nor put them into practice to bring about real unity and peace. Instead we bring more divisions and wars and suffering.

We are still, as collective humanity, going through the phase of adolescence or the end of childhood: very selfish and self-absorbed, untrusting and competitive, emotional and over-zealous, fiercely independent and alternately defensive and aggressive. Our collective maturity means becoming less self-centred and starting to work towards the well-being and betterment of all, and making sacrifices and taking responsibility. Our world is characterized by people, religions, nations and ideologies in conflict. Everyone is part of the rat race or the dog-eat-dog world, competing for wealth, trying to build up riches and buying over-elaborate houses and cars, while others struggle to put food on the table and educate their children.

We are fully occupied with chasing our own pleasures and desires in everything we do. We are pleasure seekers in the lower carnal sense like animals, but also through our higher capacities we are just running around in circles seeking sense gratification and stimulation. We hunger for entertainment and distraction. There is division within the world on every conceivable level, from the nations to the leaders and groups within a nation, to the communities and neighbourhoods, to the families and finally even within the heart of the individual. Senseless wars occupy the energies and wealth of our nations and peoples. There are such great things that we can achieve if we just turn to God and pattern our lives according to His teaching. To bring unity to the world it is necessary to address every level of human existence to begin the process of the maturity and healing of humanity. In truth, it is an ongoing process, like the education of a young child, which proceeds in stages.

> And the Earth We have spread out . . . and produced therein all kinds of things in due balance . . . and there is not a thing but its sources and treasures inexhaustible are with Us; but We only send down thereof in due and ascertainable measures. (Q 15:18–21)

> Leave Me alone with such as reject this Message: by degrees shall We draw them on, little by little, from directions they perceive not. A long respite will I grant them: Truly powerful is My Plan. (Q 68:44–5)

> We send down, stage by stage, of the Qur'án that which is a healing and a mercy to those who believe: to the unjust it causes nothing but loss after loss. (Q 17:82)

> What is the matter with you that ye are not conscious of God's Majesty? Seeing that it is He that has created you in diverse stages? See ye not how God has created the seven heavens one above another, and made the moon a light in their midst, and made the sun as a glorious lamp? And God has produced you from the earth growing gradually, and in the end He will return you into the earth and raise you forth. (Q 71:13–18)

> Ye shall surely travel from stage to stage. (Q 84:19)

The education of mankind is a long process – we cannot fathom how long but it can best be described as progressive revelation or the evolution of God consciousness, and all of humanity is involved in this awakening to the awesome presence of God, the creator and sustainer of all mankind and all the universe. To change the heart of the world He must change the heart of every one of the billions of people living on this planet, according to each one's measure and capacity. The process of revelation is the same and unchanging, as God says: 'No change wilt thou find in the Way' (Q 17:77; 30:30); and no one there is who can fathom the mysteries of God, not even His chosen Messengers and angels who are but spotless mirrors reflecting His brilliance and love.

The universe is so vast and so magnificent that we ponder and speculate upon the very basis of its material characteristics and we marvel at the great depths and silent majestic treasures scattered all through deepest, farthest space. Yet this is just the outer symbol of God's glory, it is but the outer physical material garment. What of the splendour of truth and the good? What about the spiritual realms, the heavens, which are also God's creation? The billions of creatures and organisms on this earth all co-existing – what of the countless other living beings on countless other worlds? What of the countless luminous beings, the spirits, the Messengers, the angels? How far exalted is God beyond human explanation? God alone knows. Ours is to follow His commandments as He reveals them in every season and to cultivate ourselves, to ponder His greatness, to become virtuous and loving and kind and to engage in the praise, remembrance and worship of the Lord. Ours is to seek inspiration in this life, for to be inspired is to be filled with the spirit of life and love, and to partake of the living waters.

The great purpose of religion has never been to divide mankind but rather to unite it, to guide us with laws and teachings and, most importantly, to inspire us to aspire to virtue and righteousness, to be good and kind, and to love one another. The condition of man without revelation would be very dark and full of suffering. Religion helps us to look beyond ourselves and to progress towards a vision of perfection.

The Light of Revelation Extinguished?

The continuity of revelation is explained quite simply in the Qur'án:

> Any revelation We cause to be superseded or forgotten, We replace with something better or similar. (Q 2:106)

The following verse is quite startling in its implications. The surah Emissaries (Al-Mursalát, or Those Sent Forth) begins with an adjuration implying the progressive nature of revelation and then refers to the Day of Judgement and the destruction of 'future' generations:

> By Those Sent Forth one after another (to man's profit) . . .
> Assuredly, what ye are promised must come to pass . . .

> Then when the stars become dim; When the heaven is cleft asunder; When the mountains are scattered (to the winds) as dust; And when the messengers are (all) appointed a time (to collect) – For what Day are these (Portents) deferred? For the Day of Sorting out. And what will explain to thee what is the Day of Sorting out? Ah woe, that Day, to the Rejecters of Truth! Did We not destroy the men of old (for their evil)? So shall We make later (generations) follow them. (Q 77:1, 7–17)

And the surah finally speaks, quite clearly, of future revelations:

> Woe on that Day (of Sorting Out) to those who denied the Truth! In what revelation (message) after this will they believe? (Q 77:49–50)

When we consider that the fall of wicked nations that reject revelation is always linked with the appearance of a Messenger, we can better understand the events of the Last Day.

> We never punish until We have sent a messenger. (Q 17:15)

In another surah the Qur'án links the Last Day with a Messenger:

> The Day the earth and the mountains will be in violent commotion and the mountains will be as a heap of sand poured out and flowing down. We have sent to you, O men, a Messenger, to be a witness concerning you even as We sent a messenger to Pharaoh. (Q 73:14–15)

In the surah The Heights ('Al-Araf'), God addresses mankind:

> O Children of Adam, when messengers come to you from among yourselves, reciting My revelations to you, for those

> who are conscious of God and live righteously, there will be no fear, nor will they grieve. But those who reject Our revelations and arrogantly scorn them are the people of the fire, and there will they remain. Who is more wrong than the person who invents lies against God or rejects His revelations? . . . The gates of heaven will not be open to those who reject Our revelations. (Q 7:35–40)

These verses clearly speak of the future. They warn the followers of Muhammad that there will be revelations to come in the future, and this is confirmed by the numerous warnings in the Qur'án that there will be no change in the way that God sends His Messengers:

> (This is Our) Way with the messengers We sent before thee: Thou wilt find no change in Our ways. (Q 17:77, 30:30)

These verses also clearly tell us that this is the way of God, past, present and future. That is to say, in previous dispensations, in the Revelation of Muhammad, in the future, at the Last Day and in the dispensation of Rúḥ Alláh, Jesus returned.

During the Night Journey and his ascension to heaven, Muhammad was shown the Sacred Tree of Revelation, the point beyond which there is no passing. This is something very difficult to describe and very few references exist to clarify what it is but I understand it to refer to the divine source and heart of revelation – vast, splendid, glorious and unimaginable.

> By the Star when it goes down . . . Behold the Sidratul-Muntaha [Sacred Tree of Revelation] veiled in that which enshrouds . . . verily he saw one of the greater signs (revelations) of his Lord. (Q 53:1, 16–18)

Muhammad was a mercy and his Revelation was perfect

and complete in itself. His was a universal message for all but its scope was ultimately limited. It was not intended that Moses, Buddha, Jesus or Muhammad would be the one to unite all people of the world under the banner of Islam or true religion. Indeed, Muhammad advised tolerance and forbearance with regard to religious differences and he confirmed that there are many who are veiled and yoked who will not believe. He told the unbelievers:

> Say: O ye that reject Faith! I worship not that which ye worship, nor will ye worship that which I worship. And I will not worship that which ye have been wont to worship. Nor will ye worship that which I worship. To you be your way and to me be mine. (Q 109:1–6)

Sayyidiná Samurah ibn Jundub related:

> Muhammad said: There is a pond for every Prophet. They vie with each other to see which of them has the most number of people coming to their pond and I hope to have the most[7] . . . it is cool, whiter than milk, sweeter than honey, more fragrant than musk, and he who drinks from it will never again feel thirsty but he who turns away from it will never be quenched.[8]

This is clearly a reference to the great houses, ponds or religions – Judaism, Christianity, Islam, Hinduism, Buddhism, Chinese religion, Zoroastrianism and traditional / tribal religion – that will have to share the world stage until the time of the Last Day when Jesus returns to unite all, to bring all into one fold and replace all man-made ideologies with true religion. The great honour of uniting the world's people under the banner of one common faith has been reserved for Jesus Rúḥ Alláh, who will renew the true religion of God and bring lasting peace and felicity to the world, as we will discover in the next chapter. The Qur'án makes very brief references to the return of Christ but we have many authenticated *ḥadíth* confirming and elaborating this theme:

> By Him Who has my life in His hand, surely the son of Maryam (Mary) will descend soon as a just judge . . .[9]

It seems quite obvious that Jesus in his second coming will be a Messenger of God but somehow the matter has become complicated and confused. Most Muslims believe that Jesus will return but that he will not be a Messenger and that the door of revelation is forever shut. In the following *ḥadíth*, reported by al-Nawwás ibn Sam'án, after we learn of the killing of Dajjál (Antichrist) by Ḥaḍrat 'Ísá (Jesus returned) at the gate of Ludd, in the times of the Last Day, we are told:

> At that time God will send Revelation to Isa ibn Maryam (Jesus).[10]

Having established that the imagery of the light in the Qur'án is to be associated with divine revelation, we read conclusively in the Surah of Time (or Man, Al-Dahr) about the light that will shine during the Last Day and also about the time of irreligion or darkness which must precede it:

> Hath there ever come upon man (ever) any period of time in which he was a thing forgotten? . . . But God will deliver them from the evil of that Day, and will shed over them a Light of Beauty and a blissful joy! . . . glorify him a long night through. (Q 76:1, 11, 26)

Blessed are the Meek

The station of the Messenger of God is the highest rank known to mankind. It is not like other designations of humans that can be revoked or changed. A man may change his name or his job, may even change his religion, but there are some things that simply cannot be changed. It is the absolute purity of the soul that makes a man fit to serve his Lord as a Messenger, and to be given the glorious title of Rúḥ Alláh, Spirit of God, is indeed indicative of a very high station. The Messenger is defined by the trust that God has placed in him. In order for him to teach the Word of God he must be pure and show no trace of self or personal desire. He must manifest the attributes of God, which are all that is good. One who is pure in this way is ever a channel for God's grace to mankind. He is spirit and the nature of his spirit is purity and service, it is the essence of mercy and sacrifice. He cannot cease to be who he is. He cannot cease to be the Messenger of God.

> He (Jesus) said: 'I am indeed a servant of God: He hath given me revelation and made me a prophet; And He hath made me Blessed wheresoever I be . . .' (Q 19:30)

Many imagine that Christ will return not as a Messenger of God but as a military leader who will fight many wars and lead the Muslim armies to victory over the entire world. Such thinking is the legacy of the ancient mind set given to perpetual warfare and also flows from the ambiguity of references and personalities in the *ḥadí<u>th</u>* and from the embattled history of Islam. We recognize now that war only leads to more war. There is no such thing as fighting fire with fire. The history of the world is characterized by wars of ever increasing magnitude, death and bloodshed on ever larger scales, and the great killing or '*harj*' mentioned in the *ḥadí<u>th</u>* overshadowing the Last Day. Peace on earth is not to be established through the instrumentality of war. War only ever engenders deeper resentment and fuels retaliations and vengeance. It was because Jesus taught these truths that he was not recognized for who he was.

In Jesus' first mission people were eagerly awaiting his appearance as the Saviour (Christ) but were deluded by their leaders, who held fast to a literal interpretation of the signs and were awaiting the 'King of the Jews'. However, Jesus eschewed the material world. When questioned and ridiculed by the Roman authority, Jesus replied: 'My kingdom is not of this earth.' People who were suffering under the yoke of Roman dominance were hoping for a great warrior to win victories and bring them glory, so despite the exhortation of John the Baptist, despite Christ's love and grace, despite his miracles and healing, despite his fulfilment of literal and metaphorical signs and prophecies, they ridiculed and rejected him because he was a simple and poor man with no earthly symbols of power, who said to his disciples: 'I am not come to destroy, but to fulfil.' (Matt. 5:17)

It is said that in his second coming Jesus will repeal certain laws and traditions, implied by the *ḥadíth* that he will 'break the cross, kill the swine, and abolish the jizyah'. Many people have taken this to mean that he will kill the Jews and Christians but this interpretation is illogical and counterintuitive and has no basis in the Qur'án or *ḥadíth*. The Prophet Muhammad always preached tolerance and acceptance of the people of the Book, including Jews and Christians. He fought wars in self-defence but never condoned the wanton killing of anyone, and he and the caliphs after him always gave religious freedom to the people of the Book. They did not even take property from them, let alone injure or kill them, and it was through this freedom that many embraced Islam. It is absurd to think that Christ would return to kill those who love him most.

Muhammad had to fight many battles to safeguard his growing religion, while Jesus had a very different destiny. Muhammad loved all people and was the essence of kindness and mercy. When he went alone to take his message to the people of Taif they stoned him such that blood streamed from his body and filled his boots but he forgave them and sought no revenge. In fact, he begged God not to destroy them that perchance one person from that town might accept his religion. Eventually the entire town of Taif became Muslim.

God had chosen Muhammad's destiny and ensured his dominion. The spread of Islam was a continuous struggle and battle against the forces of ignorance. The teaching of Christ was meant to spread in a different way. The circumstances surrounding his Revelation were very different and so Jesus never had to fight anyone; his ministry was characterized by meekness and submissiveness. The progress of his religion was through his disciples and their efforts. The Qur'án tells us more about his station and his return:

> And I was a witness over them while I dwelt among them, but when You did take me, You were the watcher over them . . . (Q 5:117)

> . . . and on the Day of Resurrection he will be a witness against them. (Q 4:159)

On the Day of Judgement he will be a 'witness', just as he was before. He will be a Messenger, just as he was before. Jesus was the Prince of Peace and the essence of kindness and mercy, the manifestation of healing, both inwardly and outwardly. One of his well-known teachings is 'whosoever shall smite thee on thy right cheek, turn to him the other also' (Matt. 5:39); that is to say, instead of retaliating, you should offer your other cheek to be struck as well. When a woman was accused of adultery and the people wanted to stone her to death, Jesus said, 'He that is without sin among you, let him first cast a stone at her.' (John 8:7)

Other well-known teachings of Jesus underscore this approach:

> And as ye would that men should do to you, do ye also to them likewise. (Luke 6:31) ('Do unto others as you would have done to you.')

> Thou shalt love thy neighbour as thyself. (Matt. 22:39)

> . . . see that ye love one another with a pure heart fervently . . . (I Peter 1:22)

We read in the Bible that the priest Zacharias prophesied, speaking of John the Baptist and Jesus, saying that they would

> . . . give light to them that sit in darkness and in the shadow of death, to guide our feet into the way of peace. (Luke 1:79)

Despite all the abuse and torture to his blessed person, Jesus never once retaliated or even uttered a harsh word. Rather, he prayed for his tormentors saying, 'Father, forgive them; for they know not what they do.' (Luke 23:34) His love and meekness are legendary and he was the very antithesis of violence and killing. We can discern this from the following saying of Jesus in which he explains how his followers should behave, and in so doing describes his own nature, for he was their exemplar:

> And seeing the multitudes, he went up into a mountain: and when he was set, his disciples came unto him: And he opened his mouth, and taught them, saying, Blessed are the poor in spirit: for theirs is the kingdom of heaven. Blessed are they that mourn: for they shall be comforted. Blessed are the meek: for they shall inherit the earth. Blessed are they which do hunger and thirst after righteousness: for they shall be filled. Blessed are the merciful: for they shall obtain mercy. Blessed are the pure in heart: for they shall see God. Blessed are the peacemakers: for they shall be called the children of God. Blessed are they which are persecuted for righteousness' sake: for theirs is the kingdom of heaven. Blessed are ye, when men shall revile you, and persecute you, and shall say all manner of evil against you falsely, for my sake.

> Rejoice, and be exceeding glad: for great is your reward in heaven: for so persecuted they the prophets which were before you. Ye are the salt of the earth: but if the salt have lost his savour, wherewith shall it be salted? it is thenceforth good for nothing, but to be cast out, and to be trodden under foot of men. Ye are the light of the world. A city that is set on an hill cannot be hid. Neither do men light a candle, and put it under a bushel, but on a candlestick; and it giveth light unto all that are in the house. Let your light so shine before men, that they may see your good works, and glorify your Father which is in heaven. (Matt. 5:1–16)

This is a teaching of kindness, humility and forbearance, but also of courage and boldness. The theme is echoed by the saying of our beloved Prophet Muhammad:

> Ḥárith ibn Wahb reported that Muhammad said: 'Shall I not inform you of the inhabitants of Paradise? They are every meek person who is regarded as helpless – if he swears by God then God will fulfil his oath. Shall I not inform you about the deserving of Hell? He is every stern, arrogant, unfaithful.[11]

There are a few paradoxical spiritual truths such as true wealth in poverty, true movement in stillness, and true power in humility. Meekness, kindness, patience, humility and forgiveness are the qualities of the Messengers of God and the attributes that are praiseworthy in the Books of God. Lasting peace and prosperity will be established upon these foundations.

> Abú Hurayrah narrated that Rasúl Alláh (Muhammad) said that the poor will overtake the rich on the Day of Resurrection by half a Day, which is five hundred years.[12]

This suggests that it will take five hundred years, or half

the Day of Resurrection, to change the world. Looking at the world today we realize that it is not easy to establish peace on earth or to address the vast economic imbalance that holds so many of our brothers and sisters in poverty and suffering. The world is filled with far-reaching divisions, hatred and warfare that are, sadly, on the increase. We have witnessed world wars and atrocities of mass murder in which weapons of mass destruction are hurled at civilians in order to murder the maximum number of people in the most brutal and violent way possible. More war is not the solution. We have the beginnings of a global consciousness, or culture, in the modern modes of communications and transportation, yet we are still so divided among ourselves.

There are superficial differences among people which appear very deep to the materialistic and narrow-minded. These differences include race, religion, gender, language, nationality, class and wealth. In truth we are all spirit souls, created by God equal but different. We are beginning to realize that racial differences are irrelevant, or rather that they add to the diversity of consciousness, like many different flowers in a garden; that all religions are from God and speak the same universal spiritual language of truth and submission; that male and female are complementary natures made by God equal but different; that the world has been such a vast place that people have developed separately their individual languages yet we are able to communicate; and that the earth is continuous and there are no borders except for the ones that exist in our minds and hearts. We are beginning to understand that God has created the earth and all it contains for our advancement and not so that we can pile up and hoard wealth and resources; that God has created diversity in humanity and that some will be leaders and some followers, some will be wealthy and some poor; but He does not like the leaders to misguide their people and the wealthy to withhold their riches from the poor.

Kahlil Gibran explains some of the causes of divisions in humanity:

> Selfishness, my brother, is the cause of blind superiority, and superiority creates clanship, and clanship creates authority which leads to discord and subjugation.
>
> The soul believes in the power of knowledge and justice over dark ignorance; it denies the authority that supplies the swords to defend and strengthen ignorance and oppression – that authority which destroyed Babylon and shook the foundation of Jerusalem and left Rome in ruins. It is that which made people call criminals great men; made writers respect their names; made historians relate the stories of their inhumanity in manner of praise.[13]

We live in a world fascinated by violence and competition. We live in our minds obsessed with our own ego's self-drama and its consequent power struggles. In order to bring abiding peace to the world a fundamental change in the heart of the entire body of humanity and every one of us must be made. Confucius explains this dynamic process:

> Things being investigated, knowledge became complete. Their knowledge being complete, their thoughts were sincere. Their thoughts being sincere, their hearts were then rectified. Their hearts being rectified, their persons were cultivated. Their persons being cultivated, their families were regulated. Their families being regulated, their states were rightly governed. Their states being rightly governed, the whole kingdom was made tranquil and happy.
>
> From the Son of Heaven down to the mass of the people, all must consider the cultivation of the person the root of everything besides.
>
> It cannot be, when the root is neglected, that what should spring from it will be well ordered.[14]

It is our collective ignorance that creates warfare and division. People must be given a more encompassing vision of mankind, one that embraces all as one family and gathers all together, which brings all under the universal canopy of one common faith, the true faith, the eternal faith. Only then will the hearts, minds and spirits of the peoples of the world be aligned and in harmony: we will share a common understanding of reality and earthly purpose and a vision of our destiny and future. Peace on earth has to come about very gradually through negotiation, arbitration, cooperation, love, education, kindness and charity. These will eventually change the attitude of the nations, leaders, governments and the people and lead to unity in diversity, a true global consciousness, economy and culture. Above all, peace requires acceptance, tolerance, love, understanding, compassion and mercy, not violence and more killing and more hatred. Those who cannot see this will never recognize the beauty of God and His Messengers. Without such understanding, we will continue to create our hell on earth and call heaven on earth a dream or an unattainable ideal. To enable us to grasp this vision, Jesus revealed a beautiful prayer:

> Our Father which art in heaven, Hallowed be thy name.
> Thy kingdom come. Thy will be done in earth, as it is in heaven.
> Give us this day our daily bread.
> And forgive us our debts, as we forgive our debtors.
> And lead us not into temptation, but deliver us from evil:
> For thine is the kingdom, and the power, and the glory, for ever. Amen. (Matt. 6:9–13)

These words of Jesus put us in mind of the first surah of the Qur'án, the Surah of the Opening (al-Fátiḥah), which Muslims recite during their prayers.

> In the name of God, the Most Gracious, the Most Merciful
> Praise be to God, the Cherisher and Sustainer of the Worlds
> Most Gracious, Most Merciful, Master of the Day of Judgement
> Thee alone do we worship and thee alone do we ask for help
> Guide us on the straight path,
> The path of those who have earned thy favour
> Not the path of those who earn thy anger,
> Nor of those who go astray, Amen. (Q 1:1-7)

Others call the Kingdom of Heaven on earth the 'Golden Age'. It is something that will take a long time to establish and it will endure, as the term clearly implies, for an age – a very, very long time.

How far we are from our great destiny and the beauty that is locked away inside us! The confused and self-contradictory picture that many people have of the Last Day is due to the accumulation of faulty ideas and interpretations over centuries, people adding things to the simple beautiful promise of Rasúl Alláh (Muhammad) and Rúḥ Alláh (Jesus) that in the fullness of time, when their followers have sunk under the fog of worldly ways and there is great confusion and killing in the world, God will guide and inspire Imam Mahdi to pave the way for the coming of Rúḥ Alláh, the 'return' of Christ, who will guide a small community of followers that will grow in strength and number. 'True religion' will return, as it always does, but this time it will eventually fill the entire earth, as water fills a vessel.

Many people are unable to envision our glorious future of unity, peace and harmony because they resign their intelligence within the primitive, animal tendencies and instincts that engender division and conflict as integral and fundamental aspects of the physical, natural form. But in truth the whole purpose of religion and life on this earth has been to transform ourselves and to gradually realize our higher, or true, nature by subduing and overcoming our lower, false nature. It is a very slow and painful process but eventually we will come to see ourselves and other people very differently, not merely tolerate and co-exist, but rather love with radiant hearts and truly care and show real compassion and kindness. This is the essence of our beliefs and all the rituals and dogmas, superstitions and myths must fade into the background so that we can focus on the important aspects of faith.

We know that God loves us and wants what is best for all His creation, and not just for some people in some places. He wants us to love and worship Him and to bring lasting peace and unity to the world. The people of the world do not realize this at first because this knowledge is so far exalted above them. But this love is so pure that it attracts the hearts of the faithful and overthrows worldly powers and religious authorities. So subtle and gentle is His plan that He is able to preserve the freedom of human thought while introducing the world to higher knowledge.

The return of Christ does not imply the return of the selfsame human body as existed two thousand years ago. Rather it portends a similar unfolding of events and guidance and truth: the return of the same spirit – Rúḥ Alláh – the Spirit of God, the spirit of love, peace and unity. Mankind is learning the utter futility of war and hate. We are ready for a new way. According to prophecy, as we shall see later, Christ will return to the land of his first coming, the Holy Land, that is, the currently disputed territory Palestine/Israel. Fearless and courageous, he was called the Lion of Judah yet he was the essence of humility and meekness and thus known as the Lamb of God. He was the unfailing standard of righteousness for he revealed right from wrong.

> Blessed is the man that walketh not in the counsel of the ungodly . . . the ungodly shall not stand in the judgement, nor sinners in the congregation of the righteous. For the

Lord knoweth the way of the righteous: but the way of the ungodly shall perish. (Ps. 1:1–6)

Say: 'God does not command disgraceful deeds. How can you say about God things that you do not know?' Say: 'My Lord commands righteousness.' (Q 7:29–31)

Blessed are the meek: for they shall inherit the earth . . . Blessed are the peacemakers: for they shall be called the children of God. (Matt. 5:5, 9)

Blessed are the Strangers

The following *ḥadíth* is very significant for our exploration:

> Muhammad said: 'Islam began as a stranger and will return to its state of stranger as it had begun. So blessed are the strangers.'[15]

At first reading this is a very unusual *ḥadíth* but upon further investigation it makes more sense.

What does it mean that Islam will return as a stranger? To truly understand this very potent concept we must appreciate the meaning of 'Islam' and what it means to be a 'Muslim', what 'return' means and what a 'stranger' is in this context.

Who is a Muslim and What is Islam?

The famous musician Cat Stevens, better known after his conversion as Yusuf Islam, explains:

> I did not come into contact with any Muslim before I embraced Islam. I read the Qur'án first and realized no person is perfect. Islam is perfect and if we imitate the conduct of the Holy Prophet . . . we will be successful.

Abu Aaliyah Surkheel Sharif explains this concept further in his introduction to Shaykh 'Abd al-Raḥmán al-Sa'dí's *The Exquisite Pearl*:

> . . . as the servant embodies and internalizes obedience to Allah, and as his spirit is elevated and his ego debased, he is filled with a deep concern for people's welfare and for being in their service; aiding, guiding, counselling, and supplicating for them. It is here, in the absence of the ego, that the effusions of true altruism pour forth from the servant, exemplifying the prophetic concern and conduct.[16]

Appearance and allegiances, names and cultural customs are not the defining qualities of a Muslim. Rather it is actions and behaviour that define a Muslim, a person who has submitted to the Will of God, which is what Islam means. All those who follow God's commandments and who submit to His Will, who recognize His Messenger in his Day, are the followers of the true religion, are the followers of Islam and are Muslims, as consistently confirmed in the Qur'án. The followers of Moses considered themselves Muslims:

> . . . take our souls unto Thee as Muslims (who bow to Thy will). (Q 7:126)

Similarly, the disciples of Christ testified that they were Muslims when they spoke to Jesus:

> They said: 'We have faith, and do thou bear witness that we bow to God as Muslims.' (Q 5:112)

The believers of other previous Revelations have similarly declared:

> Indeed we have been Muslims (bowing to God's will) from before this. (Q 28:53)

The Qur'án also declares:

> It is He (God) Who has named you Muslims, both before and in this (Revelation) . . . (Q 22:78)

Jesus did not name his followers Christians, nor did he label his teaching 'Christianity'. These names come from man and not from God. But the Qur'án calls the followers of Muhammad Muslims, as it does the followers of all the Messengers of God who have believed in him throughout history. The Revelation of Jesus was Islam. While each era requires different laws and rituals in accordance with the changing capacities and qualities of mankind and its societies, the essential and eternal religion is '*Lá iláhá ilá Alláh*' ('There is none worthy of worship besides God'), and through each successive Revelation humanity is brought nearer to truth and closer to God, is made more conscious and is drawn deeper into 'submission' (Islam). Islam is not a static form or concept, it is not a pattern of rituals and limited beliefs and concepts; it is an ever-growing and developing relationship with God. Islam is not a separate religion; it is progressive revelation itself.

> Say: 'We believe in God, and in what He has revealed to us and what was revealed to Abraham, Ismail, Isaac, Jacob, and the tribes and in the Books given to Moses, Jesus, and the Prophets, from their Lord; we make no distinction between one and another among them and we are Muslims (bowed in submission) unto Him (God).' (Q 3:84)

> So set thou thy face truly to the religion being upright, the nature in which God has made mankind: no change (there is) in the work (wrought) by God: that is the True Religion: but most among mankind know not. (Q 30:30)

> O believers, say, We believe in all the prophets of the world

> and make no distinction between them by accepting some and rejecting others. (Q 2:136)

The veils that keep us from the presence of God are many and are subtly and deeply interwoven with the fabric of our being such that they are only gradually lifted. Muhammad said that the Prophets are all true because they reveal truth from one source. The following *ḥadí͟th* confirms this teaching. Sayyidiná Abú Hurayrah reported that God's Messenger said:

> The prophets are brothers (in that they diffuse the light of Shariah from one single lamp). Their mothers are different, but their religion is one. And I am nearest of men to Isa ibn Maryam because there has been no prophet between him and me. He will descend. When you see him do recognize him ... He will invite the people to Islam, and in his times, God will destroy all the *umam* except Islam. And in his times, God will destroy Al-Masih Al-Dajjál. Then there will be peace on earth, and the black (serpent) will graze with the camel, the leopard with the cow and the wolf with the sheep, and the children will play with snakes . . .[17]

This is a very important *ḥadí͟th*. Besides enhancing our understanding of what Islam really is, it also goes on to explain some important prophecies pertaining to the Last Day and the return of Rúḥ Alláh, the Spirit of God, Jesus, who will bring unity and lasting peace. He will destroy the forces of evil and disunity and leave nothing but the true religion of God, which is the eternal religion of monotheism which has always been 'submission to the Will of God'. The analogy of the animals is used to convey a future in which the strong are at peace with the weak, the wicked reconciled with the righteous, the arrogant in harmony with the meek. But a literal interpretation is also possible. Through the instruments and methods of breeding and domestication wild animals have been tamed and even used for entertainment. Similarly, we now know which snakes are harmful and which are not and so children have harmless snakes as pets and are given them to hold at snake parks as an amusement.

So if the Prophets are brothers shining the same light of revelation in great cyclical periods, then it makes sense that the people of the Book (or those who follow the teachings of the true Prophets) should be united in their faith and not divided into different religions and sects:

> And dispute ye not with the people of the Book, except in the best way, unless it be with those who do wrong. But say: 'We believe in the Revelation which has come down to us and in that which came down to you; Our God and your God is One; and it is to Him We submit (in Islam). (Q 29:46)

> O ye messengers! Enjoy all things good and pure, and work righteousness: For I am well acquainted with all that ye do. And verily this Ummah of yours is a single Ummah, and I am your Lord and Cherisher: therefore fear Me and no other. But people have cut off their affair of unity between them, into sects: each party rejoices in that which is with itself. But leave them in their confused ignorance for a time. (Q 23:51–4)

The true religion is that which God establishes in each time and place. God loves all people, in all places, at all times. His guidance is always the truth but because it appears in such diverse conditions, in different languages, it takes shape through the forces of human imagination as distinct religions; but the light of revelation ever flows from one effulgent, brilliant source. What the Qur'án describes as Muslim is quite different from what we imagine the word 'Muslim' to mean in the world today. Similarly Islam, as the true revelation of God, is different from what is called by the name of Islam. Islam is not a name or set of practices and rituals. It is more than an ideal, a goal and a hope. It is the call to humanity to raise its consciousness and standard and enter into a more mature relationship with God. It is an invitation to recognize that all things depend on God and that success in life is a matter of submitting to His Will whether or not we understand it. It is a cyclical repetitive process.

> Do they expect anything but what happened to earlier people? You will never find any change in God's practice, you will never find any deviation there, no turning off wilt thou find in God's Way of dealing. (Q 35:43)

With this deeper understanding of what the Seal of Prophethood means and what Islam is we can better understand Muhammad's closing statement in his final sermon – 'No prophet or apostle shall come after me and no new religion shall be born' – and recognize that it does not preclude the return of Christ. No new Prophet shall arise until the coming of Christ and no new faith shall arise because what Christ will teach is the same eternal message, which is the true religion.

What Does it Mean to Return and How Can Islam be a Stranger?

Hindus await the 'return' of Krishna as the Kalki Avatar; Buddhists await the 'return' of Buddha as Meteyya; Jews await the 'return' of ben Joseph and ben David, or Elijah and Isaiah; Christians and Muslims await the 'return' of Christ (the Saviour); and the whole world collectively awaits the return of revelation. Different interpretations abound concerning 'return'. Some view it in terms of incarnation or reincarnation; some in terms of the physical return of the self-same person; and others as a 'return' of the same essence, love, purity and wisdom, the return of the same spirit with a similar unfolding of events and transformation in the world of man.

The souls of those who depart from the physical realm go to the spiritual realm and leave behind on earth the material vehicle that is the human body. To imply that the physical body can protrude into the spiritual reality is an absurd suggestion, similar to suggesting that when someone who is driving his car reaches his home, instead of climbing out he continues to drive his car into the kitchen, bathroom and shower. Heaven is not another planet in space; it is a more subtle plane of existence. The organic machinery of the physical body enables one to participate in the game, or the drama, or the school, of life. After death the material body returns to the earth and the spirit soul returns to the spiritual reality. A physical body can only exist and have meaning in the physical world.

The Messenger of God is by nature far exalted in every way above the masses of the people. His mind, behaviour and use of language are radically different, and only a few – those who have spiritual susceptibilities – rise to the level of recognizing truth in the being of this person. The rest are either indifferent or actively arise to persecute and injure him. The Messengers come to unite people and they are the essence of kindness and humility. They are the closest to God that we can experience. They come from a place of closeness to God and they call on all people to transcend selfishness, the idea or experience of the separative self and ego. The true Messengers are thus one light and reality. When a Messenger appears it is fair to say that the previous Messenger has returned. Not only do the same qualities and virtues appear but there is a similar unfolding of events. The Messenger is recognized by a few but persecuted by the authorities. He becomes a stranger to his people and culture, since his practices, teachings and ideas are strange to them. The true revelation from God always returns as a stranger or, rather, the true Messenger from God always returns as a stranger. In the Bible the theme of Christ returning as a stranger is portrayed in somewhat different language:

> . . . the day of the Lord will come as a thief in the night . . . (II Peter 3:10)

> And this know, that if the goodman of the house had known what hour the thief would come, he would have watched, and not have suffered his house to be broken through. Be ye therefore ready also: for the Son of man cometh at an hour when ye think not. (Luke 12:39–40)

The thief in the night is a stranger and comes unannounced and the Bible uses this analogy to explain how the Last Day and the return of Christ will be unexpected and strange. A similar meaning to the above biblical verses is conveyed in the Qur'án:

> And (Jesus) shall be a Sign (for the coming of) the Hour (of Judgement): therefore have no doubt about the (Hour), but follow ye me, this is a straight way . . . Do they only wait for the Hour – that it should come on them all of a sudden, while they perceive not? (Q 43:61, 66)

Jesus in his first coming was rejected by the authorities and many of the people in his day, and his disciples had to break away from their people. Prophet Muhammad similarly became a stranger to his own people, just as did almost every other Messenger. When Muhammad declared his mission his people could not comprehend it nor smell the sweet fragrance of the divine words he uttered. He gathered a small following, which grew slowly. He and his followers were reviled and persecuted, in the same way that every Messenger of God – from Noah, to Abraham, to Moses and Jesus – was. The religion they taught was always Islam and it always returned as a strange, new phenomenon. It is the cyclical nature of things. It is how we come to understand that each revelation is a Day, a complete cycle or alternation of light and darkness from one extreme to the other.

It is only a few who are able to recognize the Messenger of God at the dawn of his Day and who follow and help him; but in time everyone, whether they understand or not, is illumined by the Revelation and begins to grow morally and spiritually.

> Neither too soon nor too late, shall a people reach its appointed time. Then sent We Our messengers in succession: every time there came to a people their messenger, they accused him of falsehood: so We made them follow each other: we made them as a tale that is told. So away with a people that will not believe! . . . do they not ponder over the Word of God or has anything new come to them that did not come to their fathers of old? Or do they not recognize their messenger that they deny him? Or do they say: 'He is possessed'? Nay he has brought them the Truth, but most of them hate the Truth. (Q 23:43–44, 68–70)

Ibn Májah, one of the respected compilers and commentators on the *ḥadíth,* offers his interpretation on our opening *ḥadíth*: 'Islam began as a stranger and will return to its state of stranger as it had begun.'

> . . . Another interpretation of the *ḥadíth* has been given by those well-versed in the science of *ḥadíth*. According to this interpretation, Islam at its advent was deemed to be a strange institution as the concepts and practices propounded by Islam were entirely different from those believed and practised by them [pagan Arabs]. Islam thus emerged on the scene as a strange code of life. According to this interpretation, the Islamic ideals will, with the passage of time, be adulterated with anti-Islam ideologies and notions and the tenets of Islam will go to the wall. The overwhelming majority of Muslims will abandon the duties prescribed by Islam; only a negligible minority will observe them. The people will consider Islam's life code to be outdated and

thus impracticable and thus Islam will be reduced again to a strange phenomenon.[18]

Decline of the Muslim *Ummah*

There are many signs pertaining to the Last Day and we shall explore them in greater detail as we go along. We will begin to see that the fulfilment of prophecy is upon us and that the times foretold have come:

> There will come a time for my people when there will remain nothing of the Qur'án except its outward form and nothing of Islam except its name and they will call themselves by this name even though they are the people furthest from it.[19]

In the compilation of his articles and works entitled *First Things First*, Khalid Baig reports a saying of Shaykh al-Hind Mawláná Maḥmúd al-Ḥasan, and explains:

> 'I gave a lot of thought to the causes of the sorry state of the Ummah (followers of Muhammad), during the years of my captivity in Malta,' said Sheikh-ul-Hind Maulana Mahmood-ul-Hasan. It was 1920, and at 69, not only was he one of the most distinguished scholars of his time, he had also spent a lifetime in political struggle. His audience was a gathering of ulama (religious leaders), eager to hear the lessons of a lifetime of study, struggle, and reflection. His conclusion: 'Our problems are caused by two factors: abandoning the Qur'án and our infighting.'[20]
>
> A very large number of our internal battles are the result of narrowly defined self-interests. Islam could have been the force that helped us overcome that. Unfortunately, instead of letting it fulfil that role, today we have made even religion provide us with additional and irresolvable points of

conflict. We fight over petty issues of '*fiqh*'. We fight over fine points of religious interpretation. We turn minor points of religious law into big battlegrounds while the most important and fundamental teachings or religion are violated . . .[21]

The author of an email message I received from the contemporary Islamic forum 'Muslims at Work' tried to answer the question: 'Why are the Muslims suffering?':

The Qur'án mentions:

Corruption has spread in the land and sea due to what the hands of people have earned so that God can make them taste the effect of some of their actions in order that they may refrain. (Q 30:41)

This verse clearly mentions that disasters and calamities occur when the laws of God are broken. We can infer from this that peace and tranquillity will reign when the orders of God are fulfilled. When we look at the world today we see that Muslims as a whole are oppressed and persecuted. Muslims are suffering even in Muslim countries. According to the verse quoted above we need to reflect on this. For how long can we continue to blame our enemies for our problems? Are the enemies forcing us to indulge in sin? As true Muslims we need to search for deeper, internal causes within ourselves.

We have to admit that many Muslims have become westernized. Many Muslims have unfortunately become steeped in sin. How many times have we heard Muslim names in connection with fraud, hijacking syndicates, drug-peddling, theft and murder? In the business world some Muslims are flagrantly violating the commands of God by participating in interest deals, conventional insurance and stolen goods. Our *masájid* [mosques] are empty on normal days but full on Jum'ah [Friday] and Eid [holy day]. The number of pious

> and devout Muslims are few when compared to the majority. If the majority of Muslims do not revert to a life of piety and obedience to God hoping for God's mercy upon the *ummah* [Muslim community] it will continue to remain a deception.

The world today is desperately in need of enlightened virtuous leadership but it is clear from the prevailing conditions of competition, corruption and manipulation that the leaders are following low and corrupt inclinations: 'The Hour will come when leaders are oppressors.'[22] Religious leaders issue edicts and fatwas that contradict not only Islamic law but also morality and common sense. The Muslim nations are in turmoil from Iran and Iraq to Afghanistan and Pakistan to Palestine and its neighbours. More recently, historic revolutions have shocked the globe and rocked the Islamic world from Tunisia to Egypt, Yemen and Bahrain to Libya. The people have arisen in unison to oust long-term dictators with a view to establishing modern democratic governance in their countries. Reminiscent of the European and Asian revolutions that overthrew outdated monarchies, revolution spread like wildfire around the Islamic world.

The 'Arab spring' was sparked by one man, a young seller of vegetables named Muḥammad Bú 'Azízí who was so disempowered and humiliated by the government officials and systems in Tunisia and was reduced to such utter poverty and hopelessness that he poured fuel on his body and set himself alight, burning to death in front of the government buildings. This spark ignited the smouldering discontent of the masses and the winds of change did the rest. Within a short time the dictator Ben Ali was toppled and similar mass uprisings erupted in Egypt and Yemen, and then Bahrain and Libya, leading to many deaths and much destruction as these leaders tried to hold onto power. Hosni Mubarak, president of Egypt for 30 years, was the next to fall. He was captured and is being tried for corruption, abuse of power and the murder of peaceful protestors; and there is also an inquiry into his involvement with the assassination of his predecessor Anwar as-Sadat in 1981. Sadat, the former president of Egypt and Nobel prize winner for his work in the democratization of Egypt and a historic peace treaty negotiation, averred, 'Peace is much more precious than a piece of land . . . let there be no more wars.' He also asserted:

> He who cannot change the very fabric of his thought will never be able to change reality, and will never, therefore, make any progress . . . It is not the strongest of the species that survives, nor the most intelligent that survives. It is the one that is the most adaptable to change.

Harun Yahya, the prolific and dynamic Islamic writer/producer, explores very thoroughly the *ḥadíth* pertaining to the condition of the Muslims during the 'End Times' in his work *Signs of the Last Day*.[23] In his introduction to one of his sub-themes, 'The Rejection of the True Religion and the Moral Values of the Qur'án', he explains that

> We can understand from the *ḥadíths* of the Prophet (SAWS) that the first stage of the End Times is a period that seems to be religious, but one that almost completely rejects God's religion and the moral values of the Qur'án. It is a period in which that which has been clearly indicated in the verses of the Qur'án are overlooked, non-Islamic judgements are given by using the name of God, religion falls into discord, worship is performed for show, and religion is used as a means for profit and gain. It is a characteristic of this time that faith does not depend on knowledge and study but on imitation. In this time, so-called Muslims are in the majority, while real scholars and sincere Muslims are in the minority . . . signs revealed by the Prophet (SAWS) 14 centuries ago, and which are coming true in the age in which we live.[24]

This is a sad realization and it is hard to admit but it is the fulfilment of the prophecy and is unavoidable. The decline of the Muslim *ummah* was foreseen. Its term was fixed and cannot be lengthened. It is a cyclical pattern which prevails in every Revelation.

Signs of the Times

These are some signs of the Last Day, summarized here from authentic and accepted *ḥadíth*:

Knowledge (religious knowledge) will be diminished
Ignorance will be common
Indecency and adultery will be commonplace
Wine and alcohol will be widely consumed
There will be much *harj'* (killing and homicide)
The signs of Islam/true religion will fade
Plague and drought will afflict people
Trials, calamity, famines, hardships and earthquakes will occur
Music and singing girls will be patronized
The most unworthy and worst of men will be leaders/prominent
There will be many oppressive kings
Knowledge of subjects other than religion will be acquired
Trust and justice will be lacking
People will compete in building high-rise apartments
Men will enjoy men and women will enjoy women
Women will assist their husbands in trade
The strong will devour the weak
False prophets will appear
There will be much illusion and trickery
There will be much temptation, perversity and nudity
Islam will survive in name only
The mosques will be decorated and will serve as a platform for worldly speeches
People will compete with each other regarding mosques

People will turn graves into mosques
The birthrate of illegitimate children will increase
Financial interest will be paid and earned by most people
Gambling will be common
Marketplaces will be near each other
Time will seem to pass swiftly
Great distances will be traversed in short spans of time
Literacy will increase
The earth will give up its hidden treasures (gold, diamonds, etc.)
The Arabs will be wealthy and their lands will have green fields (deserts will transform)
A battle will take place between Muslims and Jews

Clearly, many of these signs are now evident. Their fulfilment also correlates well with the prophecies and traditions of other faiths, particularly those concerning the Age of Darkness, Ignorance or Confusion, as it has been variously called. Of course, it can be said that some of these signs also refer to earlier times but the point is that now, together, they can refer to no other time but the present and confirm that the Last Hour is near, or even here. When asked about the Last Hour, the Prophet sometimes admonished the questioner, saying that it was something that he would not live to see (it is yet far away) and that the questioner should focus on the clear and the present; but at other times the Prophet himself warned people and was very much agitated, even moved to tears, saying: Beware!

Harun Yahya, in the conclusion to his work *Signs of the Last Day*, summarizes his exploration of this theme:

> The verses of the Qur'án and the *ḥadíths* examined throughout this book have clearly presented a number of facts regarding the promises of God. The period in which we live is one in which a large part of these signs of the Hour have come to pass. Today's world is witnessing, for the first time

in history, the evident fulfilment of these divine promises, one after the other. Surely these are the most important developments since the time of the Prophet (SAWS). To view these divine signs dismissively, to neglect them or reject them is a great loss. So we can understand that the twenty-first century marks the beginning of a totally new era in world history. God's promises are certainly true. No one can change His promises or prevent their fulfilment.[25]

By returning to the authentic verses of the Qur'án and *ḥadíth* we return to what is originally from God; but by holding onto the limited perceptions and traditions of the self-appointed authorities of our day, from whom the light of knowledge has faded, we allow ourselves to be deflected from true understanding. We shall explore further the symbolic signs of the Last Day in the following chapters but for now we can cite one instance which has a literal as well as symbolic fulfilment in our times:

> O mankind! Fear your Lord! For the convulsion of the Hour of judgement will be a terrible thing. The Day ye shall see it: Every mother giving suck shall forget her suckling babe, and every pregnant female shall drop her load, thou shalt see mankind as in a drunken riot, yet not drunk: but dreadful will be the chastisement of God. (Q 22:1–2)

This tells us of the chaos of those times in metaphors. But it can also be seen to be literally true, as many women will no longer suckle their children and there are many miscarriages and abortions, and much thoughtless, barbaric behaviour.

The following is a collection of authenticated *ḥadíth* pertaining to the conditions of the *ummah* in the end times of the Last Day. These have been confirmed by their fulfilment in our time.

Concerning knowledge and the recitation of the Qur'án:

> There will come a time upon the Ummah when people will recite the Qur'án, but it will not go further than their throats (into their hearts).[26]

> There will come a time when the Qur'án will be read as if singing a song, and when a person is well thought of for reading in that way, even though he is not learned.[27]

> In the final times there will be many people who read the Qur'án and seek their reward from other people.[28]

> Ziyad said: 'Rasúl Alláh, how can knowledge vanish when we are reciting the Qur'án and teaching its recitation to our children and our children will teach its recitation to their children up to the Day of Resurrection?' Thereupon the Prophet (SAWS) said: 'Ziyad, do not many of the Jews and Christians recite the Torah and the Bible but not act according to what is contained in them?'[29]

> There will come a time for my people when there will remain nothing of the Qur'án except its outward form and nothing of Islam except its name and they will call themselves by this name even though they are the people furthest from it.[30]

In the Qur'án it is stated that the Prophet Muhammad will lament on that 'Day' that his people have abandoned the Qur'án:

> O my Lord! Truly my people treated this Qur'án with neglect . . . (Q 25:30)

And regarding the moral condition of the *ummah*:

> A time will come when a man will not care about how he obtains things, whether lawfully or unlawfully.[31]

Wolves will give readings in the End Times. Let those who come to see those times seek shelter from their evil in God. They will be very corrupt people. Hypocrisy will prevail, and nobody will be ashamed of it and its manifestations.[32]

Muhammad (SAWS) said: In the End Times men will come forth who will fraudulently use religion for worldly ends and wear sheepskins in public to display meekness. Their tongues will be sweeter than sugar but their hearts will be the hearts of wolves.[33]

The Hour will come when leaders are oppressors.[34]

In the End Times of the community of the faithful people, those who adorn the mosques but leave their own hearts in ruins, who fail to look after their religion as much as they do their clothes, who forsake their religious obligations for the sake of their activities in this world, will increase in number.

The Last Hour will not be established until there will remain those people who will neither be aware of the virtues nor prevent the vices.

A time will come upon people when they will use the masjid as a meeting place.

Anas reported the Prophet (may peace be upon him) as saying: The Last Hour will not come until people vie with one another about mosques.[35]

No doubt a time will come when no one will withhold himself from receiving interest [on money]. Even if a person does not benefit directly from interest, he will not escape its effects, which will inevitably reach him.[36]

> A time will come when the rich go on pilgrimage for purposes of travel, the comfortably-off for business, the worldly-wise for boasting and to show off, and the poor to beg.

The following *ḥadíth* elaborates on the theme of the decline of the Muslim *ummah*. Abú Idrís Khawlání reports that he heard Sayyidiná Hudhayfah ibn al-Yamán narrate:

> People used to ask Rasúl Alláh (the Messenger of God) about good, but I asked him about evil, being apprehensive that I might become involved in it. I asked him, 'O Rasúl Alláh, we lived in Jáhiliyyah (the dark time of ignorance and confusion before the Prophet's revelation) and evil till God brought to us this good (Islam). Will this good be followed by evil?'
>
> He said, 'Yes!'
>
> I asked, 'Will there be good after the evil?'
>
> He said, 'Yes! Yes, but it will be smoky (lacking sincerity).'
>
> I asked, 'How will it be smoky?'
>
> He said, 'Some people will lead others to ways other than my guidance. You will recognize something to approve and something to reject.'
>
> I asked, 'Will that good be followed by evil?'
>
> He said, 'Yes, those standing at the gates of hell will invite others to them and when they respond to them they will cast them into it.'
>
> I requested him to describe them to us. He said, 'They will belong to us and speak our language.'
>
> I asked him, 'What is your command for me should it happen in my life time?'
>
> He said, 'Stick to the true community of Muslims and their Imam (leader).'[37]

In his work entitled *Smaller Signs of the Day*, Muhammad bin Bayyumi writes:

> The Prophet's companions were trustworthy; fewer people from the next generation were trustworthy, and fewer still from the generation that followed, and so the situation has declined until our time, when very few trustworthy people can be found. And, no doubt, some of the future generations will be worse off than us in this regard. The messenger of God informed us about this progressive degeneration.[38]

> When trust will be lost then wait for the Hour.[39]

> When the affair will be entrusted to those who do not deserve it then wait for the Hour.[40]

> Abdullah narrated: The Prophet said, 'Just before the hour there will be days in which knowledge will disappear and ignorance will appear, and there will be much killing.'[41]

> Sayyidiná 'Abd Alláh ibn Amr narrated: God's messenger said, 'The Last Hour will not come till God takes away His Shariah [Law] from the earthlings. So, only the worst of people and disobedient will remain there. They will not know piety, nor will they reject evil.'[42]

These signs are upon us and only our pride prevents us from realizing the sad state of the Muslim *ummah*. The leaders of our communities compete to put up richly-decorated and elaborate mosques on every second street, mosques which usually attract only a single row of worshippers for all prayers except Jum'ah (Friday) prayer. Many of our youth are taught to read the sounds of Arabic without any meaning or understanding. Many of the Ḥáfiẓes are taught to memorize the entire Qur'án as a long collection of sounds which they do not know the meaning of, let alone understand and receive guidance, assurance and tranquillity from; and then they recite it in melodic tones to the delight of many listeners who take no interest in the meaning and understanding of the verses. We speak to God and we do not know what we are saying! Many people think that the rigid application of Arab custom equals piety. Unless one invests himself with sincerity and devotion and the power of his mind and heart in his prayer, then going to the mosque five times a day is just a custom, a habit or a form of exercise, and the mosque becomes a place for the men of a community to socialize and discuss worldly matters. Sometimes more effort is put into looking like the Prophet in clothing and cut of beard than in actually behaving like him in virtue and high moral standards.

Many Muslim youth of my community are becoming increasingly distanced not only from Arab custom but also from Islamic culture and teachings. They are being alienated by the primitive attitude of the leaders of so-called Islamic institutions and are becoming immersed in decadent, irreligious, western pop-culture and the idols of the 'West', that is, the modern way. This involves entertainment and the seeking of every pleasure, including promiscuity and adultery, consuming alcohol and abusing drugs and becoming lost in the wilderness of worldly things. They are far away from the light of divine guidance. The condition of the Muslim *ummah* and the confusion around the matter of the Last Day are themselves signs of the Last Day and demonstrate that the 'stars' have indeed fallen and lost their lustre.

> The Prophet said, Surely you will follow the ways of those nations who were before you.[43]

> Rasúl Alláh [Muhammad] said, Before the Last Hour there will be commotions like pieces of a dark night.[44]

Significantly, Muhammad said that:

> The signs are like beads arranged in a thread. When the thread snaps, they follow one after another.[45]

This is a weighty statement. If the conditions mentioned and the signs foretold are already upon us, then what about the other signs and events? Are we living in the Last Hour, are we at the dawn of the Last Day? Is the appearance of Mahdi and Christ imminent or has it perhaps already happened? Is it possible that we are living in the Day of Judgement and Resurrection?

7

THE DAY OF SORTING

The Day of Resurrection

> The blind and the seeing are not alike, nor are the depths of darkness and the Light; nor are the (chilly) shade and the (genial) heat of the sun: nor are alike those that are living and those that are dead. God can make any as He wills to hear; but thou canst not make those to hear who are (buried) in graves. (Q 35:19–22)

Belief in the Last Day is a very important aspect of faith. The people of the Book are also considered to be believers in God and the Last Day and thus belief in it is a universal aspect of faith. It does not form a part of the *Shahádah* or 'Bearing Witness' but it is repeatedly mentioned in the Qur'án that the Muslims are those who believe in God and His Messenger and the Last Day. In fact, every day Muslims all around the world in their *ṣaláh* repeat the title of God as in the first two verses of the Qur'án:

> All Praise is due to God, Sustainer, Cherisher of the Worlds, Master of the Day of Judgement. (Q 1:1–3)

Numerous references are made to the Last Day in the Qur'án and *ḥadíth* and it is a firmly established belief that is shared with people of all other faiths as well. This is because the Last Day is the common destiny of all humankind and all the Prophets told their people about it. Because Muhammad is the 'Seal of the Prophets' and because his mission and the Last Day are closely connected – the one follows on the heels of the other – his Revelation contains a more complete description and meaning of these events than do earlier scriptures. There is a great wealth of information concerning the Last Day but before we explore it, let us try to understand more completely the purport of its many names so that we may unravel the true meaning.

The Last Day has many names: the Day of Reckoning, the Day of Sorting, the Day of Gathering or Assembly, the Day of Recompense, the Day of Resurrection, the True Day, the Day of Reality, the Day of Clamour, the Day of Distress, the Day of Decision, and the Overwhelming Event, among others.

A vision of the Prophet Ezekiel recorded in the Hebrew Bible, a parable, illustrates very vividly the imagery of the resurrection and puts the literal against the metaphoric meaning:

> The hand of the Lord was upon me, and carried me out in the spirit of the Lord, and set me down in the midst of the valley which was full of bones, and caused me to pass by them round about: and, behold, there were very many in the open valley; and, lo, they were very dry. And he said unto me, Son of man, can these bones live? And I answered, O Lord God, thou knowest. Again he said unto me, Prophesy upon these bones, and say unto them, O ye dry bones, hear the word of the Lord. Thus saith the Lord God unto these bones; Behold, I will cause breath to enter into you, and ye shall live . . . So I prophesied as I was commanded: and as I prophesied, there was a noise, and behold a shaking, and the bones came together, bone to his bone. And when I beheld, lo, the sinews and the flesh came up upon them, and the skin covered them above: but there was no breath in them. Then said he unto me, Prophesy unto the wind,

> prophesy, Son of man, and say to the wind, Thus saith the Lord God; Come from the four winds, O breath, and breathe upon these slain, that they may live. So I prophesied as he commanded me, and the breath came into them, and they lived, and stood up upon their feet, an exceeding great army. Then he said unto me, Son of man, these bones are the whole house of Israel: behold, they say, Our bones are dried, and our hope is lost: we are cut off for our parts . . . And ye shall know that I am the Lord, when I have opened your graves, O my people, and brought you up out of your graves, And shall put my spirit in you, and ye shall live . . . (Ezek. 37:1–14)

Here we are given a graphic description of bringing back to life the bones of the dead, but in the end we are told that the account is a parable and that the dead represent the fallen people of the Jews who have lost hope and faith. Ezekiel says that the people who speak thus and are very much alive in the physical sense will be brought out of their graves, for unbelief equals spiritual death, and this is the true meaning of the resurrection. The Spirit of Life and breath are likened to Rúḥ Alláh (Spirit of God), Jesus, the Holy Spirit and Revelation. If we take the resurrection literally we might imagine that on that day people will dig their way out from six feet below the earth and stand again as they did before they died; that after having been reduced to dust and bones and their spirits withdrawn from their bodies and the earth, they will return from the graves. If we apply ourselves to unravelling the intended symbolic meaning then we will come to know the true import of the resurrection. In a beautiful passage which recounts the simple signs of God we learn that:

> It is God who causeth the seed-grain and the date-stone to split and sprout. He causeth the living to issue from the dead. And He is the one to cause the dead to issue from the living. That is God: then how are ye deluded away

> from the truth? He it is that cleaveth the day-break (from the dark): He makes the night for rest and tranquillity, and the sun and moon for the reckoning (of time): Such is the judgement and ordering of (Him), the Exalted in Power, the Omniscient. (Q 6:95–6)

The date is in itself a marvellous sign of God. It is the fruit of the desert tree, which grows in perhaps the harshest earthly condition, where there are very few nutrients in the soil, precious little water and the sun is scorching. Although there are many types of fruit, the date is unique in its taste and texture. Its outer skin is a thin membrane that preserves the inner contents fresh and moist for months and even years, but is itself very fragile and easily broken through with the teeth. Its flesh is sweet and nutritious and goes a long way. It is a great blessing, especially in the desert.

The date stone is perhaps the toughest seed, hard as stone – hence the name – preserving the potential of life and countless fruits and unlimited providence within its solid lifeless shell. When the time is right the stone breaks open and life grows from it, drawing water from the earth, air from the sky and energy from the sun. Similar to how the living issues from the lifeless is how the dawn breaks forth from the dark. The following brief extract from the works of Kahlil Gibran in an essay titled 'Resurrection' helps to put this theme into perspective:

> Beloved, was not my soul yesterday like unto the tribes of Israel? Did I not wait in the silence of the night for the coming of my Saviour to deliver me from the bondage and evils of time? Did I not feel the great thirst and the spirit's hunger as did those nations of the past? Did I not walk the road of life like a child lost in some wilderness, and was not my life like a seed cast upon a stone, that no bird would seek, nor the elements split and bring to life?[1]

This lamentation recalls the parable of the sower through which Jesus instructed his people and disciples on the subjects of understanding, belief and growth. The parable is linked with the Last Day, the resurrection. The parable of the sower tells of a man who went out to the land scattering seeds:

> . . . And when he sowed, some seeds fell by the way side, and the fowls came and devoured them up: Some fell upon stony places, where they had not much earth: and forthwith they sprung up, because they had no deepness of earth: And when the sun was up, they were scorched; and because they had no root, they withered away. And some fell among thorns; and the thorns sprung up, and choked them: But other fell into good ground, and brought forth fruit . . . (Matt. 13:4–8)

It was said of Jesus that he was that sower and that he gave life to the dead, in both the literal and symbolic senses. The following verses explain the symbolism:

> But now we are delivered from the law, that being dead wherein we were held; that we should serve in newness of spirit, and not in the oldness of the letter. (Rom. 7:6)

> But God, who is rich in mercy, for his great love wherewith he loved us, Even when we were dead in sins, hath quickened us together with Christ, (by grace ye are saved;) And hath raised us up together, and made us sit together in heavenly places . . . (Eph. 2:4–6)

> In him was life; and the life was the light of men. (John 1:4)

And this verse from the Qur'án echoes this tradition and belief of the Christian peoples:

> Then will God say: 'O Jesus the son of Mary! Recount My favour to thee and to thy mother. Behold! I strengthened thee with the Holy Spirit . . . And behold thou bringest forth the dead by My leave . . . (Q 5:110)

In the Qur'án we are told:

> O Mankind! If ye have a doubt about the Resurrection . . . thou seest the earth barren and lifeless, but We pour down rain on it, it is stirred (to life), it swells, and it puts forth every kind of beautiful growth (in pairs). This is so because God is the reality; it is He Who gives life to the dead and it is He Who has power over all things. (Q 22:5–6)

The resurrection is repeatedly likened to an outpouring of life-giving waters that bring new life from the barren earth:

> It is God Who sends forth the winds, so that they raise up the clouds, and we drive them to a land that is dead, and revive the earth therewith after its death: even so will be the Resurrection! (Q 35:9)

> It is He Who sendeth the winds like heralds of glad tidings, going before His Mercy: when they have carried the heavy-laden clouds. We drive them to a land that is dead, make rain to descend thereon, and produce every kind of harvest therewith: thus shall We raise up the dead: Perchance ye may remember. (Q 7:57)

> . . . and prove me now herewith, saith the Lord of hosts, if I will not open you the windows of heaven, and pour you out a blessing, that there shall not be room enough to receive it. (Mal. 3:10)

Taken literally we would imagine that the resurrection implies that the dead will rise up out of their graves and live again. But the descriptions given in the Qur'án use this analogy to convey a theme of the renewal of humankind. That is to say, just as the rain falls to the dry earth and renews the slumbering potential of life, so the shower of divine bounties, revelation and inspiration brings new life to those who are as dead, spiritually dead, and causes them to live again. And so the Resurrection Day means the renewal of the religious and spiritual life of man, as the following verses clearly state:

> Whoever works righteousness, man or woman, and has faith, verily, to him will We give a new life, a life that is good and pure, and We will bestow on such their reward according to the best of their actions. (Q 16:97)

> Can he who was dead, to whom we gave life, and a light whereby he may walk amongst men be like him who is in the depths of darkness? (Q 6:122)

Life equals light equals righteousness. Resurrection equals revelation equals the return of Christ. This makes a lot more sense than the idea that all the people who have lived and died on this earth will spend many, many years in a grave locked within the frame of a rotting corpse and then one day rise up out of their graves and stand around waiting to be judged. This notion is the result of literal interpretations by materially minded men who have difficulty understanding spiritual reality and symbolism. The spiritual afterlife transcends matter and space and time. The soul at physical death relinquishes the body and ascends to its personal judgement.

What then is this symbolic death in which people are physically alive?

> For they that are after the flesh do mind the things of the flesh; but they that are after the Spirit the things of the

> Spirit. For to be carnally minded is death; but to be spiritually minded is life and peace. (Rom. 8:5–6)

Thus we can be physically living in the world but be spiritually dead if we are devoted to all our selfish desires and the things of the world and not to God and goodness, if we live only for ourselves, chasing wealth and pleasure, without faith, love and peace. Albert Einstein eloquently explains this:

> The finest emotion of which we are capable is the mystic emotion. Herein lies the germ of all art and all true science. Anyone to whom this feeling is alien, who is no longer capable of wonderment and lives in a state of fear, is a dead man. To know that what is impenetrable for us really exists and manifests itself as the highest wisdom and the most radiant beauty, whose gross forms alone are intelligible to our poor faculties – this knowledge, this feeling . . . that is the core of the true religious sentiment.

We can see very clearly from the following verses how belief is equivalent to life and unbelief to death:

> Then behold O man! The tokens of God's mercy! How he gives life to the earth after its death: verily the same will give life to the men who are dead: for He has power over all things . . . So verily thou canst not make the dead to hear, nor canst thou make the deaf to hear the Call, when they show their backs and turn away. Nor canst thou lead back the blind from their straying: only those wilt thou make to hear, who believe in Our Signs and submit (their wills unto God) . . . and this is the Day of Resurrection but ye, ye did not know! . . . Verily we have propounded for men, in this Qur'án every kind of parable, but if you bring to them any sign, the unbelievers are sure to say, 'Ye do nothing but talk vanities.' Thus does God seal up the hearts of those who understand not. (Q 30:50–8)

> And coin for them the similitude of the life of the world as water which We send down from the sky, and the vegetation of the earth mingleth with it and then becometh dry twigs that the winds scatter . . . the good deeds which endure are better in thy Lord's sight for reward, and better in respect of hope. And (bethink you of) the Day when we remove the hills and ye see the earth emerging, and We gather them together so as to leave not one of them behind. And they are set before thy Lord in ranks (and it is said unto them): Now verily have ye come unto Us as We created you at the first. But ye thought that We had set no tryst for you. (Q 18:45–8)

> . . . a gathering together, quite easy for Us. (Q 50:44)

The Day of Gathering

The Last Day is so frequently and consistently described as a great gathering that this subject warrants deeper exploration.

> Say: 'It is He who has created you and made for you the faculties of hearing, seeing, and understanding: Little thanks it is ye give.' Say: 'It is He who has multiplied you through the earth, and to Him shall ye be gathered together.' They ask: 'When will this promise be fulfilled?' Say: 'As to the knowledge of the time, it is with God alone: I am a plain warner.' At length when they see it close at hand, grieved will be the faces of the unbelievers, and it will be said to them: 'This is the promise fulfilled, which you were calling for!' (Q 67:23–7)

When we die our souls pass beyond the mortal veil and our corpse is left behind to rot in the ground. The quality that we call life is removed from the human frame and it journeys to a realm very different. This theme of the gathering ties in with the theme of the resurrection and judgement and should be thought of as the same process, for the purpose of the gathering is to pass judgement and the purpose of the judgement is to resurrect to life. In the next section we explore the judgement in more detail but here point out that there are two types of judgement. The one is personal and the other affects the whole of humanity.

Regarding the personal individual judgement that every soul must experience, the Qur'án tells us:

> And your creation or your resurrection is in no wise but as an individual soul: For God is He Who hears and sees (all things). Seest thou not that God merges Night into Day and he merges Day into Night . . . (Q 31:28–9)

In a compilation entitled *The Signs Before the Day of Judgement* Ibn Kathír explains that:

> Some *ḥadíth* report that the Prophet (SAWS) was asked about the 'Hour'. He looked towards a young boy and said: 'If he lives he will not grow very old before he sees your last hour coming to you.' By this he meant their death and entering the hereafter, because everyone who dies enters the hereafter; some people say that when a person has died his judgement has begun. This *ḥadíth* with this meaning is *ṣaḥíḥ* [correct].

Several *ḥadíth* and Qur'ánic verses reiterate this point of the personal or individual judgement.

> Say: 'The death which ye flee will truly overtake you: then will ye be sent back to the Knower of things secret and open: and He will tell you the things ye did!' (Q 62:8)

After the death of the body, the soul ascends and returns to its Creator to be judged as an individual soul. Everyone will experience the hereafter, or the Spiritual Reality, when their body dies. It is a place very different from this reality. In fact we cannot even call it a place, for time and space are contingent terms dependent on materially-orientated perception, while the Spiritual Reality is a formless realm of being and knowing. When you die you leave your body behind but your soul continues and retains its essential and enduring qualities of consciousness, will, thought and intuition. If we do good deeds in our earthly lives and we recognize God and hold fast to His command, His presence and His love, then when we enter into the afterlife we will have no fear and we will abide forever in the garden of God's glory, the placeless heaven of His beauty.

The second type of judgement is that which affects the whole of humanity collectively. The Qur'án refers often to the day when we shall all be gathered together:

> One Day We shall remove the mountains, and thou wilt see the earth as a level stretch, and We shall gather them, all together, nor shall We leave out any one of them . . . They will find all that they did, placed before them: and not one will thy Lord treat with injustice. (Q 18:47–9)

> . . . He will gather you unto the resurrection day, there is no doubt therein; but most men do not know. God's is the kingdom of the heavens and the earth, and on the day when the Hour shall arise, on that day shall those who call it vain be losers! And thou shalt see each nation kneeling, each nation summoned to its book. Today are ye rewarded for that which ye have done. (Q 45:26–8)

It is clear, then, that we will be called to account individually but also as peoples, nations and humanity as a whole. This is the grand judgement of the Last Day, when all mankind will be judged. Yet we are informed that:

> He does take account of them (all), and hath numbered

> them (all) exactly. And every one of them will come to Him singly on the Day of Judgement. (Q 19:94–5)

> So make no haste against them, for We but count out to them a (limited) number (of days). That Day We shall gather the righteous to (God) Most Gracious, like a band (presented before a king for honours) . . . (Q 19:84–5)

We have understood the resurrection to mean the renewal of true religion through revelation and it is in this light that we can put the above verses into context. In the same way that every Messenger was recognized by individuals, one at a time, who gathered together to follow the teaching, so in the Last Day will the gathering of the righteous take place. So also it is necessary for there to be a dividing line between those who believe and those who do not:

> Those who disbelieved among the people of the scripture and idolaters could not have left off erring till the clear proof came unto them. A messenger from God, reading purified pages, containing correct scripture. Nor were the people of the scripture divided until after the clear proof came to them. (Q 98:1–4)

> But set thou thy face to the right religion, before there come from God the Day which there is no averting: On that Day shall men be divided in two. Those who reject faith will suffer from that rejection and those who work righteousness will make provisions for themselves in heaven . . . (Q 30:43–4)

After the parable of the sower Jesus recounted the parable of the field in which the sower sowed good seeds but a wicked person came and sowed tares (weeds) among them. When the seeds grew the servants asked if they should pull up the tares but the sower said 'no' in case they pulled up the wheat as well:

> Let both grow together until the harvest: and in the time of harvest I will say to the reapers, Gather ye together first the tares, and bind them in bundles to burn them: but gather the wheat into my barn . . . As therefore the tares are gathered and burned in the fire; so shall it be in the end of this world . . . Then shall the righteous shine forth as the sun in the kingdom of their Father. (Matt. 13:30–43)

> Say, 'It is He who sowed you in the earth, and unto Him shall ye be gathered!' (Q 67:24)

Jesus explains the Kingdom of Heaven (the Last Day). This passage weaves together the themes of resurrection, gathering and judgement with simple yet exquisite metaphors that help us to understand the meaning of the signs:

> The kingdom of heaven is like to a grain of mustard seed, which a man took, and sowed in his field: Which indeed is the least of all seeds: but when it is grown, it is the greatest among herbs, and becometh a tree, so that the birds of the air come and lodge in the branches thereof . . . The kingdom of heaven is like unto leaven, which a woman took, and hid in three measures of meal, till the whole was leavened.
>
> . . . the kingdom of heaven is like unto treasure hid in a field; the which when a man hath found, he hideth, and for joy thereof goeth and selleth all that he hath, and buyeth that field. Again, the kingdom of heaven is like unto a merchant man, seeking goodly pearls: Who, when he had found one pearl of great price, went and sold all that he had, and bought it. Again, the kingdom of heaven is like unto a net, that was cast into the sea, and gathered of every kind: Which, when it was full, they drew to shore, and sat down, and gathered the good into vessels, but cast the bad away.
>
> So shall it be at the end of the world . . . (Matt. 13:31-3, 44-9)

The Day of Gathering now makes more sense. The revelation is the dividing line which sorts the believers from the non-believers (the wheat from the tares, the good fish from the bad). The following verses from the Holy Qur'án confirm this:

> (A voice will say,) 'This is the Day of Sorting Out, whose truth ye (once) denied!' (Q 37:21)

> Say: 'Our Lord will gather us together: then will He judge between us in justice; for He is the Judge, the Knowing!' (Q 34:26)

The Day of Judgement and the Cosmic Signs

> We create man in the finest state then reduce him to the lowest of the low, except those who believe and do good deeds; they will have an unfailing reward. After this what makes you (man) deny the Judgement (to come)? Is God not the most decisive of Judges? (Q 95:4–8)

The 'Doomsday'–Last Day–Apocalypse scenario that has captured the imagination of many generations holds that the world will come to a sudden, abrupt end in a violent catastrophe that causes the destruction of the universe. This view arises from a literal interpretation of the symbols and signs of the prophecies. It has been established that there will be no true believers but for the community led by the Mahdi and then Jesus. However, the pop-prophecy belief of many is that they will wage a great war that subjugates the world and kills off Jews and Christians; then suddenly there will be peace and plenty in the world; and then again suddenly there are no Muslims left and then suddenly the world comes to an end and everyone is brought back to life from their graves and then judged on a grand platform together and sent either to Heaven or to Hell for all eternity for the actions of a single simple lifetime lived unconsciously and in ignorance and confusion.

None of this makes sense!

This is not the 'way' of God. We were warned in the Qur'án that we will find no change in His way. How did the confusion come about? It comes from a few things: alterations and additions and not adhering to the Qur'án and the true authentic *ḥadí<u>th</u>*; not appreciating the allegory and symbolism of scripture; and unworthy people seeking to explain things they do not understand and then imposing this interpretation on others. So what then do these cosmic catastrophic signs or metaphors imply if not the destruction of the physical world? We discover from the Qur'án, *ḥadí<u>th</u>* and the Bible that the last hour will be hard to perceive.

> Do they only wait for the Hour – that it should come on them all of a sudden, while they perceive not? (Q 43:66)

> But the day of the Lord will come as a thief in the night; in which the heavens shall pass away with a great noise, and the elements shall melt with fervent heat, the earth also and the works that are therein shall be burned up. (II Pet. 3:10)

A thief in the night is quiet and unknown, imperceptible, yet there will be great chaos and noise and upheaval. How can we account for such a scripture? How can the frightful, terrible signs of the Last Day go unnoticed? How can we not perceive the destruction of the physical world? The answer lies in understanding those parables that the Qur'án tells us about. A parable is a story or analogy whose symbolic meaning is significant but whose literal meaning is not. This is not an opinion but the guidance given by the Qur'án itself and we have seen this often enough to appreciate it not as a special case but rather as a continuous theme. The Qur'án helps us to understand the imagery employed in it to describe the awesome power of the Word of God. The verse that follows is one of the central verses in bringing this entire work into focus:

> If there were a Qur'án with which mountains were moved, or the earth were cloven asunder, or the dead were made to speak, this would be the one! But truly the command is with God in all things! Do not the believers know, that had God so willed, He could have guided all mankind? (Q 13:31)

This single verse aptly frames the discussion that follows, and indeed this whole exploration, and allows us to appreciate the fantastic imagery and symbolism that the Qur'án uses to describe the events of the Last Day. It is the Word of God which moves mountains and cleaves the earth and resurrects the dead.

> Mankind was one single people, and God sent Messengers with glad tidings and warnings; and with them He sent the Book in truth, to judge between people . . . (Q 2:213)

> By Him Who has my life in His hand, surely the son of Maryam will descend soon as a just judge . . .[2]

We know that the Word of God is a judge because it decides between the believers and non-believers, the good and bad, the righteous and wicked. But what does it mean to be a witness?

> There is not one of the people of the scripture but will believe in him (Jesus) before his death and on the Day of Resurrection he will be a witness against them . . . (Q 4:159)

This is used to describe the Prophets of old and it is used many times to describe Muhammad: 'O Prophet! Truly We have sent thee as a witness . . .' (Q 33:45). In this verse Jesus speaks to God:

> And I was a witness over them while I dwelt among them, but when You did take me, You were the watcher over them . . . (Q 5:117)

In the modern court of law a witness gives testimony or evidence. Upon the completion of their mission the Prophets have always declared that their work is done and that they have perfected religion for their people. They testify and confirm those who follow their teaching and are a witness against those who reject the Word of God.

Sayyidiná Abú Hurayrah narrated that Muhammad said: 'We are the last, the first on the day of Resurrection.'[3] Another version says: 'Our judgement will begin before all the creatures.'[4]

Sayyidiná Ibn 'Abbás narrated that the Prophet said: 'We are the last of the *umam* and the first who will be judged.'[5]

The *ummah* (followers) of Muhammad will be the first to be judged on the Day of Judgement because the dispensation of Muhammad was the one immediately preceding the Last Day (the return of Christ). So Christ will return among the Muslims and be a witness against them, as he was a witness against the Jews, and he shall be a just judge who separates the believers from the unbelievers. Every Messenger of God has been a witness and every Revelation has been a day of judgement.

> Every community (people) is sent a Messenger, and when their Messenger comes, they will be judged justly; they will not be wronged. (Q 10:47)

> It was We Who revealed the Law (to Moses); therein was guidance and light. By its standard have been judged the Jews, by the Prophet who submitted/bowed to God's Will . . . (Q 5:44)

> The Day the earth and the mountains will be in violent

> commotion and the mountains will be as a heap of sand poured out and flowing down. We have sent to you, O men, a Messenger, to be a witness concerning you even as We sent a messenger to Pharaoh. (Q 73:14–15)

As we saw earlier, each one of the divine Revelations is a day in the life of humankind. Each Manifestation of God's light and mercy was as a shining spiritual sun over the horizon. Each came in the dark of night and steadily rose to illumine the world and, having reached the height of his powers and influence, affected a complete change in the sky of human thinking and endeavour, awakening the slumbering souls and bringing to life the spiritually dead. Afterwards the forces of human ignorance and greed beclouded their radiance and caused the orb of true guidance to decline back into obscurity. The world once again plunged into gloom, then gradually prepared itself once more for the rising of that next Sun of Truth. Thus each Revelation is a Day of Resurrection and Gathering. We have established that the 'Day' is to be taken as a long period of roughly a thousand years, and that each 'Day' in spiritual terms refers to the rising and setting of the Divine Luminary, the Day Star of Revelation, the Messenger of God. In many surahs and verses the events and explanation of the last 'Day' are set forth in the unfolding of great celestial signs, signs linked with the related themes of resurrection, gathering and judgement:

> When the sun (with its spacious light) is folded up; and when the stars fall (losing their lustre), When the mountains vanish (like a mirage) . . . So verily I call to witness the Planets that recede, go straight or hide; and the night as it dissipates; and the Dawn as it breathes away the darkness; verily this is the word of a most honourable messenger. (Q 81:1, 15–19)

The literal meaning of this surah is fantastic and incomprehensible. A tradition mentions that the sun will rise in the West and be darkened. Of course, nothing is impossible for God but a literal interpretation of such verses is not in keeping with natural rhythms or the harmony of nature and such events have no parallel in human experience. An ancient mind might imagine the stars falling because the stars look like they are hanging in the sky – little pinpricks of light. A meteor streaking across the sky looks like a 'shooting star'. But those with scientific minds recognize that stars only appear to be small – they are in fact massive and distant. They have very long lives in which they first coalesce from primordial stellar gas and begin the process of fusion and start radiating light and energy until they have exhausted their fuel, change their nature and evolve into different forms, a process that takes many billions of years. These physical stars cannot 'fall'. Where would they fall to?

So what does it mean that the stars shall fall? How do we understand such a statement? The imagery consistently used in the Qur'án gives us the formula for decoding such signs: light = revelation; Sun = Messenger; star = teacher/religious leader. This imagery was also used by the Prophets of old because it is a universal description:

> And they that be wise shall shine as the brightness of the firmament; and they that turn many to righteousness as the stars for ever and ever. (Dan. 12:3)

The Qur'án gives not merely a description of God's gifts but 'Signs for those who give thought'. (Q 30:21)

> . . . and by the stars (men) guide themselves. (Q 16:16)

Yusuf Ali explains this in a note to his translation of the Qur'án:

> As there are beacons, landmarks, and signs to show the way to men on the earth, so in the spiritual world . . . Then

> we have the examples of Great Men as further sign-posts: 'Lives of great men all remind us. We can make our lives sublime.' In long-distance travel, the pole star and the magnetic needle are our guides; so in our long-distance journey to the other world, we have ultimately to look to heavenly guidance or its reflection in God's Revelation.[6]

The stars and the constellations have been used by navigators in all places and ages in order to determine their direction at night and plot a course in the darkness. Not only do they enable us to find our bearings from their universal and unchanging patterns but they are also physically so beautiful and inspiring that they draw us to contemplate the universe and the mysteries of God. In like manner, for our spiritual growth there are Messengers and Prophets and lesser luminaries gifted with wisdom and inspiration: the teachers, saints, leaders and pious ones who are guides after the Messenger has passed away.

A verse from Surah of the Star (Al-Najm) links directly the setting of the star and the rise of revelation, using imagery understandable to the pagan Arabs of the time, who worshipped and venerated the 'Mighty Star', Sirius, which shines bright in the night sky:

> By the star when it goes down, your companion is neither astray nor being misled, nor does he say (aught) of (his own) desire. It is no less than inspiration sent down to him: he was taught by one mighty in power, endued with wisdom: for he appeared (in stately form) while he was in the highest part of the horizon . . . That he hath promised a second creation . . . That He is Lord of the Mighty Star (Sirius). (Q 53:1–7, 47, 49)

The Surah of the Mountain (Tur) opens with this appeal:

> By the Mountain (of Revelation); By a Book inscribed, in a

> parchment unfolded; By the much frequented house, by the canopy raised high, and by the oceans filled with swell. Verily the chastisement of thy Lord will indeed come to pass. There is none can avert it, on the Day when the firmament will be in dreadful commotion, and the mountains will move. Then woe that Day to the rejecters of Truth! (Q 52:1–11)

Yusuf Ali explains:

> The mountains are a type of firmness and stability. But things that we think of as firm and stable in this material life will be shaken to pieces, and will be no more substantial than a mirage in a desert.[7]

It is mentioned in some verses in the Qur'án that the mountains will be made to flow, that they will be like wool, that they will be scattered, that the earth will be pounded to dust, 'When the earth is shaken violently and throws out its burdens' (Q 99:1–2), and that the mountains will float away or move. These symbols explain the destruction of something mighty and well-established as if it were a mere plaything. They are inconsistent with each other if taken literally and so only the symbolic explanation makes sense.

We must try to understand the meaning of these signs and the imagery used so that we can appreciate more fully the description given in these Qur'ánic verses to the Last Day. The beauty of the description is that it uses the frightening imagery of the end of the physical world and reality to bring to our attention the significance of the fading of that shining, spiritual sun of revelation. When the sun of revelation has been removed from the world, the lesser lights – the teachers and inspired authorities (stars) – have fallen from the heights of knowledge and all that man has established which seems so mighty (mountains) is suddenly overthrown, then the earth will be plunged into darkness and error: these are signs of the Day. In the Surah of the

Overthrowing (Al-Takwír), the dawn 'as it breathes away the darkness' is called to witness revelation. (Q 81:18)

In the next surah the theme is continued:

> When the heaven is cleft asunder, and when the stars are scattered. When the oceans are suffered to burst forth . . . and what will explain to thee what the Day of Judgement is? Again what will explain to thee what the Day of Judgement is? (It will be) the Day when no soul shall have power (to do) aught for another: For the command, that Day, will be (wholly) with God. (Q 82:1–3, 17–19)

Here it is shown that every person will stand on his or her own. This is not meant to imply that we will be isolated and apart from other people but rather that we will each be responsible for our deeds and actions. There will be no spirits or gods, angels or idols that can intercede, nor priests or leaders or *mawlánás*, nor saints, family or friends – none shall stand between a person and God, and all shall be laid bare. In the traditions we are told that the Prophets will be able to intercede for their *ummah* (people) on the Day of Reckoning but even that is only by the leave and command of God and so none have power to do anything for anyone save by the Will of God. The following *ḥadíth* reflects this:

> Sayyidiná Anas reported: There will be none of you but will be spoken to by his Lord, there being no interpreter between them.

The Surah of the Moon (al-Qamar) opens with a clear and grave forewarning:

> The Hour (of Judgement) is nigh, and the moon was cleft asunder . . . they reject the warning . . . therefore, (O Prophet) turn away from them (and wait for) the Day that the Caller will call (them) to a terrible affair. (Q 54:1–6)

When the hour of judgement is near, the moon is cleft asunder. It is a commonly held tradition that this is what happened in the day of the Prophet Muhammad himself. Thus if we examine the symbolic meaning of this verse we realize that the light of the moon is the pale reflection of the sun. When the shining sun disappears then the moon is the light of the night, which reflects the sun's light but only dimly, not with its full radiance. By this description we can understand that the 'moon' as used frequently in the metaphorical sense in the Qur'án, is none other than the religion that each Messenger or Heavenly Luminary leaves behind him in the dark world of man, as a reflection of his splendour, and so the splitting of the 'moon' is the decline and then the renewal of religion.

The term '*shaqqah*', which is translated as 'cleft asunder' or the 'splitting' in line with the doomsday scenario, is more appropriately translated as 'the ploughing' (as translated by some authoritative translators and by Harun Yahya, who claims that this prophecy finds literal fulfilment in man's physical landing on the moon) or 'the digging', as a farmer would split the earth in order to uproot weeds and plant new seeds.[8] In the literal reading it makes no sense to say either that the moon will be split or that it will be ploughed; only the figurative meaning allows us to understand the true significance of the term. The previous religion that has fallen into decline is uprooted and replaced, or rather it is harvested and the new seeds of the new season are planted. This has been the way of God's progressive revelation in the past and we are told that we will find no change in His way. Just as the moon fades with the rising of the sun, so the past dispensation and its religion are cleft asunder and replaced by the bright effulgence of revelation and divine Light.

The 'Caller' mentioned in the above verse from the Surah of the Moon is referred to many times in the Qur'án, so we will undertake a deeper study of that theme in chapter 8 but for now let us continue to consider the majestic metaphoric signs of the Last Day:

> When the sky is rent asunder and hearkens to (the Command of) its Lord, and it must needs (do so); and when the earth is flattened out, and casts forth what is within it and becomes (clean) empty, and hearkens to the command of its Lord, and it must needs (do so); (then will come the full Reality) . . . So I do call to witness the ruddy glow of Sunset; the Night and its homing, and the moon in her fullness, ye shall surely travel from stage to stage. (Q 84:1–5, 16–19)

The sky cannot physically be rent asunder for it is but space, and the earth cannot truly be flattened out for it is a sphere. This is a metaphor to describe the revitalization and renewal of the sky and the earth, or the lives, culture, minds and hearts. The world becomes the true reflection of God's command and Will, and all that is human contrivance is cast out. Later, the approaching gloom and the night and its moon reflecting the hidden sun are called to witness that we will progress and be taken to ever higher levels. How sweetly the imagery is interwoven to draw us into an appreciation of the Last Day and its dawning reality. But we are also cautioned:

> The Day the heavens shall be rent asunder with clouds . . . (Q 25:25)

The clouds in our physical experience have many meanings. They are lakes of vapoury moisture suspended in the air which pour out water onto the earth, bringing new life and cleansing. At times that pouring out of water is violent and brings destruction, sweeping away buildings and mighty human constructions. But most importantly for the significance of our theme, the clouds obscure the light of the sun and the moon, they darken the world, and make it such that even though it is day and there is light, we are unable to see the sun itself and witness its radiance. It is in this meaning that this verse can best be understood. The symbolism is meant to convey the idea that the world of human understanding – not the physical world – will be affected in these ways by the Word of God. This is confirmed in more direct language in the following verses:

> The Day that We roll up the heavens like a scroll rolled up for books (completed); even as We produced the first creation, so shall We produce a new one: A promise We have undertaken: Truly shall We fulfil it. (Q 21:104)

> The Day when the earth will be changed to other than the earth and the heavens (also will be changed) . . . (Q 14:48)

> . . . and they were judged every man according to their works. (Rev. 20:13)

> And I saw a new heaven and a new earth: for the first heaven and the first earth were passed away . . . (Rev. 21:1)

These potent verses once again imply the renewal of humankind rather than the destruction of the world. This theme is then expanded in even more direct language, and in more detail:

> No just estimate have they made of God (they esteem not God with the true esteem due to Him): on the Day of Judgement the whole of the earth will be but His handful, and the heavens will be rolled up in His right hand: Glory to Him! High is He above the partners they attribute to Him! The trumpet will (just) be sounded, when all that are in the heavens and on earth will swoon, except such as it will please God (to exempt). Then will a second one be sounded, when, behold, they will be standing and looking on! And the Earth will shine with the Light of its Lord . . . (Q 39:67–9)

Yusuf Ali elaborates on this:

> It will be a new Earth. All traces of injustice or inequality, darkness or evil, will have gone. There will be the one universal Light, the Glory of God, which will now illuminate all. Falsehood, pretence, and illusion will have disappeared. Everything will be seen in its true light.[9]

Al-Naqúr (the Trumpet), al-Ṣúr (the Bugle) and al-Sakhah (the Mighty Trumpet Blast) refer to the horn that is blown to announce, to warn, to frighten, and to gather people together and stir them into action. When the trumpet is sounded the first time it will be a great shock and all will be utterly bewildered except for a chosen few, but after the second blast of the trumpet the earth will be illumined by the Glory of God. This event is sometimes described as an 'awful cry' or the 'mighty blast' or 'terrible noise'. In the context of the ancient people of the desert, a trumpet could be used to communicate, to announce the arrival of an army or travelling group, to rally and excite troops to common action, and to strike fear into the hearts of opponents on the battlefield. In the old imperial context it was often used to announce the arrival of the emperor before the people and had the effect of silencing the masses and turning the attention of everyone to the emperor as a central figure.

A modern parallel would be the loud hooter or horn of a vehicle such as a train or ship, or a siren or alarm at a school or factory. It is a clear loud blast that is stunning, gets everyone's attention and communicates a message of warning to them. We know, furthermore, that every word of the Qur'án is carefully chosen and so the clear reference to not one but two blasts of the mighty trumpet is not insignificant. Its interpretation is simple. The twin blasts refer to the announcement of Al-Mahdi, the forerunner, and then Al-Masih, Jesus Christ, in quick succession.

In the Bible we are given a simple explanation of this symbol:

> If when he seeth the sword come upon the land, he blow the trumpet, and warn the people; Then whosoever heareth the sound of the trumpet, and taketh not warning; if the sword come, and take him away, his blood shall be upon his own head . . . So thou, O son of man, I have set thee a watchman unto the house of Israel; therefore thou shalt hear the word at my mouth, and warn them from me . . . Therefore, O thou son of man, speak unto the house of Israel . . . (Ezek. 33:3–10)

> The great day of the Lord is near, it is near, and hasteth greatly, even the voice of the day of the Lord: the mighty man shall cry there bitterly. That day is a day of wrath, a day of trouble and distress, a day of wasteness and desolation, a day of darkness and gloominess, a day of clouds and thick darkness, a day of the trumpet and alarm against the fenced cities, and against the high towers. (Zeph. 1:14–16)

Some who are bound by the literal interpretation of scripture have held fast to the notion of a physical blowing of some giant material trumpet that is supposed to destroy the world. They imagine that an angel, a being of spirit, will blow the trumpet, a physical object, and cause doomsday. This interpretation is once again inconsistent with the complete picture of the Last Day that the Qur'án and *ḥadí<u>th</u>* are describing. To understand the trumpet as a symbol makes more sense and ties together *ḥadí<u>th</u>* and the Qur'án.

***

At times the Bible and the Qur'án explain the purpose of the imagery used but often it is difficult to appreciate the meaning of the signs and symbols. The symbolism of the scriptures is a dividing line between those with a material and literal mind who can only accommodate what occurs to them through sense-orientated perception, and those who can penetrate to the true meaning through intelligence and symbolic imagination. The symbolism applied in world scriptures is part of the power of the Word of God to draw us into higher consciousness. It is this very quality, this human faculty of symbolic imagination and moral spiritual awareness, which equips us for ascent into the Kingdom of Heaven. In fact it is that very faculty which enables us to have a real relationship with God who is not physically seen or heard by us but is perceived and experienced nonetheless. It is only when we enter that spiritual kingdom and become self-realized in God consciousness that virtue will shine from each individual and the physical earth will be transformed into the Kingdom of God. Those who are materially minded will not grasp such concepts, images and prophecies. They will remain bound to the literal and material and the primitive past. The affair of the Last Day will continue to be complicated and phantasmagorical for those with a literal mind set but for those with spiritual susceptibilities the truth of the Last Day is simple and can be summed up in a single brief sentence: When religion has become obscured God will send Mahdi to prepare the world for the coming of Al-Masih Jesus Christ, Rúḥ Alláh, the Spirit of God, who, through revelation, will remake the earth into a true reflection of God's glory, thereby bringing abiding peace and unity. This is the essence of our beliefs and traditions which is resolving into focus and emerging from the quagmire.

8

CLEARING AWAY THE CONFUSION

There is much confusion and no real consensus among people as to what the Last Day is all about. There are layers of veils enclosing the truth and what we have thus far discussed has helped to unravel the mystery to a certain extent. Part of the challenge, as discussed in an earlier chapter, is that prophecy is, by its very nature, vague and non-specific. At this point in our exploration the Last Day is beginning to make more sense and the essential aspects of it are resolving into focus. However there is another layer, or a certain class of misinformation, which tends to cloud people's understanding of the Last Day and fuels speculation which could prove most destructive to the coherence we are trying to achieve. So now we have to clear up the other complicating factor which is the multiplicity of personalities and battles mentioned in the *ḥadíth*.

The Prophet Muhammad spoke of the future many times, sometimes briefly and at other times at length. Usually people remembered what he said and told others what they had heard. Sometimes he spoke about the near future and the leaders and events affecting his *ummah*, and at other times he spoke of the far future, the Last Day, and the conditions of the time, and the coming of the Mahdi and the return of Christ. Eventually over time the *ḥadíth* compilers put all these reported sayings together in a vast category called prophecies. The confusion comes in when people fail to recognize this time line through the rise, growth, struggles, triumphs, development, expansion, and then decline and degeneration, leading up to the Last Hour, but rather they consider them all to be simultaneously applicable to the calamitous 'end of the world'.

These combined factors have complicated the matter and led to misconceptions regarding the Last Day and the coming of Mahdi and Christ. We have already dealt with many of these and explored sincerely and closely the Qur'án and what it teaches us about the nature of 'Revelation', 'Islam', and the 'Day'. We were able to shed light on the fantastical cosmic signs but there is still much confusion regarding the future personalities and events mentioned in the *ḥadíth*. There have been many mahdis, or pious leaders, but there is only one Mahdi. There are many *dajjáls*, liars, but there is only one Al-Dajjál. There have been many false pretenders to the title of Prophet, Messenger or saviour but there is only one true Al-Masih, the promised Messiah. There is talk of the frightful one-eyed Antichrist, vague mention of strange beasts, chained-up monsters, marauding cannibals and donkeys with heads 40 cubits wide.

The Good, the Bad and the Ugly

The confusion arises, in part, when the Mahdi of the Last Day is confused with the other pious leaders who have fought battles in the name of the expansion of Islam. For example:

Ibn 'Umar (*Raḍí Alláhu 'an hu*) said to Ibn Hanafiyyah: 'Al-Mahdi is a title which one would use for a pious person. If a person is pious (*ṣáliḥ*), he will be called Mahdi.' According to this interpretation a number of people will be called Mahdi.

Walid ibn Muslim reports: 'I heard a person stating to the Muslims that Mahdi will be three [different persons], [The first will be] Mahdí al-Khayr 'Umar ibn 'Abdu'l-'Azíz, [the second will be] Mahdí al-Damm, he will be the one in whose era bloodshed will end [and the third will be] Mahdí al-Dín, 'Ísá ibn Maryam.'

Ibráhím ibn Maysarah says that he asked Táwús if 'Umar ibn 'Abdu'l-'Azíz was the Mahdi. He replied: 'He was a Mahdi, however, not THE Mahdi. During his ['Umar ibn 'Abdu'l-'Azíz's] era there did not exist total justice (as will be the case in Imam Mahdi's era).'

These *ḥadíth* are not very authoritative because they are the reported sayings of people other than the Prophet; in fact, they cannot rightly be called *ḥadíth* but they serve the purpose of illustrating my point all the better. There is a great deal of confusion regarding the coming of Al-Mahdi and Christ owing to the blind belief in traditions that have been added over and above the Qur'án and authentic *ḥadíth*. Al-Mahdi of the Last Day is not to be confused with the actions and wars of the pious leaders who have gone before. Often a *ḥadíth* begins simply with 'A man from Medina will . . .' and even though it makes no mention of Mahdi, interpreters take it as a reference to the Mahdi. There are numerous stories of wars and battles citing various enemies of Islam, including the Romans, and even though the Romans are no more, people still associate those references with the events and personalities of the Last Day. There have been many wars and battles during the turbulent history of Islam, wars with the Romans/Byzantines, Persians, Egyptians, Spanish, North Africans and central Asians. There was also a devastating civil war.

Similarly bound up with these wars are the opponents of Islam and their leaders, who are evil and liars. There are also many other liars – it is said in a tradition that there will be some 30 *dajjáls* before Al-Masih Al-Dajjál (the Antichrist). Thus there have been many personalities involved in battles and sieges who were *dajjáls* – liars and enemies of the faith – and false prophets and thus the prophecies referring to these personalities have already been fulfilled. The Prophet occasionally said that there were those amongst his companions who would live to see a *dajjál*. Among the many false prophets and alleged enemies of Islam that have appeared throughout its history are: Musaylima, Al-Aswad al-'Ansí, Al-Ḥarith ibn Sa'íd, Muḥammad ibn Sa'íd al-Maṣlub, Maḥmud ibn al-Faraj, Bayán ibn Sam'án al-Tamímí, Háshim ibn Ḥakím, 'Abdu'lláh ibn Mu'awiyah, Mughíra ibn Sa'íd al-'Ijlí, Abu'l-Khaṭṭab al-Asadí, Mu'ammar ibn Kaytham, Muḥammad ibn Nuṣayr al-Namírí, Muḥammad Aḥmad (al-Mahdí), Ibn Túmart. These false prophets were resisted and many were executed. Rumi, exploring the theme of hypocrisy in his *Mathnavi* eulogizes: 'They give the title of Muhammad to false Musaylima. But Musaylima retained the name of "Liar" (Dajjál) and Muhammad that of "Sublimest of beings".'

There are groups or sects amongst the Muslim *ummah* who claim that Mahdi or Christ is hidden somewhere, or has already appeared. Among these are the Ithná Ash'arís who hold the firm belief that the final Imam, Muḥammad ibn Ḥasan 'Askarí, disappeared many centuries ago and is still in hiding in a cave until his reappearance in the Last Day as Al-Mahdi. There are others who believe that 'Alí was the Prophet of God, giving him even greater preeminence than Muhammad. The Qadiyánís or Ahmadiyya declare Ghulam Ahmad of Qadian to be a reformer Messenger. The Nation of Islam claims that Wallace Fard Muhammad and Elijah Muhammad were Messengers of God. There are also non-Muslim groups with similar claims. The Rastas claim that Haile Selassie was God. The American guru Avatar Adi Da claims to be the promised god-man for our age, and the Indian gurus Caitanya and more recently Sai Baba advanced similar claims in the East. The founder of the Unification Church, Sun Myung Moon of Korea, claimed to be the messiah of the second coming. Joseph Smith revealed a hidden gospel called the Book of Mormon, setting in motion the Church of Jesus Christ of Latter-day Saints, while Guru

Nanak inspired the Sikh religion in India. Bahá'ís claim that al-Báb ('the Gate') and Bahá'u'lláh (the 'Glory of God') are the promised Mahdi and Christ respectively.

A few have made the fantastic claim of divine inspiration. Some of these figures have inspired movements that grow and reform certain communities. Divine inspiration is subtle and not easy to explain and thus also not easy to decisively refute. However, to assert that someone is a Messenger of God is a weighty claim and must be demonstrated with proofs: not miracles but inspiring teachings, civilizing principles and a legacy of love and beauty that grows with time rather than diminishes or disintegrates into divisions and darkness.

A few radical and dangerous cult leaders had brief ministries that ended in shocking mass suicides such as the Branch Davidians at their compound in Waco, Texas, under the leadership of David Koresh; the followers of Luc Jouret in Canada and Switzerland; a group in Uganda led by an unknown 'holy man'; and the worst of the lot involving nine hundred followers of Reverend Jim Jones, the leader of the Peoples Temple, whose bodies were found in a South American forest. The followers of Muḥammad ibn 'Abdu'lláh ['Abdu'lláh Ḥamid Muḥammad Al-Qahtání], under the tutelage of his conniving consort Juhayman [Juhaymán ibn Muḥammad ibn Sayf al-'Utaybí], seized the holiest mosque in Mecca and the Ka'bah for several days and held hostage a large group of *muṣallís* (worshippers), resulting in many deaths. There have been others who have not achieved such infamy and notoriety who have advanced similar claims and attracted such cult following. But these false claimants, or false prophets, who led lost souls into terrible darkness, all faded, like creepy spiders, into the obscurity from whence they emerged. Many such liars simply retracted their claims at the threat of torture and death, whereas the true Mahdi and Christ will be recognized in the same way that John the Baptist and Jesus Christ were recognized – by their absolute certainty, courage and sacrifice, even in the face of torture and death, and by the freedom and beauty they inspired. Moses of Crete, Asher Lamlein, Sabbatai Zevi, Ann Lee, Bernhard Müller, Billy Meier, Samael Aun Weor, Nirmala Srivastava, André Matsoua and Arnold Potter are reported to have advanced similar claims. Frightful figures like Hitler, Lenin, Mao and other mass murderers and political figures in the Christian West have been considered possible Antichrist Dajjál candidates.

The *ḥadíth* inform us that the true messiah will slay the anti-messiah (*Dajjál*). The Qur'án makes no mention of this diabolical *dajjál* personality but God does explain to us the purpose of such enemies of the faith:

> Thus have we made for every prophet an enemy among the sinners: but enough is thy Lord to help and guide. (Q 25:31)

Hence every Prophet was opposed by a wicked anti-Prophet. In the time of the return of Christ it will be the Antichrist, Al-Dajjál, who is mentioned in numerous *ḥadíth* in direct and symbolic descriptions. It is said that he is a man who will claim divinity, that he will be one eyed (or have a bulging eye), that the back of his head will be like a network of roads and that he will possess powers to beguile and attract followers. He will be able to revive the dead. He will reach all places and he will have the power to bring prosperity to some and misery to others. His followers will live in luxury. His water will be fire and his fire will be cool water, his Hell will be Paradise and his Paradise will be Hell. He will have a great abundance of things. Inscribed between his eyes will be the word 'unbeliever'. He will be an enemy of the cause of God. It is said that Dajjál and his followers will dissolve at the mere sight of Christ or Rúḥ Alláh. Again it is said that every disbeliever who perceives Christ's sweet smell will die and that his breath will reach as far as his sight falls, and that Christ, Rúḥ Alláh, will finally deliver a deathblow to Dajjál in Palestine, near the gate of Lut.

Again, it is not easy to make sense of this affair because it is overlain with much that is symbolic and much that belongs to the past and other *dajjáls* or enemies of faith, and perhaps much that is human fabrication. But even knowing this, it is still difficult to explain. As we have seen with many other signs of the Last Day, literal and symbolic signs are often intertwined to convey layers of meaning. This is the only possible interpretation because many of the *ḥadíth* are plainly descriptive of a human being while others are fantastic and describe something beyond human. So the literal signs refer to personalities who will appear between the time of the Prophet Muhammad and the time of Al-Masih Ḥaḍrat 'Ísá, while the more fantastical signs refer to the Great Liar or the Antichrist. In a sense such signs also refer to the decadent and materialistic modern culture. Since the Qur'án makes no reference to this wicked person and the *ḥadíth* are vague at best, we shall not enter into a detailed study of this subject.

Gog and Magog

There are numerous *ḥadíth* and a Qur'ánic verse referring to a depraved race, Yajuj and Ma'juj or 'Gog and Magog', that will break through a mighty barrier many times reinforced and wreak havoc in the world. These references are more closely linked with the Last Day than many other prophecies about future wars. The Qur'án says:

> There is a ban on any population which we have destroyed: that they shall not return, until the Gog and Magog (people) are let through (their barrier) and they swiftly swarm from every hill. Then will the true promise draw nigh . . . (Q 21:95–7)

> . . . on that Day we shall leave them to surge like waves on one another. The trumpet will blow and we shall gather them all together. (Q 18:99)

The implication is that all the wicked people of the world will return at the time when the Gog and Magog are let loose. This image of chaos and war corresponds well with *ḥadí<u>th</u>* and with events of recent times.

The earliest reference to Gog and Magog is given in the Old Testament:

> . . . prophesy and say unto Gog, Thus saith the Lord God; In that day when my people of Israel dwelleth safely, shalt thou not know it? And thou shalt come from thy place out of the north parts, thou, and many people with thee, all of them riding upon horses, a great company, and a mighty army: And thou shalt come up against my people of Israel, as a cloud to cover the land; it shall be in the latter days, and I will bring thee against my land, that the heathen may know me, when I shall be sanctified in thee, O Gog, before their eyes. (Ezek. 38:14–16)

This account from the Prophet Ezekiel refers to a leader called Gog from a northern place called Magog. This legend already existed some one thousand years before the Prophet Muhammad, in a different land, and so by the time of Muhammad these prophecies persisted as ancient tales that plagued the minds of many people. Being a very firmly established legend it is certainly one of the signs of the Last Day but if we are to recognize these people then we must look carefully into history.

Later they are mentioned in the Book of Revelation but there they seem to be 'the nations which are in the four corners of the earth' (Rev. 20:8). By the time we encounter the first Qur'ánic reference (18:94–101), Gog and Magog appear as a terrible duo who are held behind a mighty barrier by a noble and pious king of the past, referred to in the Qur'án as Zul-Qarnayn (the Two Horned), but when they break through and advance with a vast army (with bows and arrows) they will bring much killing, oppression, exploitation of man and nature, violence and destruction. Their expansion and conquests will also precede the Last Day. The account given in the Qur'án is at once a parable and a description of a personality from the past. In the Surah of the Cave (Al-Kahf) some of the stories that had captured the imagination of the people and were a source of some debate and controversy are discussed, including that of the 'sleepers' of the Cave who took refuge in God from the wicked pagans of their time; the parable of the two men and their gardens and how the one who waxed proud against God was brought low; and the story of Moses and the pious sage whose actions Moses questioned to his own detriment.

It is in this surah that the Qur'án also relates the tale of Zul-Qarnayn. A great king, he travelled first to the place of the setting of the sun and found it set in murky waters, and he brought justice to the people there. He then travelled to the land of the rising of the sun and found there a people who had no covering to protect them from the sun, and he left them as they were. Then he followed another way. There he found a people who did not understand him but who asked his help against Gog and Magog. He helped them to build a mighty barrier, a gate of iron, to keep them at bay, but he warned them also that they would be released in the Last Day. (Q 18:83–100)

The story instructs us in noble leadership, explaining how Zul-Qarnayn punished the wicked and rewarded the good, and how he observed people in different lands in different conditions. Literally, the 'setting sun' is the West – the lands of Egypt, Babylon, Greece and Africa – and the 'rising sun' is the East – Persia, India and China. The rising sun, according to the imagery of light and the 'Day', is a land where revelation has dawned and the people had no covering protection, that is, they did not have any veils between themselves and the sun of truth and so Zul-Qarnayn left them to their ways, understanding well their condition. The setting sun is a place where religion has fallen and the light of revelation has been removed, and so Zul-Qarnayn found there a people in murky waters without guidance or order. In the third case he found a people he could not understand – so whoever Zul-Qarnayn was, these people were complete foreigners to him, with a unique language. They lived in a valley between two mountains and asked for his help. He erected a mighty barrier to keep the barbaric invaders out.

There were many great emperors of the past like Zul-Qarnayn who conquered various lands and travelled widely, and even built mighty fortifications and did works like those described in this story. The legend of Zul-Qarnayn and enemies coming from the North might refer to any of them.

The description of a mighty wall in the mountains immediately brings to mind the Great Wall of China, which is a massive structure built to prevent the barbaric northern peoples from raiding and invading the civilization of China. It is thought that the original section of wall was built by a powerful leader of the Chinese, Emperor Shih Huang Ti (Qin Shi Huang), sometime around 200 BCE. It literally is a massive wall, built of stone, but in it are gates of iron. This barrier kept out the vicious northerners until they eventually broke through under the leadership of Genghis and Kublai Khan, plundering, murdering and conquering throughout China, India, Asia Minor and Byzantium, even to the borders of Africa and Europe. They were cruel and their effect on the people was devastating, so they seem to fit the description of Gog and Magog.

Interestingly, the period of the first building of the wall coincides with the conquests of the enlightened and inspired Emperor of the Persians, Cyrus, who also freed the Jews from Babylon and helped them return home and rebuild their city. His empire stretched from India to Ethiopia and from the Caucasus Mountains to the Arabian Sea. Chinese might well be the language that Zul-Qarnayn could not understand, with Babylon the place of the setting sun, and India the place of the rising sun.

Alternatively, Gog and Magog could refer to certain northern Germanic tribes of the European lands who were held at bay for many centuries by the efforts of the Romans, a mighty impregnable barrier, metaphorically described as a wall of metal, and so perhaps Zul-Qarnayn is one of the just and fair-minded Roman emperors. Eventually the barbaric Germanic northerners broke free when the Roman Empire crumbled, and they wreaked havoc on Europe and, by extension, on the broader world, through the horrors of colonialism and, more recently, Nazism and the terrible events and killings of the Holocaust.

Interestingly enough, many people seem to think that Zul-Qarnayn was Alexander the Great. He was a very charismatic, inspired, dynamic and vibrant leader, extending religious tolerance to all in his dominions and envisioning a great free empire. His exploits were quite well known and there is nothing that confirms the story of the mighty iron wall but after his conquest of Egypt he was known as the two-horned and was even pictured on coins as having two horns, symbolic of his dominion.

Another possibility for Gog and Magog is the rapid expansion of the Russian Empire, which came down from the north attacking and conquering the realms of Islam in the early 19th century. They defeated the Ottomans repeatedly, annexing the Crimea and much of the European part of the Ottoman Empire and provinces of northern Iran and much of central Asia. A *ḥadí<u>th</u>* narrates that the Yajuj and Ma'juj will be so boastful and vainglorious after their conquests they will say: 'Indeed we have slain all on earth. Come! Let us kill those in heaven.' They will shoot arrows at the sky. Taken literally this could refer to missiles that are launched into the sky, or it could be viewed figuratively as the atheistic doctrine that came out of communist Soviet Union. Coincidentally the self-imposed barrier or blockade that the Soviets later established became known as the 'Iron Curtain'.

These are just opinions and possible interpretations; admittedly, they may sound a little contrived but the point is that the legend of Zul-Qarnayn and Gog and Magog relates to some event in the past and is bound up with history and symbolism. Our view of past events is not so clear but our view of present events is much clearer owing to telecommunications, television, the Internet, other media and globalization. The world is quite well known to us now and there is no great iron wall that holds some barbaric race captive. We would certainly know about it if there were. The swords, bows and arrows, and horses used in battle have been replaced by guns, heat-seeking missiles and stealth bombers. There are a few *ḥadíth* that describe warring peoples and their conditions but they are foot soldiers of old, not modern paratroopers and soldiers. The world is still groaning under the weight of barbaric warmongers, so we need not look forward into the future for that aspect of the legend. There are references made to wars that will be fought with the Romans, and sieges and battles, but all these things belong to the past. There is no longer a Holy Roman Empire; there is but a small city within a city in Italy, the Vatican in Rome. Gog and Magog do not belong to the future; they belong to the past and the present. Swarming, chaotic barbarians are today running riot throughout the world killing each other; that is the prophecy of Yajuj and Ma'juj, Gog and Magog.

In the Last Day, Al-Mahdi and Al-Masih, the return of Christ, will fight only a spiritual war against ignorance and arrogance and in so doing conquer the hearts, minds and souls of all human beings and bring them back to God; and after conquering the nations with love and patience they will remake this fragmented global village into one world, thus ending the Gog Magog psychosis.

> ... and they shall beat their swords in to ploughshares, and their spears into pruning hooks: nation shall not lift up a

> sword against nation, neither shall they learn war any more . . . all people will walk every one in the name of his god, and we will walk in the name of the Lord our God for ever and ever. (Mic. 4:3–5)

A *ḥadí<u>th</u>*, as we have already seen, confirms this verse from the Hebrew Bible:

> . . . Peace will be restored . . . swords will be put aside . . .[1]

This can only be accomplished through love and kindness and those noble qualities that are the hallmark of the chosen ones of God. We, humankind, stand on the threshold of our maturity and we are meant to leave behind all our childish bickering and divisions, selfishness and mistrust and to begin to heal, to create true unity. All the beautiful qualities loved by God – generosity, truthfulness, sincerity, patience, loving-kindness, trustworthiness, charity, mercy, friendliness, prayer, devotion, respect, humility, etc. – are things that cause unity and bring people together. These will characterize the divine civilization of the future because God has the power to transform us into that which He loves and not to leave us to fall into that which He does not love. Millions pray daily, 'Guide us on the straight path, the path of those who earn thy favour, not the path of those who earn thy anger, nor of those who go astray.' (Surah 1) In his remarkable work entitled *Abraham* Bruce Feiler records a conversation with a friend at dusk as they overlook the city of Jerusalem:

> 'You could not have written a script that would say that today, after thousands of years with all our technology and sophistication, we would still be fighting a war over this place, over the legacy of Abraham. But the reason is that this is the place of relationship. This is not only the spot where it is possible to connect with God, it's the spot

> where you can connect with God only if you understand what it means to connect with one another. The relationship between a person and another human being is what creates and allows for a relationship with God. If you're not capable of living with each other and getting along with each other, then you're not capable of having a relationship with God.' He gestured up at the Wall, the Dome, the Churches. They were illuminated in man-made light now, their brilliance a little too sharp.[2]

Killing and war are the antithesis of peace and can never lead to peace. And so it follows that if we are to hold fast to this glorious vision and destiny of the purification of man, of the love of God and the promise of lasting peace, then we must relinquish certain misconceptions or remain confounded.

> Wert thou to follow the common run of those on earth, they will lead thee away from the Way of God. They follow nothing but conjecture: they do nothing but lie. (Q 6:116)

Beauty and the Beast

Another strange figure present in the traditions is the 'dabbah' or beast of the Last Day. Adding to the frightful menace of Dajjál and Yajuj and Ma'juj, this curious figure is referred to in vague and obscure *ḥadíth*. Interestingly the cosmic sign that is most frequently linked with this figure is that the 'Sun will rise in its place of setting [the West]'. There are many curious stories connected with this sub-theme but we will not consider them here because they are too strange and didactic and we should not allow ourselves to be beguiled or distracted by such misrepresentations. On the other hand, this figure is mentioned frequently in the *ḥadíth* and the Qur'án itself refers to it, so we have to consider it and its implications. Ironically, this figure is found in a Qur'ánic surah entitled the Ant:

> And when the Word (Decree, Sentence or Decision) is fulfilled concerning them, We shall bring forth a Beast of the earth to speak unto them because mankind had not faith in Our revelations. And (remind them of) the Day when We shall gather out of every nation a host of those who denied Our revelations, and they will be set in array; Till, when they come (before their Lord), He will say: Did ye deny My revelations when ye could not compass them in knowledge, or what was it that ye did? (Q 27:82–4)

And so the beast is no mere legend but, equally, it is not a literal entity. That is to say, it is not a physical animal or a frightening creature, as we shall clearly see from the descriptions in the *ḥadíth*. It is not wicked in itself and will not do terrible things and it is not to be associated with Dajjál or evil. Curiously enough, the beast is said to be a righteous judge, for it will place the mark of recognition on the believers and the unbelievers; it is said that it will bear the staff of Moses with which to mark the believers and cause their faces to become radiant, and the ring of Solomon with which to place a black dot which will blacken the faces of the unbelievers. This confirms the Qur'ánic verse mentioned above. It is said that the beast will emerge in a remote place and news of it will not reach Mecca for a long time. It will come from somewhere other than its first location and will be mentioned much in the cities before news of it arrives. It will travel in the desert and let out a mighty shriek to the East, the West (Syria) and to the South (Yemen) and will even reach Mecca. Furthermore it is said in connection with the beast that people will become partners in wealth and live in cities. But, strangely, this symbol of the beast of the Last Day is frequently associated with the rising of the 'Sun' in the 'West'.[3]

Other *ḥadíth* describe the beast as having simultaneously the features of many different animals – 'head like an ox, eyes of a pig, ears like an elephant, chest like a lion, neck like an ostrich, feet like a camel, etc.' – which is fantastical but symbolic, if at all true. The head of an ox is strong and stable, the eyes of a pig are seeking, greedy, hungry, the ears of the elephant are big and allow him to hear a lot, the chest of a lion is powerful and a symbol of dominion, the neck of the ostrich is long and raised above others, and the feet of the camel are long and strong and have unmatched endurance. At first hearing, the description of the beast conjures up frightful images from our own subconscious but as we delve into the *ḥadíth* and rightly judge the Qur'ánic verse above then we come to see that the beast will be the enforcer of the Word or Decree of God. How is that so and what is this beast if it is not an animal?

This mention of the beast immediately calls to mind the visions and prophecies of Daniel, who lived around 400 BCE (some sources seem to suggest 600 BCE) and the last book of the modern Bible entitled the Book of Revelation by the saint/Prophet John, who lived around the first, or possibly second, century after Christ. In his visions the Prophet Daniel saw beasts on earth, which were given earthly ascendancy and dominion. They were similarly fantastical figures, with bodies made up of the parts of different animals. The first beast mentioned by Daniel was like a lion, with the wings of an eagle and standing like a man. (Dan. 7:4) This reminds us of the sphinx, the symbol of ancient Egypt, and this is the first clue to understanding the imagery. The fourth and last beast mentioned by Daniel had iron teeth that devoured things and broke them into pieces, and ten horns. As Daniel watched, a little horn appeared which replaced three other horns. Then the Son of man (Jesus Christ) arrived and to him was given dominion and the beast was slain. (Dan. 7:7–14)

The interpretation of these visions was clearly given to Daniel. The beasts represented four great earthly kingdoms or empires which would, each in its own time, establish their sovereignty. (Dan. 7:16–28) The first was the kingdom of Egypt and the fourth was undoubtedly the Roman Empire, over whom the teaching of Christ eventually triumphed and which became the vehicle of his Revelation. The ten horns are the ten emperors and the one horn that replaces the three is Caesar Augustus who dissolved the triumvirate and sat on the throne as the Emperor.

In the Book of Revelation of the modern Bible St John saw similar visions confirming the visions of Daniel but also adding that the beast 'causeth all, both small and great, rich and poor, free and bond, to receive a mark in their right hand, or in their foreheads: And that no man might buy or sell, save he that had the mark, or the name of the beast, or the number of his name.' (Rev. 13:16–17)

This agrees remarkably well with the *ḥadí<u>th</u>* and the Qur'ánic verses concerning the beast. Later, John prophesied the coming of Muhammad in quite clear and lucid terms.

> And I saw heaven opened, and behold a white horse; and he that sat upon him was called Faithful and True, and in righteousness he doth judge and make war. His eyes were as a flame of fire, and on his head were many crowns; and he had a name written, that no man knew, but he himself. And he was clothed with a vesture dipped in blood: and his name is called The Word of God. And the armies which were in heaven followed him upon white horses, clothed in fine linen, white and clean. And out of his mouth goeth a sharp sword, that with it he should smite the nations: and he shall rule them with a rod of iron . . . And the beast was taken, and with him the false prophet that wrought miracles . . . And the remnant were slain with the sword of him that sat upon the horse, which sword proceeded out of his mouth . . . (Rev. 19:11–21)

These visions refer to Muhammad. The white horse reminds us of the Prophet as a warrior of God and also of Buraq, the 'winged white horse' that carried the Prophet from Mecca to Jerusalem during the Night Journey. We are also reminded of the Prophet's army of *Ṣaḥábah* (companions) in their pure white garments and of his titles 'Al-Amín', the Trustworthy, and 'Kalímu'lláh', the Word of God. John also prophesies Muhammad's victories and dominion.

In his vision John saw the Angel Gabriel come down from heaven with a key and a chain and he bound Satan for a thousand years. (Rev. 20:1–2)

> And when the thousand years are expired, Satan shall be loosed out of his prison, And shall go out to deceive the nations which are in the four quarters of the earth, Gog and Magog, to gather them together to battle: the number of whom is as the sand of the sea. And they went up on the breadth of the earth, and compassed the camp of the saints about, and the beloved city: and fire came down from God out of heaven, and devoured them . . .
>
> And I saw a great white throne, and him that sat on it, from whose face the earth and the heaven fled away . . . And I saw the dead, small and great, stand before God; and the books were opened: and another book was opened, which is the book of life . . . and they were judged every man according to their works . . .
>
> And I saw a new heaven and a new earth: for the first heaven and the first earth were passed away . . . And I John saw the holy city, new Jerusalem, coming down from God out of heaven . . . And I heard a great voice out of heaven saying, Behold, the tabernacle of God is with men, and he will dwell with them, and they shall be his people, and God himself shall be with them, and be their God. And God shall wipe away all tears from their eyes; and there shall be no more death, neither sorrow, nor crying, neither shall there be any more pain: for the former things are passed away. And he that sat upon the throne said, Behold, I make all things new . . . And I saw no temple therein: for the Lord God Almighty and the Lamb are the temple of it. And the city had no need of the sun, neither of the moon, to shine

> in it: for the glory of God did lighten it, and the Lamb is the light thereof. And the nations of them which are saved shall walk in the light of it: and the kings of the earth do bring their glory and honour into it . . .
>
> And he saith unto me, Seal not the sayings of the prophecy of this book: for the time is at hand. (Rev. 20:7–22:10)

The Book of Revelation describes in symbolic language the future, which correlates quite well with what we have experienced. Daniel prophesied the fourth beast, or Rome, and the coming of Christ; St John prophesied the coming of Muhammad and his dominion as well as the return of Christ; and Muhammad himself prophesied the beast of future times and the coming of Christ, Rúḥ Alláh. The one who sits upon the 'great white throne' is the Lamb of God, Jesus. The vision of the new Jerusalem is truly descriptive of the kingdom of heaven on earth.

Thus the beast of the Last Day is a great empire that shall have earthly dominion. Having established that many of the signs of the Last Day are upon us and that the signs all follow in quick and ordered succession, then we have to look to our own times to recognize this empire prophesied by the *ḥadíth* and the Qur'án. The expanding empire of these latter days is the so-called West.

By the 19th century the British Empire had spread to various parts of the world, establishing its ascendancy over many nations across all the habitable continents; it was a world superpower. The most attractive of its former colonies was a vast piece of the new world which drew men and women seeking liberty from the stifling order of the old world. They came in numbers – bright innovative middle-class businessmen, free-thinking aristocrats, ambitious peasants and slaves. A new nation was born that was destined to become the modern expanding empire. Thus Britain paved the way for the USA, just as the Greek expansions paved the way for the expansion and consolidation of

Rome. The difference is that although the Americans use the instruments of war to subdue other nations, they prefer to utilize the modern instruments of political, social and economic subjugation to manipulate and control rather than physically expand and occupy, and by controlling governments, international trade and the entertainment and media industries, they are fast expanding their empire, capturing the imagination of youth and the minds and hearts of the people of many nations who wish to share in this modern culture, promising liberty and democracy.

Unfortunately, the West is still very much caught up in the negative and self-serving aspects of its 'free' society and so there is much indulgence, sensuality, greed, acquisitiveness, division, selfishness, individuality, inequality, piling up of wealth, violence and injustice. This often overshadows the positive aspects which are its modern methods and systems that make improvements to our civilizations in terms of public services, clear rational thought and the scientific method, and systems of justice, separation of state powers and democratic governance which have been adopted by virtually every nation (and now continents) as the norm, not because they are forced to but because they recognize in them a better standard. But modern democracy and free market capitalism are deeply and fundamentally flawed and ultimately incapable of achieving true civilization and shared prosperity for all.

Far higher than the standard that man can conceive is the standard that God designs and reveals. Just as He made Christ to triumph over the Roman Empire so will He make Christ returned to triumph over the American empire, the West, and make it the vehicle of His Word. Thus will the prophecy 'the sun will rise in the West' be fulfilled – meaning that the light of Revelation will illumine the West, become apparent in the West and will even radiate from the West.

The return of Christ is not meant to convey the idea that the selfsame human person will return but rather that there will be a 'return' of the same spirit, the same quality, and a similar unfolding of events or destiny that is this promised Day of Reality. To summarize: Christ was a simple, humble, pure man who taught and healed and loved, and spoke words of Truth, revealing scripture for the guidance of humankind. He was preceded by a Prophet, John the Baptist or Yaḥyá, whose mission it was to prepare people even though it led to his own martyrdom. Jesus himself also sacrificed his earthly life for the sake of mankind. After many struggles, his teaching found a home in the heart of the 'beast' of his day, the Roman Empire, and triumphed over it, converted it and made it the vehicle of far greater expansion.

The return of Christ means the return of the same personality filled with love, truth and wisdom, the same beautiful spirit and, most significantly for the current discussion, a similar unfolding of events. Just as Jesus was heralded by John the Baptist, so will Rúḥ Alláh be announced by the Mahdi. Rúḥ Alláh and the Mahdi will challenge the leaders of their time just as John and Jesus did, and they will be persecuted and threatened with imprisonment, torture and death, just as John and Jesus were. This enigmatic figure of Rúḥ Alláh will preach a message of love and unity destined to unite all people under one faith. This teaching will be fiercely resisted by the people to whom it comes but in time it will prevail over the dominant empire of that era – the 'beast' of the 'day' – and it will spread to all parts of the world, filling the earth like water gradually fills a vessel.

This story brings to mind the well-known and much-loved children's story in which the beast is a terrible and ugly monster that holds Beauty captive. But as he gets to know her, so the softness and sweetness of Beauty transforms the beast's personality and appearance and softens his hard heart, and he becomes the kind and loving prince. And they live happily ever after.

The Caller

A further sign and personality of the Last Day is the herald or forerunner. Yaḥyá, as he is known in the Qur'án, or John the Baptist, travelled throughout the land preaching a message of warning and preparation for the coming of one whose shoestrings he was not worthy to untie. John was a Prophet and a Caller or Witness and he baptized people with water, stirring them up to an awareness of a greater one to come who would baptize them with the Holy Spirit. He baptized Jesus in the river Jordan and Jesus experienced the Holy Spirit descend upon him.

When Jesus' mission began, John's ended. He was seized by the authorities and executed for his teachings. His death is a symbol of the truth of his message. What kind of person would give up his life to deliver an announcement or warning? Only a true Prophet would do so because only a true Prophet would be so selfless and detached from the world and so submissive to the Will of God that he would endure ridicule, pain and death for the sake of God's decree. So the relationship of Al-Mahdi to Al-Masih Christ returned is like that of John the Baptist to Jesus Christ. Mahdi is, in a sense, the return of Yaḥyá. In the Surah of Mary (Maryam) God said to John the Baptist:

> 'O Yahya! take hold of the Book with might': and We gave him wisdom . . . and purity . . . So peace be upon him the day he was born, the day that he dies, and the day that he will be raised up (again)! (Q 19:12–15)

Later in this surah we find that Jesus the son of Mary says:

> So peace is on me the day I was born, the day that I die, and the day that I shall be raised up to life (again)! (Q 19:33)

This is one of the rare instances when the resurrection or

return of an individual person is spoken of in the Qur'án. It is spoken first of Yaḥyá and then of Jesus. Such rare and specific references to a return to life give us an indication that we can connect Yaḥyá, or John the Baptist, with Imam Mahdi. Furthermore we are told that Christ frequently referred to John the Baptist as the return of Elijah but during his lifetime Christ spoke with Elijah in the spirit. The Qur'án gives us yet a further clue to this connection by linking these three figures together in this verse: 'And Zakariyah and John, and Jesus and Elijah: all in the ranks of the righteous . . .' (Q 6:85) Why would an earlier Prophet be mentioned after John and Jesus if not to highlight this connection?

> So also was Elijah among those sent (by us). Behold, he said to his people, 'Will ye not fear (God)?' Will ye call upon Baal and forsake the Best of Creators, God, your Lord and Cherisher and the Lord and Cherisher of your fathers of old? But they rejected him, and they will certainly be called up (for punishment.) Except the sincere and devoted Servants of God (among them) and We left (this blessing) for him among generations (to come) in later times: 'Peace be unto Elijah!' (Q 37:123–30)

Elijah was the herald or forerunner of Elisha. The above verse says that Elijah was left for future generations. Elijah, John the Baptist and the Mahdi are thus linked. It behoves us to be watchful, for we are told that the coming of Al-Mahdi and Al-Masih in the Last Day will be something very subtle and hard to perceive.

We now explore the traditions regarding this enigmatic personality of the Last Day, the Mahdi. The name Mahdi is derived from the root *hudá* meaning 'guide' as used in '*muhtadí*' (rightly guided) and *hidáyah* (guidance). Mahdi thus means 'one who is rightly guided', while 'Imam' means 'leader', and so this person will be a rightly guided leader of men in the end times. The Mahdi will have 'inspired knowledge' and he will be exalted in a single night. He will have to be recognized by the pure of heart and those with understanding minds. As with every rightly guided one he will face the resistance of his people and the persecution of the authorities.

Sayyidiná 'Abdu'lláh narrated:

> We were in the company of the Prophet when his eyes filled with tears and the colour of his face changed. We asked: 'O Messenger of God! Why do we see signs of anxiety on your face?' He said: 'We are the people of the house for whom God, the Exalted, has chosen the Hereafter over this world. The people of my house will face anxieties and trouble after me, so much so that a company of men with black standards will come from the east. They will ask for bread during their journey but people will not give them any, so they will fight and gain victory so that they will be given what they demand but they will not accept it till they give it to a man of the people of my house. He will fill this land with justice while it was first filled with oppression. If one of you finds him then you must go to him even though you have to drag yourself on ice.'[4]

This *ḥadíth* describes a significant event in the life of Mahdi and his followers and gives a very clear indication that the Mahdi will be a descendant of Muhammad – from 'my house'. This is confirmed in several other *ḥadíth*:

> Umm Salamah, Umm al-Mu'minín narrated: The Prophet (peace be upon him) said: The Mahdi will be of my family, of the descendants of Fatima.[5]

And in case we were uncertain as to whether it is the Mahdi of the Last Day that is referred to, another confirmation is added:

> 'Abdu'lláh ibn Mas'úd narrated: The Prophet (peace be upon him) said: 'If only one day of this world remained, God would lengthen that day till he raised up in it a man who belongs to me or to my family . . . who will fill the earth with equity and justice as it has been filled with oppression and tyranny.'[6]

This *ḥadí<u>th</u>* provides further confirmation and another clue to the Mahdi's mission:

> Abú Sa'íd Al-<u>Kh</u>aḍrí narrated: Rasúl Alláh said: 'The Mahdi will be of my stock . . . and he will rule for seven years.'[7]

If we seek more direct references from the Qur'án to the events of the Last Day then, as we have already seen, there are many, albeit couched in symbolic language, but if we seek specific references to the personalities involved then we will not be satisfied for such references are vague and rare. For example, there is no specific mention made of Dajjál and only a few instances where the return of Christ is clearly mentioned but no detail is given. The following verse, however, can be taken as a reference to Al-Mahdi or the 'morning star' of piercing brightness:

> The Hour (of Judgement) is nigh, and the moon was cleft asunder. But if they see a sign they turn away . . . Therefore (O Prophet!) turn away from them, (and wait for) the Day that the Caller will call (them) to a terrible affair. They will come forth – their eyes humbled – from (their) graves, (torpid) like locusts scattered abroad, hastening with eyes transfixed, towards the Caller! 'Hard is this Day!' The unbelievers will say. (Q 54:1–8)

This surah explains that many people throughout time have disbelieved in the signs and Messengers of God so Muhammad is advised to turn away from them and wait for the Last

Day when the Caller will bring them to life. In this instance unbelief is clearly linked to death, so the resurrection is a spiritual one, a bringing back to faith, that is implied, as we have seen earlier. The Qur'án also counsels us:

> And listen for the Day when the Caller will call out from a place quite near – The Day when they will hear a (mighty) Blast in (very) truth: that will be the Day of Resurrection. (Q 50:41–2)

The Caller (al-Munádí) is one who 'calls' or invites people to faith. It is used in this context in other verses of the Qur'án as in: 'Our Lord! We have heard the Call of one Calling (us) to faith . . .'(Q 3:193) This description is also used of the Prophet Muhammad himself: 'Call all to the Way of thy Lord with wisdom and beautiful preaching' (Q 16:125) and 'Call (them to the Faith) and stand steadfast . . .' (Q 42:15) The Prophets and Messengers are at various times called 'Warners', 'Witnesses' and 'Bearers of Glad Tidings', designations synonymous with the title 'Caller'. 'Caller' is also used in the sense implied by the *a<u>dh</u>án* as a 'call to prayer'. The Caller is one who stands apart from others and delivers a clear message to the people that they may gather and hear an announcement with a message. It is quite certain, then, that every Prophet of God was a Caller.

Commentators are not clear to whom the term refers but they quite rightly link it with the blast of the Trumpet because these symbols portray the same thing. But while the Trumpet is an inanimate material object that calls to mind the act and the sound of a mighty blast, the Caller evokes the image of a living, breathing human being. Both the Caller and the Trumpet are symbols pertaining to the Last Day that foretell the coming of Al-Mahdi and Al-Masih. The above verses very clearly link the Caller, the mighty blast, the Trumpet and the return to life, or Resurrection, with Al-Mahdi and Al-Masih.

> . . . when the trumpet shall sound surely that Day will be a Day of Anguish . . . over it are Nineteen . . . (Q 74:8–9, 30)

The place that is 'quite near' from which the Caller will call is not specified in the Qur'án but allusions to this place have been made by the Prophets of old and also in the *ḥadí<u>th</u>*, as we have seen above, indicating that he will come from the East.

> 'Abdu'lláh ibn al-Ḥári<u>th</u> ibn Juz'al-Zubaydí narrates that Rasúl Alláh said: 'A people will come out of the East who will pave the way for Al-Mahdi.'[8]

The most striking of these *ḥadí<u>th</u>* very clearly indicates a location:

> Thawbán reported that Rasúl Alláh said: 'When you see Black Standards coming from Khorasan go to them for God's Caliph, the Mahdi, will be among them.[9]

In the past Khorasan referred to the lands of Persia and central Asia. In more modern times Khorasan is a large province of eastern Iran.

The Bible also provides some clues to the location of the Caller:

> In that day also he shall come even to thee from Assyria . . . (Mic. 7:12)

> And, behold, the glory of the God of Israel came from the way of the east . . . (Ezek. 43:2)

> For as the lightning cometh out of the east, and shineth even unto the west; so shall also the coming of the Son of man be. (Matt. 24:27)

Thus from the scriptures and from the *ḥadí<u>th</u>* we know much about the Caller who will announce the Messiah. He will call out as a mighty blast that disorientates people but attracts the faithful and he will come as a flash of lightning, brightening the world briefly. He will be a rightly guided leader and will gather a small following whom he will send as emissaries to invite people to the truth. They will ride one day in a small band from the land of Khorasan bearing a black standard. The Caller will teach a message of love, unity, peace and progress and will introduce Al-Masih the return of Christ to the world. He will suffer greatly for this, enough to bring tears to the eyes of our beloved Muhammad, who exhorted his *ummah* to wait and be ready, to recognize and give allegiance to the Mahdi, even if they have to suffer great agony for his cause.

***

By using for our analysis only authentic verses of the Qur'án and *ḥadí<u>th</u>* we achieve a greater coherence and a clearer picture of the Last Day. The fear and fuzziness that surrounds this subject can confuse many people but this has never been the purpose of revelation. Revelation leads us towards certainty and higher consciousness, so it is up to each of us individually and independently to consider these matters and judge for ourselves. Our great, uniquely human, power of choice is what distinguishes us from the rest of the natural world and lifts us into a higher realm, but only if we use this power and choose. At a time when the 'stars' of religion have fallen, that is to say, when the leaders controlling public opinion and interpreting scripture are no longer reliable sources, true believers must return to the authentic Qur'án and *ḥadí<u>th</u>* and exercise their faculties of reason, understanding, judgement and intuition in order to make sense of the Last Day. The purpose of this chapter has been to present information and to weave together the concepts into a coherent framework. Ultimately, however, it is the reader's task to clear away the confusion and seek Truth.

9

THE BREAK OF DAWN

The Last Surahs

The following is the series of surahs towards the end of the Qur'án whose titles give us a sense of an arrangement implying again the extended theme of the Last Day. The names in bold highlight the rising and setting sun.

Al-Mudaththir	'The Cloaked One' or 'One Wrapped Up'
Al-Qiyámah	**'The Resurrection'**
Al-Dahr or Insán	'Time' or 'Man'
Al-Mursalát	'Those Sent Forth' or 'The Emissaries'
Al-Nabá	'The Great News' or 'The Tidings'
Al-Názi'át	'Those Who Tear Out' or 'Those Who Drag Forth'
Al-Takwír	'The Folding Up' or 'The Overthrowing'
Al-Infitár	'The Cleaving Asunder' or 'The Cleaving'
Al-Inshiqáq	'The Rending Asunder' or 'The Ploughing'
Al-Burúj	**'The Mansions of the Stars' or 'Constellations'**
Al-Taríq	**'The Morning Star' or 'The Night Comer'**
Al-A'lá	'The Most High'
Al-Gháshiyyah	'The Overwhelming Event'
Al-Fajr	**'Dawn'**
Al-Balad	'The City'
Al-Shams	**'The Sun'**

Al-Layl	**'Night'**
Al-Ḍuḥá	**'The Glorious Morning Light'**
Al-In<u>sh</u>iráḥ	'The Expansion' or 'Solace'
Al-Tín	'The Fig'
Iqrá or Al-'Alaq	'Read' or 'The Clot'
Al-Qadr	'[The Night of] Power'
Al-Bayyinah	'The Clear Proof'
Al-Zilzal	'The Convulsion'
Al-'Ádiyat	'Those that Run' or 'The Coursers'
Al-Qári'ah	'The Day of Clamour'
Al-Aṣr	**'The Declining Day' or 'Time through the Ages'**
Al-Naṣr	'Help / Victory'

It is not difficult to see the thread that is the Dawning of the new 'Day'. These later surahs are either about the Last Day or they contain clear references to the Last Day and they are interspersed with the themes of revelation, resurrection, judgement, gathering, punishment of past peoples who rejected faith, Heaven and Hell, and vivid symbolic descriptions of the renewal of the world. Following the Surah of the Mansion of the Stars and the Surah of the Morning Star, Abdullah Yusuf Ali, in his introduction and summary to the symbolically significant Surah of Dawn surmises that:

> Its mystic meaning is suggested by contrasts – contrasts in nature and in man's long history. Thus does it enforce the lesson of faith in the Hereafter to 'those who understand'. Man's history and legendary lore show that greatness does not last and the proudest are brought low.
>
> . . . When all the things on which his mind and heart are set on this earth shall be crushed to nothingness, he will see the real glory and power, love and beauty, of God, for these are the light of the Garden of Paradise.[1]

> In respect both of beauty and terror, of hope and inspiration, of suddenness and continuing increase of light and joy, this 'holy time' of night may well stand as the type of spiritual awakening from darkness to Faith, from Death to Resurrection.[2]

Surah of Dawn (Fajr)

> By the Dawn; and the ten Nights; and the Even and the Odd and the night when it passeth away, this surely is an oath for thinking man. (Q 89:1–5)

Here a cryptic reference to a period of time is given which some take as a reference to the ten days of Hajj at the beginning of the last Islamic month. For many it is more applicable to the last ten nights of Ramadan, wherein the Night of Power (Laylat al-Qadr) is concealed between the odd and even nights. So what then is the oath or promise? We know that Dawn refers to the beginning of revelation or the appearance of the Messenger and in the context of the Last Day it refers to the 'return' of Jesus and so the oath is concerning his appearance. Adding ten nights, and the even (two) and the odd (one), and the night as it passeth away (one), this gives us 14 nights before the rising of the sun of revelation. But what are these 14 nights?

> Abú Bakr Siddiq narrated: Muhammad said: '. . . seventy thousand will enter paradise without reckoning, their faces like the moon on the fourteenth night, their hearts like one man's heart. I asked my Lord, the Mighty, the Glorious, to increase. So he gave me an increase of seventy thousand for every one.'[3]

First, literally, 14 nights is the period of time between the new moon and the full moon, and also between the full moon and the next crescent moon. The physical moon on the fourteenth night is in the height of its fullness and radiance. According to our analogy, the sun symbolizes direct revelation and the moon symbolizes the religion that the Messenger leaves behind him to guide mankind and so this further reinforces what we have learned from *ḥadíth* about the decline of the Muslim *ummah* and the appearance of Mahdi and Christ. Seventy thousand multiplied by seventy thousand is almost five billion, 70 per cent of the population of the earth today, so again it is linked with the Last Day and universal common faith.

We will see later the full significance of the metaphoric meaning which seems to give a period of time before the Dawn of the Last Day because this surah is clearly linked with the Surah of [the Night of] Power (Al-Qadr), the night that the revelation of the Qur'án began.

Intervening surahs continue the theme of the Last Day with titles like the Sun and the Glorious Morning Light, leading up to the Surah of Read or the Clot (Iqrá or Al-'Alaq) which was revealed during Ramadan on the Night of Power (Laylat al-Qadr) – and it is to the Surah of [the Night of] Power we must look to find the solution:

> We have indeed revealed this Message in the Night of Power (Glory): and what will explain to thee what the Night of Power (Glory) is? The Night of Power (Glory) is better than a thousand months! Therein come down the angels and the Spirit by God's permission, with all decrees. Peace! . . . This until the break of Dawn! (Q 97:1–5)

The reference to time, the 'night' and the 'break of dawn' links this passage with the earlier surah of this progression discussed above – the Surah of Dawn (Al-Fajr) – in which an oath is made, the oath of the ten nights and the even and the odd and the night as it passes away. This is a clear reference to the Night of Power (Laylat al-Qadr) which is hidden among the odd nights of the last ten nights of Ramadan.

But also in its reference to the 'Dawn' or the rising of the sun on the Last Day the link between these two surahs is enhanced. We see that it is also an oath concerning a period of time which must elapse before the great event of the appearance of Christ. That is to say that there are 14 'nights' to pass before the dawning of the Last Day. So what then is the duration of a 'night'? The Surah of [the Night of] Power answers that question emphatically: the night of Glory is better than a thousand months.

So, beautifully, they come together here: the first revelation in the holy month of Ramadan and the blessed Night of Power. A thousand months (84 years) is given as the equivalent of the Night of Power. We were given the oath in the Surah of Dawn (Al-Fajr) that the dawn will come to pass after 14 nights and so by elementary mathematics we get 84 x 14 '1176 years until the dawning of the day. Taking the date of the Prophet's passing behind the veil, the setting of the sun of Muhammad's light, 632 CE, as the beginning of the 'Night', then we can place the dawn of the Last Day at approximately 1808 CE as the date for the rising of the sun of Al-Masih Rúḥ Alláh, known as the return of Christ. So although it is somewhat vague and cryptic, the Qur'án gives an indication of the time, and as we shall see, the events surrounding the 'Dawning'. This further confirms our 'Day' that is 'as a thousand years'.

The last surah in the sequence is the Surah of the Declining Day, a reminder of the decline of the *ummah* leading up to the Last Day:

> By the Declining Day. Lo! Man is in a state of loss, save those who believe and do good works, and exhort one another to truth and exhort one another to endurance. (Q 103:1–3)

A Time and a Place

> They see the Day indeed as a far off event: but We see it quite near. (Q 70:6–7)

A day of revelation is as a thousand years in earth terms and the oath of the cryptic Surah of Dawn (Al-Fajr) and of [the Night of] Power (Al-Qadr) tells us that the dawn will appear after 1176 years, or on a date around 1808 CE. So it is either already upon us or it is quite near indeed. Having reviewed the lesser and greater signs we can confidently say that the Last Day is upon us.

Masjid Al-Aqsá in Palestine/Israel has always had a special significance for Muslims, as well as for Christians and Jews. The 'furthest mosque' or Al-Aqsá was where Muhammad led the prayer of all the Messengers and then ascended to Heaven during his Night Journey. It was also the first Qiblah to which the followers of Muhammad prayed before they were commanded to turn unto the Ka'bah in Mecca. In this is a sign. Furthermore there are numerous *ḥadíth* that seem to establish a location or area:

> Abú Hurayrah says that Rasúl Alláh said: '(Armies carrying) black flags will come from Khorasan. No power will be able to stop them and they will finally reach Ilia (the Holy Land/Palestine/Jerusalem) where they will erect their flags.'[4]

> Ibn Ḥawála said: 'Choose for me (a place to go), O messenger of God, if I should reach that time [the Last Day].' Muhammad said: 'Get thee to Syria for it is God's chosen land and for it He has selected His most favoured servants . . . for God has taken special charge of Syria and its inhabitants on my account.'[5]

In the Qur'án we read:

> If ye turn *back* (from the path), He will substitute in your stead another people; then they would not be like you! (Q 47:38)

And this *ḥadí<u>th</u>* explains:

> Abú Hurayrah said: Some of the companions of Rasúl Alláh said: O Rasúl Alláh! Who are those people about whom God has said that if we turn back (from the path), He will substitute in our stead another people and they would not be like us? And Salman (the Persian) was beside Rasúl Alláh and Rasúl Alláh struck him (on the thigh) and took Salman and said: 'This man and his people. By the One in whose hand is my soul! Were faith to be suspended in the Pleiades men from among the Persians would attain unto it.'[6]

> There will come a time for the people when there will not be a believer upon the earth except those who cleave to Syria.[7]

And most significantly, in *Al-Futúḥát al-Makkiyyah*, Muhyi ad-Dín Ibn al-'Arabí records the following *ḥadí<u>th</u>*:

> The Mahdi will emerge at a time of decline in religion. God will constrain through him what was not constrained through the Qur'án, such that a man who is ignorant, cowardly and miserly one evening will be transformed to being learned, brave and generous on the morrow . . . He will witness the most mighty battle, the banquet of God, upon the plain of 'Akká. He will banish tyranny and those who espouse it and he will revive religion . . . His martyrs will be the best of martyrs and his trusted ones the most excellent of trustees . . . his supporters whom God has caused to help him . . . will follow in the footsteps of those of the companion of the Prophet who held true to the covenant that they had made with God. And they will all be Persians, there being no Arabs among them, but they will speak Arabic . . .

> They are the most favoured of the supporters and the most excellent of the trustees . . . and all of them will be killed except one who will be upon the plain of 'Akká, the divine table that God has laid out for His creatures.[8]

It is said of Al-Masih Jesus returned that he will descend near the 'White minaret of eastern Dimishq [Damascus, Syria]'[9] but Ibn Kathír in his work entitled *Before and After the Last Hour*[10] cautions that 'it is possible that the narrator may have changed the sequence of the words inadvertently'. Whichever is the true *ḥadíth*, it is nonetheless intriguing because we find now a convergence between the Christian and Muslim traditions concerning a time and a place for the appearance of Christ. Dimishq is very near to 'Akká and Mount Carmel and in the general area of Syria or northern Palestine. We have it that Imam Mahdi will emerge in Persia, a land that is both to the east of Palestine and to the west of India, and that a small band of his followers will ride from Khorasan bearing a black flag or standard. His followers will be Persian and they will eventually be established in the Holy Land. We have the fulfilment of many signs as elaborated by all the world's great religions but more specifically by the Qur'án and the *ḥadíth*. We also have the saying that the signs will all follow in quick, ordered succession. From St John (Revelation) we know that after Muhammad there would be a period of a thousand years before the signs of the end times begin, and we have the clear reference of the Qur'án that tells us that a 'Day' is as a thousand years and then more specifically the veiled reference in the Surahs The Dawn and [the Night of] Power giving us a date at the beginning of the 19th century for the dawning of the Sun of Truth.

In his prophetic vision, Daniel gives cryptic clues, in which a day equals a year (Dan. 9:24–7; see discussion in chapter 4, above) but he continues on the topic of the desolation:

> How long shall be the vision concerning the daily sacrifice,

> and the transgression of desolation, to give both the sanctuary and the host to be trodden under foot? And he said unto me, Unto two thousand and three hundred days; then shall the sanctuary be cleansed. (Dan. 8:13–14)

Again we take it as a year for a day and so it is 2,300 years to the desolation and the cleansing. Daniel prophesied around 450 BCE. Add 2,300 years and you get 1850 CE. William Sears in his work *Thief in the Night, or The Case of the Missing Millennium* found that all the Christian prophecies, whether pertaining to events or cryptic references, converge on the 19th century and the date of 1844. He also presents a compilation of biblical prophecies regarding the Return of Christ:

1. He shall come from Persia (additional evidence).
2. He shall go to the valley of the Tigris and Euphrates rivers in the land of Babylon.
3. He shall withdraw from the city into the barren places, as Christ had gone into the desert in the day of His FIRST coming.
4. He shall openly proclaim His Mission in Babylon (or its modern equivalent), and there he shall 'redeem' Israel and the world.
5. He shall come from the Tigris and Euphrates valley to the Holy Land, Israel, as Abraham had come. He shall make the same journey from the land of the Chaldees to the promised land of Canaan.
6. He shall come from a fortified city to a fortified city on His journey to Israel.
7. He shall come out of the 'fortress' and journey to the freedom of the 'river'.

8. On His journey from the East to Israel, He shall come from 'mountain to mountain'.

9. The land of Israel shall be desolate when He comes, but it will later 'blossom as the rose'.

10. He shall dwell in the 'midst of Carmel' and from there He shall 'feed his flock' with His Teachings.

11. His ministry on earth shall last for exactly 'forty years'.

12. He shall come to the valley of Achor where He shall be found by those who 'have sought' Him in the last days.

13. The place where His feet have walked in the Holy Land, Israel, shall 'be made glorious'.

14. The place of His 'rest' or 'sanctuary' or tomb shall become beautified with trees, paths, and flowers.

15. He shall come from the 'seed' of Abraham.

16. He shall 'glorify' Christ in the day of His coming.

17. There shall be signs in the physical heavens in the day of His appearance.

18. He shall 'unseal the books' and explain their 'hidden meanings' so that all may understand (additional evidence).

19. He shall overthrow the power and thrones of wicked kings.

20. He shall set up a spiritual 'kingdom' in all parts of the world . . .[11]

Mount Carmel is that same mountain that is bound up with

the lives of the Prophets including Elijah, who brought down fire from the heavens there and challenged the wayward King Ahab and his wife Jezebel. Elijah's cave is still there to this day. It is certain that John the Baptist spent time there as well. Also Nazareth is relatively close to Mount Carmel and it is possible that Jesus prayed and taught there. Pythagoras went there as well, as it was considered a sacred mountain. It was written that Mount Carmel shall see the Glory of God and the 'new' Jerusalem.

The Time has Come

Around the beginning of the 19th century or 2,400 years after the enlightenment of the Buddha, 1,800 years after the revelation of Christ and 1,200 years after the revelation of Muhammad, there was much change and upheaval in the world. This period was a very tense time in world history, with a sudden upsurge in the progress of every human endeavour. There were developments in science and medicine and a sudden explosion in population and consequently there were dramatic social revolutions and chaos as old world social systems became untenable. It was a time of revolutions and colonial expansion and the occupation of the remote parts of the world, and the beginning of globalization and of technology and the communications age. People enjoyed increased freedom to move and settle around the earth. There was a revolution in governance, in collective living, methods and laws, ownership and trade, relations and communications. There was a new form and standard of scientific endeavour and increasing individuality and independence. The Renaissance, extending from the 14th to the 17th centuries, saw the blossoming of the pure arts, sciences and philosophy and served to awaken the powers of human imagination and fuelled the Industrial Revolution which followed it in the 18th and 19th centuries. The Industrial Revolution led to major changes in agriculture, manufacturing, mining, transportation, medicine and technology, and had a profound effect on the socio-economic and cultural conditions of the time. It was a period that saw the beginning of international travel and global communications but in most places there was a paralysing fixation on material greed and territorial conquest leading to the terrible industries of slavery and warfare. It was a tense world of peoples and nations on the verge of devastating conflict and violent struggle. Everywhere was there a clash – and to a far lesser extent, sharing – of consciousness and cultures in various forms.

It was also a time that saw the rise to prominence of atheism as the modern mind challenged the dogma, ritual, mythology and superstition which plagued the ancient religious mind set. For many centuries the 'Church' held the power to suppress science and scientists with brute force but leading up to the modern era, the practical application of science led to its emergence as a socio-economic power that rendered these religious authorities impotent. The rational, imaginative, modern philosophers and scientists challenged the existence of their ancient god with a prowess that led many to support the emerging doctrine of atheism.

A whole new world emerged, completely different from the one that faced Krishna, Moses, Christ, Buddha and Muhammad. There were attempts to establish new ways of living and new social systems, and there were also many wars and much bloodshed. The leaders of the world were drowning their people in their arrogance and ignorance. Many were trying to conquer and grasp and exploit. The leaders of religion were officiating over empty rituals and not giving the spiritual guidance of which their congregations were so in need. There were many religious entertainers and manipulators applying ancient religious traditions that they did not themselves understand to a world that they could not make sense of. Reformist movements sprang up in all parts of the world expressing this need for a return to the truth or for the development of something new. In many ways the world was becoming smaller and people were coming to have, for the first time, a truly global perspective. The world was convulsing under a great need for something new and better. This new world was desperately in need of a fresh injection of spiritual revelation and divine guidance. For the first time in the history of the world it was possible for a message from God to embrace the whole world and become truly universal.

As discussed earlier, revelation and religion are commensurate with the progressive human mind and societies. The earth stood at the brink of an enormous leap forward into a technological dimension the like of which people could scarcely imagine. Movement and communications were about to radically transform reality. Humanity was approaching its maturity. People of various races and religions were moved by the forces of global commerce and slavery to interact and there was much friction, exploitation and suffering. Many people felt comfortable only with others of the same race and religion. In every part of the world conflict was stirring. The world was in need of fresh revelation that could extend its boundaries and allegiances and help its people to become one world. This was absolutely essential if we were to survive this phase without utterly annihilating each other. We could either recognize our shared humanity and faith or continue the mistrustful, hateful, destructive patterns that had characterized those obsessed with superficial and illusory differences. Not only were we expecting new revelation because of the prophecies pointing to this period but we were desperately in need of it. God promised a long time ago to send the Rightly Guided Leader and the Saviour for the restoration of humankind and to bring peace and unity.

If we are to be true to this exploration we would have to start our search from as far back as the beginning of the 19th century because it is certainly possible that revelation has appeared in the world and that the majority of people remain unaware. So let us proceed to review the claimants, these figures through the past two centuries of Islamic and world history who have made the fantastic and awesome claim that they were Prophets and reformers or leaders sent by God. There were so many that it would divert us significantly if we were to explore all of them but since many of them are so easily recognizable as impostors we need not even mention them (like the many who led people into dark cults with strange practices and ideas). But there are others who are linked with messianic zeal who have not necessarily claimed to be the Messiah. There are some whose ideas have resulted in growth and positive values and who have made people conscious of the dire conditions of our times and the imminence of the promised revelation. Very few have actually made a clear claim to be the promised ones because two holy persons must appear in succession. It behoves us to explore these claims as Muhammad warned us to do, critically and rationally, because the true Mahdi and Masih must be recognized and followed.

Recognition is of five types. First is the fulfilment of the authentic prophecies in the Qur'án and *ḥadíth* in the unfolding of events and signs. Second, we must recognize the trials, difficulties and suffering that the two Promised Ones will endure in bringing this message to humankind. Next we must discern, in their principles and teachings, solutions that address the problems of our age and, fourth, also observe in their own lives the example or the same pattern. Finally we must observe the power which they have to inspire their followers to exemplify these principles and teachings and put them into practice.

To put it less analytically, we must smell the pure sweet fragrance of the flower of divine wisdom. We must taste the flavours of the fruit of Truth, that is to say, that a goodly healthy tree brings forth good nutritious fruit. We must look to the words but also to the actions, for actions speak louder than words. A good teacher does not merely speak about things but he actually achieves the transformation and education of his students. Only a rightly guided leader can perceive the needs of humankind and guide it aright. Only the true one from God can perceive the iniquity of our times and inspire a global social revolution that will redefine the realities of all things, transform all souls according to their measure and attract all people to a recognition of their common humanity and faith.

Throughout the early to mid-1800s there was much expectation and excitement among Christians and Muslims alike concerning the return of Christ. Many were certain that his arrival was imminent. Some even went to Palestine to wait for him and prepare for his arrival. Some built permanent waiting stations in the Holy Land. But every religious group had its own expectation, interpretation and frame of reference. William Butler Yeats (1865–1939) composed a poem which would win him lasting, worldwide acclaim – in 'The Second Coming' he described succinctly the decline of the old and the rise of the new:

> Turning and turning in the widening gyre
> The falcon cannot hear the falconer;
> Things fall apart; the centre cannot hold;
> Mere anarchy is loosed upon the world,
> The blood-dimmed tide is loosed, and everywhere
> The ceremony of innocence is drowned;
> The best lack all conviction, while the worst
> Are full of passionate intensity.
> Surely some revelation is at hand;
> Surely the Second Coming is at hand . . .

Is it possible that Christ has returned and the majority of people do not know about it? It is more than possible – it is very likely that this is the case.

The Second Coming

There have been a number of spiritual/mystical teachers who have made the fantastic claim, or their followers have claimed them, to be the Messenger of God on earth for our time.

Sri Aurobindo

Sri Aurobindo was born Aurobindo Ackroyd Ghose (pronounced and often written as Ghosh) in Kolkata (Calcutta), India, on 15 August 1872. He was an Indian nationalist and freedom fighter but also a scholar and a poet, a mystic and an evolutionary philosopher, a yogi and a guru. His followers believe that he was an Avatar, an incarnation of the Absolute. He wrote works on the spiritual journey of self-purification and yoga. Although his written works have been disseminated far and wide, no organized following exists, other than the small spiritual community of the Sri Aurobindo Ashram, which has about two thousand members, and the experimental 'city' of Auroville, also with approximately two thousand members from around the world. He lived and died in India, had no connection to the Holy Land and never claimed to be the Messiah.

Adi Da Samraj

Adi Da Samraj, a social and spiritual visionary and philosopher, founded his religion Adidam in 1972. Born Franklin Albert Jones on Long Island, New York, on 3 November 1939, Adi Da Samraj followed the eastern path of spiritual practice and eventually claimed to be fully awakened, as Buddha was. He claimed to be the spiritual guide for humanity for our times and gathered a following in the West. He wrote many books showing remarkable wisdom and insight but his focus was more on personal spiritual growth and transformation through devotional relationship with him as guru than on social transformation. His followers think of him as the Kalki Avatar or an Avatar of Vishnu as per the Hindu traditions. He has a very small worldwide following of about a thousand people. His followers profess enlightened ideals but this movement does not fulfil any of the prophecies or the criteria of the messianic model and has no connection to the Holy Land.

Sathya Sai Baba

Sathya Sai Baba was born in 1926 in India. While he made no specific messianic claim, his followers regard him as an Avatar of Vishnu sent to enlighten humanity. At a very young age he began to attract a following, owing to his charismatic, enigmatic presence which many in the West find hard to understand but which the people of India know well and do not feel the need to explain. He taught love and positive values and expressed these teachings through humanitarian work and projects. He had a global following of many millions but viewed himself as the second in a line of three Sai incarnations as gurus, Shirdi Sai, himself Sathya Sai Baba, and the third yet-to-be-fulfilled appearance or incarnation. He had no connection to the prophecies outlined above.

Haile Selassie

Rastas believe that Haile Selassie was God on earth. In Jamaica the descendants of African slaves practised a kind of mixed religion with elements of the African traditional tribal religion, colonial Christianity and Ethiopian Zionism. In the years before 1920 Marcus Garvey, a Jamaican-born human rights activist, began an extensive lecture tour of Central and North America, championing the return to Africa of those of African ancestry and predicting the rise of a great African king. Although Garvey did not do so, mystics among the Jamaican people identified this king as the charismatic Haile Selassie, one of whose titles was Ras Tafari, and began to centre their millennial zeal on him. He was a bold man, an idealist who resisted the onslaught of the Italian conquerors. He spoke for African unity and against war, hatred and oppression. He never made any claim to be divinely inspired nor did he claim to be God. He never revealed any scriptures and he never gathered a following, nor was there any religion shaped with the formative and guiding hand of his love and wisdom.

Many people think of reggae music as epitomized by Bob Marley, which is sincerely conscious and religious, and of ganja-smoking when they hear of Rasta but there is much more to its beliefs than these. Rastas are peace-loving and unity-seeking and believe deeply in the Old Testament, patterning their lives according to it. However, it is difficult to link Haile Selassie, Ras Tafari, to the Messiah of the Last Day as he never claimed to be this and was himself an Ethiopian Orthodox Christian his whole life.

Ghulam Ahmad of Qadian

Ghulam Ahmad of Qadian was born in 1835 in Qadian, a small village situated in the district of Punjab in northern India. He claimed to be divinely inspired, the Mujaddid (divine reformer of Islam), the promised Messiah and the Mahdi. He was respected as a wise teacher in his community and by several scholars of surrounding areas who came to learn from him. When he made the claim that he was the Messenger of God, many people were stunned and confused and turned against him, shunning him and his followers. His writings show that depth of perception and breadth of view that characterize the wise. He founded the Ahmadiyya movement with a vibrant community of followers, the Ahmadis or Qadianis. Although they have split into two major groupings, there are several hundred thousand followers in many countries carrying out humanitarian work in many places. In general, they are not accepted by other Muslims as being Muslims, but they consider themselves to be a movement within Islam that is meant to renew the religion of Muhammad. The community has not yet extended significantly beyond those of Indian heritage. Ahmadis do not claim that Ghulam Ahmad is the Messiah of the Last Day but consider that his role is somehow preparatory.

Guru Nanak

Ghulam Ahmad likened himself to Guru Nanak, the revered founder of the Sikh faith born in 1469. Guru Nanak was Hindu by birth but through dreams, inspiration and exploration came to accept Islam as a true religion from God as well. At the age of 30 Guru Nanak had a vision of being taken to God's court where he was given a mission to teach people to follow neither the Hindu religion nor Islam but to follow God's path. After this he was described as a Guru and the Sikh movement was begun. He travelled widely in the Indian sub-continent and even travelled to Mecca and Medina, teaching that there was but one God and encouraging people to purify their ways, abandon the caste system and do good works. He did not claim to be the Messiah.

Sun Myung Moon

Sun Myung Moon, which means 'the Word made clear', was born in Korea in 1920. When he was 15 he had a vision of Jesus praying on a mountain top in which Jesus instructed him to take up his work on earth, to establish God's kingdom and world peace. About a decade later, Moon published the *Divine Principle,* which forms the scripture of the Unification Church (now called the Family Federation for World Peace and Unification) established in 1954. Moon teaches that there is only one God, that sin must be overcome and that Christ will return in our age to combat sin and unite all people. His followers number somewhere between several hundred thousand to a few million.

Moon and his followers claim that he is the Messiah. His ideas have led to interfaith dialogue and many social and political organizations. There is no connection between Moon and the Middle Eastern line of Messengers and no connection to biblical and Muslim prophecies.

Wallace Fard Muhammad

Between 1929 and 1934 Wallace Fard Muhammad, teaching ideas based on Theosophy and Islam, developed a following in the United States. In 1930 he established the Nation of Islam, which mainly attracted African-Americans, with its mission of improving the plight of black people around the world through the principles of Islam. Wallace Fard Muhammad's followers claim that he was a Manifestation of God, the Mahdi. His chief disciple, the honourable Elijah Muhammad, also claimed to be a Messenger from God.

Initially the Nation of Islam appeared to be a radical Islamic group with separatist anti-white philosophies and teachings which gave voice to the suffering of many black people who were descendants of slaves in the West. The Nation of Islam gained a vast following, especially under the bold and charismatic leadership of Malcolm X (who left the organization in 1964) and with espousers such as the famous Muhammad Ali, the great boxing legend of the 1960s. After the passing of Elijah Muhammad leadership fell to his son, W. Deen Mohammed who reformed the movement, changed its name to the American Society of Muslims in an effort to bring it more in line with mainstream Sunni Islam and then eventually resigned, dissolving the organization. But another stream continued under the leadership of Louis Farrakhan who revived the original Nation of Islam as he understood it. As a movement it has served to carry the light of Islam to millions of Americans but its claims that Wallace Fard Muhammad was the Mahdi or Elijah Muhammad was the Messiah are not convincing in terms of the criteria discussed.

Joseph Smith

The next in our exploration is Joseph Smith, founder of the Church of Jesus Christ of Latter-day Saints, commonly known as the Mormons.

Joseph Smith was born in 1805 and as a boy moved to New York state. Here he had visions of an angel directing him to buried golden plates describing the early history of the American people and their relationship to Christianity. He translated the plates and published them in 1930 as the Book of Mormon. Smith quickly developed a following, which developed into the Church of Jesus Christ of Latter-day Saints. Today the Church has some 12 million adherents around the world who believe that it represents the restoration of the Church of Jesus Christ before his second coming.

Mormons are called to a high ethical standard of conduct and a strong family life. They believe in freedom of worship, that the New Jerusalem will be established on the American continent and that Christ will personally reign upon an earth that will be renewed.

Smith considered himself a latter-day saint or Prophet but did not claim to be the Messiah or the return of Christ, whose appearance is imminent. Some of the writings of Joseph Smith show close correlation with Islamic traditions in that he mentions two prophetic figures to come and the Son of man attired in red garments, as described in the *ḥadí<u>th</u>*.

The Glory of God

The Bahá'ís believe that the founders of the Bahá'í Faith, Al-Báb (the Gate) and Bahá'u'lláh (the Glory of God), are the promised Mahdi and Messiah. The following review of their claims and the history and teachings of the Bahá'í Faith is in greater detail than that of other claimants considered owing to the great wealth of the supporting evidence available and because the two founding figures of the Bahá'í Faith lay bold and emphatic claim to the fulfilment of the messianic promise.

The Bahá'ís are a global community of some six million people of various nationalities and races. They come from diverse religious backgrounds with adherents from all the world's great religions including Judaism, Christianity, Islam, Hinduism and so on. It is considered one of the fastest growing religions in the world today and in 160 years has become the second most geographically widespread of all the world's religions.

Bahá'ís believe that a man named 'Alí-Muḥammad was the promised Mahdi and forerunner to the promised Messiah. He was given the title Al-Báb, 'the Gate', and much like John the Baptist, who paved the way for Jesus at his first coming, so was Al-Báb the Gate by which the promised Messiah would return. 'Alí-Muḥammad was born in 1819. He was a pious young man and a Siyyid (a direct descendant of Muhammad through Fatima and 'Alí). He made this amazing declaration – that he was the herald foretold in *ḥadí<u>th</u>* – in the year 1844 in Shiraz, a town in Iran. He appointed 18 of his first followers as his 'Letters of the Living' and they went forth and spread his message of warning and preparation. He formally announced his mission between the Rukn and Maqám at the Ka'bah in Mecca. He revealed several volumes, the most central being the Bayán (Exposition). He wrote:

> In every nation thou beholdest unnumbered spiritual leaders who are bereft of true discernment, and among every people thou dost encounter myriads of adherents who are devoid of the same characteristic. Ponder for a while in thy heart, have

pity on thyself and turn not aside thine attention from proofs and evidences. However, seek not proofs and evidences after thine idle fancy; but rather base thy proofs upon what God hath appointed. Moreover, know thou that neither being a man of learning nor being a follower is in itself a source of glory. If thou art a man of learning, thy knowledge becometh an honour, and if thou art a follower, thine adherence unto leadership becometh an honour, only when these conform to the good-pleasure of God. And beware lest thou regard as an idle fancy the good-pleasure of God; it is the same as the good-pleasure of His Messenger. Consider the followers of Jesus. They were eagerly seeking the good-pleasure of God, yet none of them attained the good-pleasure of His Apostle which is identical with God's good-pleasure, except such as embraced His Faith.

Thy letter hath been perused. Were the truth of this Revelation to be fully demonstrated with elaborate proofs, all the scrolls that exist in the heaven and on the earth would be insufficient to contain them.

However, the substance and essence of the subject is this, that there can be no doubt that from everlasting God hath been invested with the independent sovereignty of His exalted Being, and unto everlasting He will remain inaccessible in the transcendent majesty of His holy Essence. No creature hath ever recognized Him as befitteth His recognition, nor hath any created being ever praised Him as is worthy of His praise. He is exalted above every name, and is sanctified from every comparison. Through Him all things are made known, while too lofty is His reality to be known through anyone but Him. The process of His creation hath had no beginning and can have no end, otherwise it would necessitate the cessation of His celestial grace. God hath raised up Prophets and revealed Books as numerous as the creatures of the world, and will continue to do so to everlasting.

> If thou art sailing upon the sea of God's Names, which are reflected in all things, know thou that He is exalted and sanctified from being known through His creatures, or being described by His servants. Everything thou beholdest hath been called into being through the operation of His Will. How can such a created thing, therefore, be indicative of His essential oneness? God's existence in itself testifieth to His Own oneness, while every created thing, by its very nature, beareth evidence that it hath been fashioned by God. Such is the proof of consummate wisdom in the estimation of those who sail the ocean of divine Truth.
>
> If, however, thou art sailing upon the sea of creation, know thou that the First Remembrance, which is the Primal Will of God, may be likened unto the sun. God hath created Him through the potency of His might, and He hath, from the beginning that hath no beginning, caused Him to be manifested in every Dispensation through the compelling power of His behest, and God will, to the end that knoweth no end, continue to manifest Him according to the good-pleasure of His invincible Purpose.
>
> And know thou that He indeed resembleth the sun. Were the risings of the sun to continue till the end that hath no end, yet there hath not been nor ever will be more than one sun; and were its settings to endure for evermore, still there hath not been nor ever will be more than one sun. It is this Primal Will which appeareth resplendent in every Prophet and speaketh forth in every revealed Book. It knoweth no beginning, inasmuch as the First deriveth its firstness from It; and knoweth no end, for the Last oweth its lastness unto It.[12]

His mission lasted six years during which he preached what was essentially a message of preparation for the one whom 'God shall make manifest', employing a style reminiscent of the way that John the Baptist had extolled the virtues of Jesus Christ over 1,800 years before.

> I swear by the most holy Essence of God – exalted and glorified be He – that in the Day of the appearance of Him Whom God shall make manifest a thousand perusals of the Bayán cannot equal the perusal of a single verse to be revealed by Him Whom God shall make manifest.
>
> . . . And know thou of a certainty that every letter revealed in the Bayán is solely intended to evoke submission unto Him Whom God shall make manifest, for it is He Who hath revealed the Bayán prior to His Own manifestation.[13]

> The purpose underlying this Revelation, as well as those that preceded it, has, in like manner, been to announce the advent of the Faith of Him Whom God will make manifest. And this Faith – the Faith of Him Whom God will make manifest – in its turn, together with all the Revelations gone before it, have as their object the Manifestation destined to succeed it. And the latter, no less than all the Revelations preceding it, prepare the way for the Revelation which is yet to follow. The process of the rise and setting of the Sun of Truth will thus indefinitely continue – a process that hath had no beginning and will have no end.[14]

Many people who either read the writings of this charismatic young man or met early believers became convinced of the truth of his mission and the beauty of his teachings. The Persian authorities and religious leaders were alarmed at the way his movement was spreading throughout their country and began to resist it furiously, systematically persecuting the followers of the Báb, brutally torturing and killing many thousands. A group of the Báb's followers rode from Khorasan carrying a black standard and encountered strong opposition from the people in the towns they entered. The authorities arrested 'Alí-Muḥammad and kept him in remote prisons until six years after his declaration, when they decided to silence him once and for all. He was shot by firing squad for refusing to recant his claims.

The most prominent of his followers was a man by the name of Ḥusayn-'Alí, known as Bahá'u'lláh (the Glory of God), born 12 November 1817. Well-known for his generosity and philanthropy, Bahá'u'lláh immediately recognized the Báb after perusing some of his writings and became a champion of his cause and comforter and protector of his fellow Bábís. He was imprisoned along with many other followers of the Báb in the worst dungeon in Tehran. It was during this time that he received an intimation of his mission in a dream, when a voice spoke to him:

> Verily, We shall render Thee victorious by Thyself and by Thy pen. Grieve Thou not for that which hath befallen Thee, neither be Thou afraid, for Thou art in safety. Ere long will God raise up the treasures of the earth – men who will aid Thee through Thyself and through Thy Name, wherewith God hath revived the hearts of such as have recognized Him.[15]

After the Báb was martyred and the riders from Khorasan were besieged and killed, Bahá'u'lláh was considered the leader of the Báb's followers. As he was from a noble family that was well-respected and well-connected, rather than being executed with the other Bábís, he was banished with his close family and friends from his home in Tehran to Baghdad. Here he settled for some time and enjoyed a degree of freedom. He made many friends and won many admirers and continued to nurture and guide the believers in Iran. His growing popularity again alarmed the Persians and they persuaded the Ottomans, in whose charge he had been placed, to banish him even further, first to Constantinople and then to Adrianople. When leaving Baghdad he gathered a group of fellow detainees and declared that he was the Promised One, the Messiah come to regenerate and unite all mankind, that he was the Messenger foretold by the Báb, and indeed by Muhammad and Jesus.

> Verily I say, this is the Day in which mankind can behold the Face, and hear the Voice, of the Promised One. The Call of God hath been raised, and the light of His countenance hath been lifted up upon men. It behoveth every man to blot out the trace of every idle word from the tablet of his heart, and to gaze, with an open and unbiased mind, on the signs of His Revelation, the proofs of His Mission, and the tokens of His glory.[16]

> Darkness hath been chased away by the dawning light of the mercy of thy Lord, the Source of all light. The breeze of the All-Merciful hath wafted, and the souls have been quickened in the tombs of their bodies.[17]

After five years in Adrianople, again Bahá'u'lláh's power and influence frightened the Persians and the Ottomans. He was then banished again, this time to the desolate prison-city of 'Akká in the desert wastelands of northern Palestine/western Syria on the edge of the Ottoman empire. Here he remained a prisoner of the Ottomans until the end of his life. But during his 40-year-long mission he wrote many books, letters and Tablets enhancing humanity's understanding of the progressive revelation of God's guidance, exploring the problems facing humankind and their solution, revealing laws and ordinances for the modern era, and describing and setting in motion a global administration system to safeguard the unity and purpose of what became known as the Bahá'í Faith, and ensuring the implementation and progress of his teachings and ideals. Bahá'u'lláh's pre-eminent scriptures are the Kitáb-i-Aqdas (Most Holy Book) and Kitáb-i-Íqán (Book of Certitude):

> In the Name of Our Lord, the Exalted, the Most High.
>
> No man shall attain the shores of the ocean of true understanding except he be detached from all that is in

> heaven and on earth. Sanctify your souls, O ye peoples of the world, that haply ye may attain that station which God hath destined for you and enter thus the tabernacle which, according to the dispensations of Providence, hath been raised in the firmament of the Bayán.

The essence of these words is this: they that tread the path of faith, they that thirst for the wine of certitude, must cleanse themselves of all that is earthly – their ears from idle talk, their minds from vain imaginings, their hearts from worldly affections, their eyes from that which perisheth. They should put their trust in God, and, holding fast unto Him, follow in His way. Then will they be made worthy of the effulgent glories of the sun of divine knowledge and understanding, and become the recipients of a grace that is infinite and unseen, inasmuch as man can never hope to attain unto the knowledge of the All-Glorious, can never quaff from the stream of divine knowledge and wisdom, can never enter the abode of immortality, nor partake of the cup of divine nearness and favour, unless and until he ceases to regard the words and deeds of mortal men as a standard for the true understanding and recognition of God and His Prophets.

Consider the past. How many, both high and low, have, at all times, yearningly awaited the advent of the Manifestations of God in the sanctified persons of His chosen Ones. How often have they expected His coming, how frequently have they prayed that the breeze of divine mercy might blow, and the promised Beauty step forth from behind the veil of concealment, and be made manifest to all the world. And whensoever the portals of grace did open, and the clouds of divine bounty did rain upon mankind, and the light of the Unseen did shine above the horizon of celestial might, they all denied Him, and turned away from His face – the face of God Himself. Refer ye, to verify this truth, to that which hath been recorded in every sacred Book.[18]

Among Bahá'u'lláh's teachings are these: that there is only one God, that all religions come from God and speak the same essential spiritual language of truth, and that revelation is progressive and never-ending. He taught the importance of the equality of all people, the equality of men and women, the harmony of science and religion, and the independent investigation of truth as the foundation for spiritual progress. Writing in the late 19th century to the leaders of the world at a time when they were heading for the most devastating war ever seen, he explained that it was essential for them to convene a world assembly of national leaders and establish a forum for discussing and seeking peace, and that through these instruments they must achieve disarmament, the cessation of hostilities, and the safeguarding of the sovereignty of all nations while working towards a world federation and commonwealth.

> The time must come when the imperative necessity for the holding of a vast, an all-embracing assemblage of men will be universally realized. The rulers and kings of the earth must needs attend it, and, participating in its deliberations, must consider such ways and means as will lay the foundations of the world's Great Peace amongst men. Such a peace demandeth that the Great Powers should resolve, for the sake of the tranquillity of the peoples of the earth, to be fully reconciled among themselves. Should any king take up arms against another, all should unitedly arise and prevent him. If this be done, the nations of the world will no longer require any armaments, except for the purpose of preserving the security of their realms and of maintaining internal order within their territories. This will ensure the peace and composure of every people, government and nation. We fain would hope that the kings and rulers of the earth, the mirrors of the gracious and almighty name of God, may attain unto this station, and shield mankind from the onslaught of tyranny . . . The day is approaching

> when all the peoples of the world will have adopted one universal language and one common script. When this is achieved, to whatsoever city a man may journey, it shall be as if he were entering his own home. These things are obligatory and absolutely essential. It is incumbent upon every man of insight and understanding to strive to translate that which hath been written into reality and action . . . That one indeed is a man who, today, dedicateth himself to the service of the entire human race. The Great Being saith: Blessed and happy is he that ariseth to promote the best interests of the peoples and kindreds of the earth. In another passage He hath proclaimed: It is not for him to pride himself who loveth his own country, but rather for him who loveth the whole world.[19]

> God grant that the light of unity may envelop the whole earth, and that the seal, 'the Kingdom is God's', may be stamped upon the brow of all its peoples.[20]

Bahá'u'lláh not only taught the noble ideals of love, unity and peace but also set in place the framework for a global system of governance destined to be the pattern of a future world order. The Bahá'í administrative system provides that Bahá'ís, in whatever locality they may reside, elect a local governing council – a Local Spiritual Assembly – of nine people to guide the community and promote the Bahá'í Faith and the interests of humankind. There are no priests or other clergy. Rather, the entire community gathers to select the nine most loving and spiritually-minded individuals who are engaged in service to humankind and who exemplify the teachings and principles in their daily lives to be their representatives and leaders. Every country elects a National Spiritual Assembly, intimately linked to its many Local Assemblies, and every five years, the Bahá'ís of the world, through their national assemblies, elect the Universal House of Justice, a council of nine who are the source of guidance to the Bahá'í world and the international head of the Bahá'í Faith. This assembly of nine individuals recognized for their good qualities and service to humanity deliberate, in an open and consultative manner, on the global growth and development of the Bahá'í Faith and on the spiritualization of the planet. In time this august institution will fulfil the role of the international federal government and so it has a very great destiny to fulfil. The Seat of the Universal House of Justice is beautifully situated on Mount Carmel in Haifa (northern Israel/Palestine) overlooking the Bay of 'Akká and near the superb Shrine of the Báb, resplendent among lovely gardens and terraces.

The succession of individuals and institutions from the Gate and the Glory of God to the Servant of the Glory and the Guardian of the Cause and finally to the Universal House of Justice, Bahá'ís believe, preserves the purity and infallibility of Bahá'u'lláh's Revelation and ensures the unity of the Bahá'í Faith.

The Bahá'ís in a locality meet every 19 days to pray together and consult on the needs of the people and strengthen the bonds within their communities. The Local Spiritual Assembly also consults and guides individuals and families and promotes the expansion of their Faith and the spiritual growth of all humankind.

Edward Granville Browne, British orientalist, requested an audience with Bahá'u'lláh and reported the meeting and the words spoken to him:

> Praise be to God that thou hast attained! . . . Thou hast come to see a prisoner and an exile . . . We desire but the good of the world and happiness of the nations; yet they deem us a stirrer up of strife and sedition worthy of bondage and banishment . . . That all nations should become one in faith and all men as brothers; that the bonds of affection and unity between the sons of men should be strengthened; that diversity of religion should cease, and differences of race be

> annulled – what harm is there in this? . . . Yet so it shall be; these fruitless strifes, these ruinous wars shall pass away, and the 'Most Great Peace' shall come . . . Do not you in Europe need this also? Is not this that which Christ foretold? . . . Yet do we see your kings and rulers lavishing their treasures more freely on means for the destruction of the human race than on that which would conduce to the happiness of mankind . . . These strifes and this bloodshed and discord must cease, and all men be as one kindred and one family . . .[21]

Bahá'u'lláh often described the nature and purpose of revelation and in so doing reaffirmed the central common substance uniting all the world religions but also redefined the very concepts of religion and revelation, as in these extracts from his writings:

> . . . they Who are the Luminaries of truth and the Mirrors reflecting the light of divine Unity, in whatever age and cycle they are sent down from their invisible habitations of ancient glory unto this world, to educate the souls of men and endue with grace all created things, are invariably endowed with an all-compelling power, and invested with invincible sovereignty. For these hidden Gems, these concealed and invisible Treasures, in themselves manifest and vindicate the reality of these holy words: 'Verily God doeth whatsoever He willeth, and ordaineth whatsoever He pleaseth.'[22]

> God's purpose in sending His Prophets unto men is twofold. The first is to liberate the children of men from the darkness of ignorance, and guide them to the light of true understanding. The second is to ensure the peace and tranquillity of mankind, and provide all the means by which they can be established.[23]

> O ye that dwell on earth! The distinguishing feature that marketh the preeminent character of this Supreme Revelation consisteth in that We have . . . laid down the essential prerequisites of concord, of understanding, of complete and enduring unity. Well is it with them that keep My statutes.[24]

Here Bahá'u'lláh explains that his is not simply another Revelation or a new religion but rather the culmination of the very purpose of all previous Revelations, progressively disclosed. Bahá'u'lláh made it very clear that only after at least a thousand years would Revelation appear again.

Bahá'u'lláh's mission drew to a close in 1892 but he left humankind with a marvellous vision of 'enduring unity' and the 'most great peace'. One factor characterizing his Revelation is the wealth of his writings, either penned by his own hand or by his secretary and signed by him, whereas the scriptures of earlier religions were collated from memory by the early followers of the Messenger.

Another unique factor that explains the 'enduring unity' of his religion was that for the first time in history a succession plan had been designed by the Messenger himself. Bahá'u'lláh appointed his eldest son, 'Abdu'l-Bahá (Servant of Glory) to succeed him after his passing. 'Abdu'l-Bahá, who was also a prisoner with Bahá'u'lláh, was freed in 1908 and spent the remainder of his life teaching the message of his father, travelling to the West in 1911 to 1913, and establishing its firm foundations in the Holy Land and abroad. 'Abdu'l-Bahá was the head of the Bahá'í Faith and both the perfect exemplar of his father's teachings and their authorized interpreter. Thus he elaborated the teachings of Bahá'u'lláh:

> . . . in this marvellous cycle the earth will be transformed, and the world of humanity arrayed in tranquillity and beauty. Disputes, quarrels and murders will be replaced by peace, truth and concord; among the nations, peoples,

races and countries, love and amity will appear. Cooperation and union will be established, and finally war will be entirely suppressed . . . Universal peace will raise its tent in the centre of the earth, and the blessed Tree of Life will grow and spread to such an extent that it will overshadow the East and the West. Strong and weak, rich and poor, antagonistic sects and hostile nations – which are like the wolf and the lamb, the leopard and kid, the lion and the calf – will act toward each other with the most complete love, friendship, justice and equity. The world will be filled with science, with the knowledge of the reality of the mysteries of beings, and with the knowledge of God.

Now consider, in this great century which is the cycle of Bahá'u'lláh, what progress science and knowledge have made, how many secrets of existence have been discovered, how many great inventions have been brought to light and are day by day multiplying in number. Before long, material science and learning, as well as the knowledge of God, will make such progress and will show forth such wonders that the beholders will be amazed. Then the mystery of this verse in Isaiah, 'For the earth shall be full of the knowledge of the Lord', will be completely evident.

Reflect also that in the short time since Bahá'u'lláh has appeared, people from all countries, nations and races have entered under the shadow of this Cause. Christians, Jews, Zoroastrians, Buddhists, Hindus and Persians all associate together with the greatest friendship and love, as if indeed these people had been related and connected together, they and theirs, for a thousand years; for they are like father and child, mother and daughter, sister and brother. This is one of the meanings of the companionship of the wolf and the lamb, the leopard and the kid, and the lion and the calf.

One of the great events which is to occur in the Day of the manifestation of that Incomparable Branch (Bahá'u'lláh) is the hoisting of the Standard of God among all nations. By this is meant that all nations and kindreds will be gathered together under the shadow of this Divine Banner, which is no other than the Lordly Branch itself, and will become a single nation. Religious and sectarian antagonism, the hostility of races and peoples, and differences among nations, will be eliminated. All men will adhere to one religion, will have one common faith, will be blended into one race, and become a single people. All will dwell in one common fatherland, which is the planet itself. [25]

Know thou that all the powers combined have not the power to establish universal peace, nor to withstand the overmastering dominion, at every time and season, of these endless wars. Erelong, however, shall the power of heaven, the dominion of the Holy Spirit, hoist on the high summits the banners of love and peace, and there above the castles of majesty and might shall those banners wave in the rushing winds that blow out of the tender mercy of God.[26]

In cycles gone by, though harmony was established, yet, owing to the absence of means, the unity of all mankind could not have been achieved. Continents remained widely divided, nay even among the peoples of one and the same continent association and interchange of thought were wellnigh impossible. Consequently intercourse, understanding and unity amongst all the peoples and kindreds of the earth were unattainable. In this day, however, means of communication have multiplied, and the five continents of the earth have virtually merged into one . . . In like manner all the members of the human family, whether peoples or governments, cities or villages, have become increasingly interdependent. For none is self-sufficiency any longer possible, inasmuch as political ties unite all peoples and nations, and the bonds of trade and industry, of agriculture and education, are being strengthened every day. Hence the unity of all mankind can in this day be achieved. Verily this is none other but one of the wonders of this wondrous age,

> this glorious century. Of this past ages have been deprived, for this century – the century of light – hath been endowed with unique and unprecedented glory, power and illumination. Hence the miraculous unfolding of a fresh marvel every day. Eventually it will be seen how bright its candles will burn in the assemblage of man.
>
> Behold how its light is now dawning upon the world's darkened horizon. The first candle is unity in the political realm, the early glimmerings of which can now be discerned. The second candle is unity of thought in world undertakings, the consummation of which will erelong be witnessed. The third candle is unity in freedom which will surely come to pass. The fourth candle is unity in religion which is the corner-stone of the foundation itself, and which, by the power of God, will be revealed in all its splendour. The fifth candle is the unity of nations – a unity which in this century will be securely established, causing all the peoples of the world to regard themselves as citizens of one common fatherland. The sixth candle is unity of races, making of all that dwell on earth peoples and kindreds of one race. The seventh candle is unity of language, i.e., the choice of a universal tongue in which all peoples will be instructed and converse. Each and every one of these will inevitably come to pass, inasmuch as the power of the Kingdom of God will aid and assist in their realization.[27]

After the passing of 'Abdu'l-Bahá, the responsibility of leading the Bahá'ís fell to his grandson, Shoghi Effendi, who was appointed the Guardian of the Bahá'í Faith by 'Abdu'l-Bahá. Shoghi Effendi wrote of the primary teaching of Bahá'u'lláh:

> Let there be no mistake. The principle of the Oneness of Mankind – the pivot round which all the teachings of Bahá'u'lláh revolve – is no mere outburst of ignorant emotionalism or an expression of vague and pious hope. Its

appeal is not to be merely identified with a reawakening of the spirit of brotherhood and good-will among men, nor does it aim solely at the fostering of harmonious cooperation among individual peoples and nations. Its implications are deeper, its claims greater than any which the Prophets of old were allowed to advance. Its message is applicable not only to the individual, but concerns itself primarily with the nature of those essential relationships that must bind all the states and nations as members of one human family. It does not constitute merely the enunciation of an ideal, but stands inseparably associated with an institution adequate to embody its truth, demonstrate its validity, and perpetuate its influence. It implies an organic change in the structure of present-day society, a change such as the world has not yet experienced. It constitutes a challenge, at once bold and universal, to outworn shibboleths of national creeds – creeds that have had their day and which must, in the ordinary course of events as shaped and controlled by Providence, give way to a new gospel, fundamentally different from, and infinitely superior to, what the world has already conceived. It calls for no less than the reconstruction and the demilitarization of the whole civilized world – a world organically unified in all the essential aspects of its life, its political machinery, its spiritual aspiration, its trade and finance, its script and language, and yet infinite in the diversity of the national characteristics of its federated units.

It represents the consummation of human evolution – an evolution that has had its earliest beginnings in the birth of family life, its subsequent development in the achievement of tribal solidarity, leading in turn to the constitution of the city-state, and expanding later into the institution of independent and sovereign nations.

The principle of the Oneness of Mankind, as proclaimed by Bahá'u'lláh, carries with it no more and no less than a solemn assertion that attainment to this final stage in this

> stupendous evolution is not only necessary but inevitable, that its realization is fast approaching, and that nothing short of a power that is born of God can succeed in establishing it.[28]

> God's purpose is none other than to usher in, in ways He alone can bring about, and the full significance of which He alone can fathom, the Great, the Golden Age of a long-divided, a long-afflicted humanity. Its present state, indeed even its immediate future, is dark, distressingly dark. Its distant future, however, is radiant, gloriously radiant – so radiant that no eye can visualize it.[29]

Shoghi Effendi, as Guardian of the young Faith, set about developing human resources, promoting and encouraging the teaching of the Bahá'í Faith in various countries, and nurturing the early foundations of the global Bahá'í world order envisaged by Bahá'u'lláh and elaborated by 'Abdu'l-Bahá.

The Universal House of Justice has published the following statement in an exposition titled *The Promise of World Peace*:

> The Great Peace towards which people of good will throughout the centuries have inclined their hearts, of which seers and poets for countless generations have expressed their vision, and for which from age to age the sacred scriptures of mankind have constantly held the promise, is now at long last within the reach of the nations. For the first time in history it is possible for everyone to view the entire planet, with all its myriad diversified peoples, in one perspective. World peace is not only possible but inevitable. It is the next stage in the evolution of this planet – in the words of one great thinker, 'the planetization of mankind'.
>
> Whether peace is to be reached only after unimaginable horrors precipitated by humanity's stubborn clinging to old patterns of behaviour, or is to be embraced now by an

act of consultative will, is the choice before all who inhabit the earth. At this critical juncture when the intractable problems confronting nations have been fused into one common concern for the whole world, failure to stem the tide of conflict and disorder would be unconscionably irresponsible . . .

A candid acknowledgement that prejudice, war and exploitation have been the expression of immature stages in a vast historical process and that the human race is today experiencing the unavoidable tumult which marks its collective coming of age is not a reason for despair but a prerequisite to undertaking the stupendous enterprise of building a peaceful world. That such an enterprise is possible, that the necessary constructive forces do exist, that unifying social structures can be erected, is the theme we urge you to examine.

Whatever suffering and turmoil the years immediately ahead may hold, however dark the immediate circumstances, the Bahá'í community believes that humanity can confront this supreme trial with confidence in its ultimate outcome. Far from signalizing the end of civilization, the convulsive changes towards which humanity is being ever more rapidly impelled will serve to release the 'potentialities inherent in the station of man' and reveal 'the full measure of his destiny on earth, the innate excellence of his reality'.[30]

The oneness of humanity, with its corollary of unity in diversity, is applicable both to the peoples and to the nations of the world. It is a practical, indeed, essential standard for ordering humankind's collective life on the planet. The oneness of humanity is at once a statement of principle and the ultimate goal of human existence. It implies more than a willingness to cooperate; it speaks to the longing of people everywhere for a world infused with such a spirit of community, fellowship and compassion that human misery and degradation, violence and oppression will become intolerable and eventually unthinkable. In such a world, peace, social and economic justice, prosperity and liberty will become the order of the day. The growing acceptance of the oneness of humanity is the single most powerful force impelling the world toward unity.

In our increasingly interdependent world, it is no longer possible for a people or a nation to achieve lasting prosperity at the expense of other peoples and nations.[31]

Faith

Though I lacked the vocabulary and knowledge to express it to myself and others, as a young man I became disillusioned with the way Islam was practised in my community and taught to us as children. We attended religious classes which mainly involved compulsory, precise recitation and memorization of sounds in a language that we did not understand and routine actions of prayer as if it were some form of exercise. I was not able to draw positive inspiring values from any source in my education, family or society, and I did not have a real connection to God nor a meaningful love and fear of Him which would cause me to do right and seek fellowship with pious people and to avoid evil and the company of the wicked and insincere. The only light for me at that young age was the stories of the life of the Prophet Muhammad and his qualities of honesty and trustworthiness, and this placed an ideal model and pattern in my heart and mind though not yet in my behaviour and actions. Unable to find inspiration in religious sources and observing suffering and violence in the world, I began to doubt Islam and the Qur'án and all religion but I continued to read a lot about various religions, seeking a path and a purpose for my life, seeking to be inspired. As a student of science I was exposed to the ideas and theories of modern science but, again, these did not inspire me to aspire to higher values but rather sought to deny intelligence and beauty and replace it with random chance and luck. Though I saw the flaws in popular pseudo-scientific theories, I still struggled to discern intelligent purpose behind what everyone called creation and religion. What kind of super intelligent Creator would devise such chaos and destruction and religious communities in perpetual conflict over His name? I was at a loss for words to articulate my crisis.

As I walked the lonely path of faithlessness my anchor was the Messengers of God – the beauty and the passion of Christ, the piety and honesty of Muhammad, the serenity and the transcendence of the Buddha – and these sustained me when I had nothing else, and the only prayer I had was '*Rabbí zidní 'ilma wa zukhní fahma*' – 'My Lord, increase me in knowledge and grant me understanding'. This was the only prayer I could utter sincerely and it gave me a glimmer of hope.

After completing my studies and working for a couple of years to pay off my student loans and having saved up enough money I sent myself on a backpacking journey up East Africa and around India for about seven months, seeking adventure but also hoping to learn and observe, to read and understand, to meet people and experience other places and cultures. During this adventure I visited many mosques, churches, temples, synagogues and sacred sites of every type, and uttered my solemn solitary prayer, and sometimes just spaced out in wonder and awe at the marvellous spectacle of human existence. I was being drawn back to some kind of faith, even though I had no words to express that feeling or force of attraction. With my intelligence I struggled to discern meaning and purpose in a world where people were fighting and killing and religions were all divided and opposing each other so fiercely, but with my heart I felt something of this human drama and the civilizing role of religion. I began to appreciate the human condition and its gradual progress and that subtle inexorable force that succeeds in moving mankind forward one day to the next . . . one generation after another . . . one millennium after another.

After three months in India it became necessary for me to apply for a visa extension and so I made my way to the populous city of New Delhi. Sitting in the government offices of the city, waiting to apply for the visa extension, I had occasion to reflect on my journey and ponder the mystery of the Messengers and how they each teach about truth and honesty. I also pondered war and peace, asking myself what we can do to change the world.

The next day I was enticed by a local tour guide to visit the Lotus Temple. I had seen images of this place before at an exhibition back home and also in the in-flight magazine and so I was intrigued. I made my way by bus and then walked through the hot, dusty, busy streets of Delhi, not really knowing what to expect. Entering the Bahá'í House of Worship was an amazing experience from the moment I walked in the gates and read the principles of the Faith carved in stone and set in a lovely grass embankment. The two which immediately appealed to me were the unity of all religions and the harmony of science and religion. As I approached the beautiful flower-shaped structure I was given a pamphlet to read about the Báb and Bahá'u'lláh and linked them to the prophecies of the Mahdi and Masih. I then spoke to the librarian and we discussed my two most burning questions. He explained the story of creation and Heaven and Hell as symbolic descriptions to help us understand the spiritual condition of mankind in this world and in the next.

I was invited to attend a prayer service and I entered the marvellous House of Worship. Inside it was quiet and clean and very pure, unlike the busy streets and places I had grown accustomed to all over India. Everyone inside was respectful and gentle, and the place was so beautiful and tranquil. It had nine upturned marble petals as entrances, and light streamed in from all sides. It was simple and elegant, without being bold and ostentatious. Upon the inner wall between each entrance was a gold plaque with an etching of a passage from the Bahá'í writings. I walked around reading these poetic words of modern scripture and marvelled at the way they touched the highest part in me. I sat in silent contemplation but my soul was ablaze. The silence shimmered as the jingling bangles on the Indian ladies' wrists and ankles, and the shuffling of the tourists and the giggling of the little children all reverberated into the timeless spaces and mingled with the shafts of light streaming in from above. Looking up at the point where the marble flower structure unfurled, I spoke to God and renewed my long-lost relationship with my Maker. I should have been very ashamed and humbled to the dust but I recall being so inspired and uplifted, so thankful, so utterly thankful and excited. The opening through which sunlight streamed in was sealed with some kind of symbol, replete with curves and stars in Arabic calligraphy. I would come to know later that this was the symbol of the Greatest Name of God, the symbol of the Bahá'í Faith. The prayer service began with a chant in the sweet melodic voice of a young Indian lady.

> Is there any Remover of difficulties save God? Say: Praised be God! He is God! All are His servants and all abide by His bidding![32]

Then there was chanting from the Holy Qur'án, a reading from the Buddhist canons and another melody, this time from the Bhagavad Gita. It was so moving that if my heart had not been hardened by so many years of unbelief I would have broken down in tears. But in truth I was far too happy to cry. The only way to describe my experience that day is to liken it to the way that a flower blossoms and in the sunlight opens and unfurls – or to that mystic bird, the phoenix, which burns itself and then rises from its own ashes. I had experienced the beauty of Bahá'í worship and the sincere expression of the principles of the unity of all religions and the harmony of science and religion. I was moved and transported. I was inspired . . . finally.

I walked around for a little while, talked to some people and just floated about, savouring the moment and the sensations within. I watched people going in and out, taking photos and talking and discussing things, and I wondered if anyone was feeling what I was feeling, if anyone was realizing what I was realizing. Do they really know where they are? Do they realize the meaning of what these people are saying? Do they get the significance of this structure, this flower that has bloomed on the tree of revelation? The world would never be the same again. My world would never be the same again. Could it be that I had found what I had always been looking for? Could it be that God had revealed that which is to rework the dark human world into that radiant vision of peace and love and truth? Could it be that I had found religion – religion renewed, religion made pure, religion made fresh and meaningful, religion cleansed of all the dust and grime of the thousands of years of limited human designs? Could it be that God is there and He loves me, and He listens to me, and He guides me?

I wasn't sure if I was dreaming or waking up from a dream, or if it was a dream coming true. Maybe it was all of them. I had to rush from there to the other end of town to collect my visa and so I took a rickshaw and hastened through the busy streets from Old Delhi to New. I don't know what I saw, what I thought. All the things that happened after that are like a continuous blur in which nothing mattered but this new knowledge, this new secret that was kindled inside me.

I returned to the city where I was residing at the time, to Jaipur, or the pink city as it is called owing to the faded pink colour of the old fortified walls surrounding the inner city and its buildings. It was still dark in the early morning and instead of going home to sleep I got a rickshaw driver to take me to the base of the old fort. There was no person or creature around and in the cold darkness of early morning I started to ascend the winding path that leads to the top of the fort. As I was walking up I heard the call to prayer from down below. It was dawn and the first muezzin sang out his lonely melodic call. Suddenly I realized that it was so full of meaning and so utterly beautiful. One by one the muezzins of other mosques also began their chanting and a beautiful chorus of *adháns* in different voices and styles filled the night sky over the sleeping city and filled my eyes with tears. The normally chaotic and bustling pink city was absolutely still and just this message filled the valley and the mountains:

God is the Greatest
There is none worthy of worship besides God.

It was such a delight to be open, to be inspired with the love of God and the wonder of His mystery. I made my *wuḍú'* (ablutions) with dust and performed my *ṣaláh* alone on the hard rocks that morning. Facing the direction of my Lord, I bowed sincerely in submission, for the first time in a long time. I climbed further still to the very top of the hill and watched the sun rise over the city and listened as the city slowly came back to life.

The same day I decided to look for the city library, hoping to find some Bahá'í books. I found out from the tourist office where the library was and I looked and searched and walked for a long time until I eventually found it upstairs in an old building. It was dark and dusty, and shafts of light made beams across the passages. The librarian seemed very busy and didn't understand what I was saying, so she pointed to a catalogue drawer near the entrance. I went up to it hopefully and pulled out the drawer labelled 'B'. I stuck my finger somewhere in the middle of the hundreds of cards and flipped the stack forward and, lo and behold, the very first card that faced me was titled *Bahá'u'lláh and the New Era* by J. Esslemont. It was like God saying, 'Yes, I am watching you, and yes, you are on the right path!'

I was so excited and overwhelmed I cannot describe it. I didn't wait for help from the librarian, who was too busy. I figured out the catalogue system and in the far back on the dusty brown shelves I found the thin little book nestled snug between thick heavy volumes. I took it out, sat down and started reading about this Bahá'í Faith. I am a slow reader at the best of times and with this book I wanted to savour every word and every idea and ponder and wonder. I read about the history of the Bahá'í Faith, the lives of its founders 'Alí-Muhammad titled Al-Báb, the Gate, and Mírzá Ḥusayn-'Alí titled Bahá'u'lláh, the Glory of God, and his son 'Abbás Effendi known as 'Abdu'l-Bahá or the Servant of Glory. I returned several times to read what was to me the most important book in the world. That library, despite its dusty appearance and coldness, became a wonderful home and sanctuary and a blessed spot. I couldn't take the book out of the library, so I came back several times and read about the teachings of the Bahá'í Faith and its beliefs and what it means to be a Bahá'í. Every page was fresh evidence of its wisdom illumining the dark passages of my mind and earth's history. I read the writings of the luminaries of the Bahá'í Faith and the language was so pure and exalted, so sweet and poetic, the ideas so transcendent and all encompassing, so loving and inviting to all. There were two prayers that I read and then scribbled into my little scrapbook:

> Purify and sanctify me.
> Give me a portion from the outpouring of holiness,
> so that sorrow and sadness may vanish,
> joy and happiness descend,
> despondency and hopelessness be changed
> into cheerfulness and trustfulness,
> and courage take the place of fear.[33]

And the other one I really liked was:

> O Thou kind Lord!
> Unite all. Let the religions agree
> and make the nations one,
> so that they may see each other as one family
> and the whole earth as one home.
> May they all live together in perfect harmony.[34]

I returned and read about the promise of world peace and the Kingdom of Heaven on earth, and the slow process of changing the hearts and minds of man. I read about prophecies fulfilled, that Baha'u'llah was the one every Prophet foretold, that he was the fulfilment of all their missions as Prophets, that he was the one they had written about, that he was the one mentioned by God in all the holy Books and Scriptures of the past. I recognized in the two founding figures of the Bahá'í Faith the promised Mahdi and Christ. I knew that I had found something, or that something had found me, and my heart opened and I spoke to God after a long time. I had so much to say – my heart sang out in wordless thanks and praise, and the feeling of peace and calm that came over me when I realized that God was really there and that He had a plan for mankind, and a plan for me, was indescribable. I didn't feel so lonely anymore.

What I read began to have a profound influence over my thinking and my understanding. My mind and heart expanded. My mind was at ease but also awakened and active. The inspiring writings and lofty exhortations caused me to redefine who I was and what this world was and to re-evaluate my life, and at long last gave me the motivation and tools to try to live a positive and virtuous life. After thoroughly exploring the Bahá'í Faith and experiencing its transformative influence I was convinced that it was the truth and that Bahá'u'lláh was indeed the Messenger of God for our age and it all made sense to me. History and the progress of mankind and religion, the chaos and confusion and hatred and destruction all resolved into a sense of purpose. God was sending His Messengers to every people in every place and time to transform the world into a better world, to change that human tendency of competition and separateness to one of love, unity and peace.

Returning to my community, I joyously shared with everyone I knew the wonderful news but soon realized that they were not as enthusiastic as I was, to say the least. Very few of my friends and relatives would listen to what I had to say and they seemed unwilling to discuss or rationalize and simply resigned themselves to a kind of foggy generic consensus of the Last Day which was vague and phantasmagorical at best – it was a path they felt unqualified to tread. Many rejected the Bahá'í Faith without knowing anything about it, simply because it didn't fit some ancient pattern or wasn't what was 'expected'. Some concerned friends and relatives made arrangements for me to meet with so-called learned muftis and *mawlánás*. Both these seemed to stumble when we began to talk about symbolism and imagery in the Qur'án and it seemed they too were unable or unwilling to venture into this territory and eventually resorted to name-calling and harsh words. Very few people were willing to enter into logical discussion but even these few seemed to be terribly misinformed because they brought forward counterclaims and accusations that were entirely untrue and clearly fabricated, with the intention of creating suspicion and doubt that would prevent any open-minded thinker from even entertaining the possibility that a Messenger of God had appeared.

At the same time I was meeting Bahá'ís and becoming part of the Bahá'í community in my city and found them to be bright and friendly people, diverse but united, and engaged in service to mankind. Every meeting and prayer gathering was inspiring and uplifting, and meeting people who accepted me and had positive outlooks and loving ways helped me to heal and grow in confidence and self worth. The nervous fear and deep-rooted paranoia which had plagued me to the extent that I was barely able to communicate with people was slowly dissipating and I was gradually building healthy, nurturing friendships and relationships. Fear was giving way to love.

I read a lot and deepened my knowledge of the principles and teachings, and a marvellous transformation gradually started taking place in my soul. I started to become a better person and the old habits that kept me chasing earthly pursuits dispersed and the old habits of thought which kept me in perpetual gloom dissolved. The redefinition of the very concept of religion and the realization of the progressive nature of revelation was like a gateway to the wisdom of all the world's religions or like a primer with which the scriptures made sense. My understanding of these religions was enhanced and the seemingly diverse rituals and social laws sank into the background as transient and necessary but the essential unity of their basic principles and teachings rose above and claimed kinship to each other. I was becoming aware of the real condition of the earth and humankind, and the forces and influences shaping their progress. I became conscious of the real solutions to the problems facing the world in the deeply philosophical but also very simple and practical sense, as well as the complex dynamics of applying these solutions to a world largely unaware, uninterested, reluctant or vehemently opposed. I started to see that we need to practise virtue and help others to do the same and that this requires overcoming our egos and attachments to worldly things so that we can become selfless and truly serve and help others. I began to realize that the Bahá'í Faith is about the growth of a shared humanity and one common universal faith that does not dismantle into divisions and sects but remains a cohesive body with one vision – a vision of peace on earth, unity of all the nations, a global commonwealth and an international federal government, ensuring the final cessation of poverty, warfare, suffering and hatred, and promoting the attainment of ever higher and higher levels of virtue and spirituality.

I also felt the need to share with others this wonderful secret, especially in my community, but was well aware of the challenges facing Muslims when confronted with the Bahá'í Faith and why it is so difficult for many people to open up to the possibility, let alone to embrace the truth of this Revelation. And so the next journey of researching and writing this book began. I wanted to liberate people from the shackles that were binding them. Personally I consider myself a world citizen and child of the universe – a Buddhist, Christian, Muslim, Bahá'í – and so I do not have any particular position to defend or promote. I simply feel obligated to share what I have found inspiring and good for all mankind and the planet. So now, having addressed many of these challenges and issues, one last task remains . . .

Knowing the Tree by Its Fruit

People have raised concerns about the Bahá'í Faith and, out of fear, some have fabricated spurious stories that foster speculation and try to discredit the Bahá'í claims. We need to consider these, independently and objectively, in the spirit of this exploration.

Owing to the fact that the Bahá'í World Centre is located in Haifa, in northern Palestine/Israel and manages to coexist peacefully with the existing government, some have raised the accusation that the Bahá'í Faith is in collaboration with the Israeli government to subvert and undermine Islam and Palestine. This allegation has no factual basis and does not correlate with objectively recorded history. It is alleged that the Bahá'ís colluded with, first the British government, then the American government, then the Israeli government to subvert and undermine the Muslims and help with the occupation of Palestine. However, the truth is very different.

Bahá'u'lláh was imprisoned by the Muslim Persians and Ottomans, arrived in 'Akká as a prisoner and remained a prisoner for the rest of his life. He was imprisoned in 'Akká in 1868, some 54 years before the British had the Mandate for Palestine in 1922 and 80 years before the founding of the state of Israel; he died in 1892, again well before either of these events took place. The challenge facing the Persians was that they could not allow Bahá'u'lláh to remain in Persia, or anywhere, for that matter, central in the Islamic lands because so charismatic and magnanimous was his presence that he won the hearts and attracted a following wherever he was exiled. So eventually he was exiled with his entire family and many of his followers to the remotest outpost, the prison-city of 'Akká, obviously not of his own volition. Some other Bahá'ís followed him to this city, fleeing the persecution in their homeland and out of a desire to be close to Bahá'u'lláh. The Bahá'ís purchased land and settled in the area and because Bahá'u'lláh passed away there and his tomb was established in Bahjí, close to 'Akká, it naturally became the centre of the Bahá'í world.

After some time the administrative headquarters of the Bahá'í Faith were also established nearby, on Mount Carmel. The Bahá'ís are peace-loving and non-violent and it is a firm principle of their Faith not to engage in political affairs. When the transition from the Ottomans to the British came as a result of the First World War, the Bahá'ís were allowed to remain in the area. The Bahá'ís were focused on the steady global expansion of their Faith and made it a firm policy not to teach their Faith or engage in any political activities in Palestine/Israel. The Bahá'ís have no connection to any governments or political parties and have as their main long-term goals the unity of all mankind and world peace. The Bahá'í properties, buildings and activities are all funded by the Bahá'ís around the world themselves, as it is also a firm law that only registered Bahá'ís may contribute to the Bahá'í fund and no Bahá'í institution or individual may accept funds from any non-Bahá'í source for Bahá'í purpose. Further, no Bahá'í may discuss, let alone engage in, party politics of any kind.

By taking fragments and extracts from Bahá'u'lláh's writings out of context some have attempted to mislead people with misinterpretations alleging that Bahá'u'lláh claimed to be God. Bahá'u'lláh in numerous writings confesses his inability even to fathom the majesty of God. He prayed to God saying:

> I am the one, O Lord, whose heart and soul, whose limbs, whose inner and outer tongue testify to Thy unity and Thy oneness, and bear witness that Thou art God and that there is no God but Thee. Thou didst bring mankind into being to know Thee and to serve Thy Cause, that their station might thereby be elevated upon Thine earth and their souls be uplifted by virtue of the things Thou hast revealed in Thy Scriptures, Thy Books and Thy Tablets.[35]

This is the general tone of Bahá'u'lláh's writings: utter submissiveness and humility before God. Anyone who reads his writings will recognize and confirm this. In the scripture revealed through Bahá'u'lláh, oftentimes God addresses mankind, just as He does in the Bible and the Qur'án and other scriptures, and this is not to be confused with the station of Bahá'u'lláh, which is the Prophet and Messenger of God. Bahá'ís refer to Bahá'u'lláh and every other authentic Messenger of God, including Abraham, Moses, Jesus, Muhammad, Buddha, Krishna and so on, as Manifestations of God because each of them is the appearance of the qualities and virtues loved by God and exemplars of the names and attributes of God; each is the voice of God or the pen of God inasmuch as the Word of God is revealed through them. The name 'the Glory of God' is an example of one such attribute. Bahá'ís do not consider Bahá'u'lláh to be God and they do not pray to him.

Bahá'u'lláh extolled the unfathomable greatness of God in one of my favourite passages:

> Praise be to God, the All-Possessing, the King of incomparable glory, a praise which is immeasurably above the understanding of all created things, and is exalted beyond the grasp of the minds of men. None else besides Him hath ever been able to sing adequately His praise, nor will any man succeed at any time in describing the full measure of His glory. Who is it that can claim to have attained the heights of His exalted Essence, and what mind can measure the depths of His unfathomable mystery? From each and every revelation emanating from the Source of His glory, holy and never-ending evidences of unimaginable splendour have appeared, and out of every manifestation of His invincible power oceans of eternal light have outpoured. How immensely exalted are the wondrous testimonies of His almighty sovereignty, a glimmer of which, if it but touched them, would utterly consume all that are in the heavens and in the earth! How indescribably lofty are the tokens of His consummate power, a single sign of which, however inconsiderable, must transcend the comprehension of whatsoever hath, from the beginning that hath no beginning, been brought into being, or will be created in the future till the end that hath no end. All the Embodiments of His Names wander in the wilderness of search, athirst and eager to discover His Essence, and all the Manifestations of His Attributes implore Him, from the Sinai of Holiness, to unravel His mystery.
>
> A drop of the billowing ocean of His endless mercy hath adorned all creation with the ornament of existence, and a breath wafted from His peerless Paradise hath invested all beings with the robe of His sanctity and glory. A sprinkling from the unfathomed deep of His sovereign and all-pervasive Will hath, out of utter nothingness, called into being a creation which is infinite in its range and deathless in its

> duration. The wonders of His bounty can never cease, and the stream of His merciful grace can never be arrested. The process of His creation hath had no beginning, and can have no end.
>
> In every age and cycle He hath, through the splendorous light shed by the Manifestations of His wondrous Essence, recreated all things, so that whatsoever reflecteth in the heavens and on the earth the signs of His glory may not be deprived of the outpourings of His mercy, nor despair of the showers of His favours. How all-encompassing are the wonders of His boundless grace! Behold how they have pervaded the whole of creation. Such is their virtue that not a single atom in the entire universe can be found which doth not declare the evidences of His might, which doth not glorify His holy Name, or is not expressive of the effulgent light of His unity. So perfect and comprehensive is His creation that no mind nor heart, however keen or pure, can ever grasp the nature of the most insignificant of His creatures; much less fathom the mystery of Him Who is the Day Star of Truth, Who is the invisible and unknowable Essence. The conceptions of the devoutest of mystics, the attainments of the most accomplished amongst men, the highest praise which human tongue or pen can render are all the product of man's finite mind and are conditioned by its limitations.[36]

Some Sunni Muslims denounce the Bahá'í Faith as an offshoot of Shi'a Islam. Bahá'u'lláh was born a Muslim in Iran just as Jesus was born a Jew in Palestine/Israel. Muhammad was the last Messenger and it makes perfect sense that the Messiah would appear among the Muslims, as confirmed by *ḥadíth* – it was inevitable as the fulfilment of prophecy, destiny and absolute necessity. The Shi'a Muslim leaders and shahs of Iran persecuted, imprisoned and tortured Bahá'u'lláh because of his Revelation. They disowned him, seized his property, exiled him and wanted absolutely nothing to do with him, hoping to see him and his followers destroyed or banished, whatever was easiest for them to accomplish.

Bahá'u'lláh in his writings not only explains the cause but also prescribes the solution to the human disease which creates division and sects in religion. It is of no significance which sect within the Muslim world or even within which of the great religions of the world Bahá'u'lláh appeared because he came to annul all religious division and to redefine the very concept of religion, revealing them all to be aspects of one reality. While reaffirming the basic principles common to the religions, his Revelation moved humankind a significant leap forward in its spiritual progress and the community that has arisen to embody his ideals cannot be considered a mere sect. Our language is limited in its ability to describe and define this Revelation and its spiritual community and the great destiny envisioned – it is something the world has never seen or experienced or even dreamed of.

Some denounce the Bahá'ís because they say they deal in financial interest and consume *ḥarám* foods and these are contrary to the teachings of Islam. During Muhammad's time moneylenders would exploit people and cause much loss, sorrow and family disintegration and so the taking and paying of interest was abolished. But in the modern day interest on capital and investment is a very different thing. It is controlled and regulated, and is thus fair and equal to all, and no inhumane penalties exist. In fact, interest from invested money is how many people are able to start businesses, own homes and cars, etc. So as a practical necessity of modern living Bahá'u'lláh has abolished this law forbidding the lending of money with interest. Similarly, during the time of Muhammad the pig was seen as a filthy animal and its meat was easily diseased in the hot conditions of the desert and led to sickness. In modern farming pigs are well-bred and kept and their meat does not lead to disease and impurity. Pork is an important part of the diet of many parts of the world and so Bahá'u'lláh has permitted it.

At present our species is still fixated on a carnivorous diet which is not suitable for us. Bahá'u'lláh explains that gradually we will evolve towards a fruit, vegetable and pulse diet. Minor social laws must also be made to fit the times to protect people from their own excesses. Thus Bahá'u'lláh upholds the prohibition on alcohol, the use of drugs, gambling, immorality and adultery (or sex outside of marriage). He strongly discourages smoking, divorce and backbiting.

Some are concerned because they have heard that Bahá'ís do not read *ṣaláh* (obligatory prayer). The Báb, Bahá'u'lláh and 'Abdu'l-Bahá did read *ṣaláh* for most of their lives. It was only when God revealed new laws with regard to obligatory prayer that the form of *ṣaláh* changed. Muhammad was given *ṣaláh* and the details of ablutions, the movements, prayers and times associated with them, and the direction to face when praying. This was something new to his people but it was the command of God, the gift of God. When Muhammad changed the Qiblah (direction of prayer) from Palestine/Israel to Mecca it was quite a challenge for many of his followers. Similarly, it is not easy to accept that Bahá'u'lláh was given new ablutions, movements, prayers, times and a new direction or Qiblah (changed from Mecca back to Palestine/Israel). Bahá'u'lláh revealed three obligatory prayers and Bahá'ís have a choice of which to use each day: the short, medium or long obligatory prayer. They must perform one of these three on any given day. The long obligatory prayer has nine *rak'ahs* (including genuflections of standing, sitting and bowing), with inspiring uplifting prayers, and must be performed once in 24 hours. The medium obligatory prayer has three *rak'ahs* with beautiful but somewhat shorter prayers, and must be performed three a times day in the morning, noon and evening. The short obligatory prayer consists of the following verses to be read once between noon and sunset:

> I bear witness, O my God, that Thou hast created me to know Thee and to worship Thee. I testify, at this moment,

> to my powerlessness and to Thy might, to my poverty and to Thy wealth.
>
> There is none other God but Thee, the Help in Peril, the Self-Subsisting.[37]

The majority of people who speak against the Bahá'í Faith are just afraid that because it is something different from 'Islam', it must be leading people away from the true religion and that if they follow it, they will be condemned. In the section entitled 'Blessed are the Strangers' in chapter 6, above, we explored what 'Islam' means and how it returns as a 'stranger'. The prophecies inform us that Islam has declined and that nothing remains of it but its name and appearance. There is much good in the Muslim world but generally speaking the prophecies have been fulfilled and the time for the renewal of humankind is at hand. We have looked at revelation as the rising of the Sun of Truth but another way of looking at this renewal is to consider that fresh revelation is like the life-giving rains and warm sunshine which bring on the springtime – new growth, flowering and the appearance of fresh fruit upon the Tree of Revelation which offers nourishing sustenance to those who partake of it. Those who eat the rotting remnants from the past season will continue to suffer with diseases like fear, sadness, anger and confusion on the personal level, as well as corruption, exploitation, bigotry and abuse on the interpersonal level and perpetual war, religious fundamentalism and terrorism on the national and global scales.

The Qur'ánic verses which state that anyone who chooses a religion other than Islam will burn in the fire of Hell are to be understood in the light of what true Islam means and what the fire of Hell symbolizes. True Islam is to submit to the Will of God by following His Messengers and the commandments they establish. Those who turn away from the Messenger of God in his day are the same as those who rejected previous Messengers. The fire of Hell is the self-imposed condition of suffering caused by separation from God, owing to this inability to recognize Him caused by the inability to cultivate ourselves in line with His teachings. We thus remain self-obsessed and divided. We need not fear this situation as a possible future because such is the current condition of many people in the world today. Bahá'u'lláh explains far more eloquently:

> The Day of Return is inscrutable unto all men until after the divine Revelation hath been fulfilled. He is in truth the One Who ordaineth whatsoever He willeth. When the Word of God is revealed unto all created things whoso then giveth ear and heedeth the Call is, indeed, reckoned among the most distinguished souls, though he be a carrier of ashes. And he who turneth away is accounted as the lowliest of His servants, though he be a ruler amongst men and the possessor of all the books that are in the heavens and on earth.[38]

> O Son of Being! Thy Paradise is My love; thy heavenly home, reunion with Me. Enter therein and tarry not. This is that which hath been destined for thee in Our kingdom above and Our exalted dominion.[39]

Salám – Peace

We have come to the end of a very comprehensive and objective survey of world religion, history and prophecy. We have looked into the Qur'án and *ḥadíth* and world scriptures for that which is essentially common to better understand what they are all saying about our future – or rather, their future, which is our present. We have reviewed many signs and prophecies and concluded that the Last Day is here and that we are living in it now at the dawn of the technological and communications era and the global village. We have clarified many misconceptions and de-cluttered our thinking about the 'Last Day' and simplified it.

We have surveyed the claims of many to the title of Mahdi and Christ, including the Bahá'í claim of divine Revelation and I have shared with you my own conclusions regarding this: the Bahá'í claim closely corresponds with the prophecies and the needs of the age in which we live. But it is up to each individual to investigate for himself what the Truth is. What is certain is that this is the Last Day and the signs of it are upon us. Those who are rigidly attached to the world and fearful of change may instinctively believe they need to stick to their traditions. I believe that by doing so they will continue to live and create a fearful and divided world and thereby delay the maturity of humankind and the glorious vision of its future which is today unfolding. Those who are actively seeking Truth will arise to investigate the matter for themselves and they will progress and be inspired and learn how to live in and create a loving reality. The world needs peace and cooperation, not more wars and divisions. The return of the Messiah and the universal peace and harmony that his second coming promises are something unimaginably wonderful and simply necessary . . . a glorious vision . . . our destiny!

Love, Unity, Peace!

BIBLIOGRAPHY

Scripture

The Báb. *Selections from the Writings of the Báb*. Haifa: Bahá'í World Centre, 1976.

Bahá'í Prayers: A Selection of Prayers revealed by Bahá'u'lláh, the Báb and 'Abdu'l-Bahá. Wilmette, IL: Bahá'í Publishing Trust, 2002.

Bahá'u'lláh. *Gems of Divine Mysteries: Javáhiru'l-Asrár*. Haifa: Bahá'í World Centre, 2002.

— *Gleanings from the Writings of Bahá'u'lláh*. Wilmette, IL: Bahá'í Publishing Trust, 1983.

— *The Hidden Words*. Wilmette, IL: Bahá'í Publishing Trust, 1990.

— *Kitáb-i-Íqán*. Wilmette, IL: Bahá'í Publishing Trust, 1989.

— *Prayers and Meditations*. Wilmette, IL: Bahá'í Publishing Trust, 1987.

— *Tablets of Bahá'u'lláh*. Wilmette, IL: Bahá'í Publishing Trust, 1988.

The Bhagavad Gita. Trans. Juan Mascaró. Harmondsworth, Middx.: Penguin Books, 1962.

Confucius. *The Analects*. Various editions.

— *The Great Learning*. Various editions.

The Holy Bible. Authorised King James Version. London: The Gideons, International, 1957.

The Holy Bible. New International Version. London: Hodder and Stoughton, 1984.

The Holy Qur'an. Translation and commentary by Abdullah Yusuf Ali. n.p.: Islamic Propaganda Centre International, 1946.

The Koran. Trans. J. M. Rodwell. London: Dent (Everyman's Library), 1963.

Pickthall, Marmaduke. *The Meaning of the Glorious Koran: An Explanatory Translation*. New York: Dorset Press, n.d.

Tao Te Ching and Hua Hu Ching. Translation and elucidation by Hua-Ching-Ni. Santa Monica, CA: Seven Star Communications, 1979.

Zend Avesta Farvardin Yasht. Sacred Books of the East, vol. 23. Oxford: Oxford University Press, 1880.

Ḥadíth

Abú Dáwud al-Sijistání al-Azdí. *Sunan*. Cairo: Maṭba'ah Muṣṭafá al-Bábí al-Ḥalabí, 1371/1952.

al-Bukhárí, Muḥammad. *Ṣaḥíḥ* Trans. Muhammad Muhsin Khan. 9 vols. Chicago: Kazi Publications, 3rd ed., 1979.

al-Ḥákim an-Naysabúrí. *Al-Mustadrak 'alá 'l-Saḥíḥayn fí 'l-Ḥadíth*. Riyáḍ: Maktabah an-Naṣr, 1968.

Ibn al-'Arabí, Muhyi ad-Dín. *Al-Futúḥát al-Makkiyyah*. Beirut: Dar Ṣádir [1968?] (Reprint of Cairo: Dar al-Kutub, 1329/1911).

Ibn Ḥanbal, Aḥmad. *Musnad*. 6 vols. Cairo: Maṭba'ah al-Maymán-iyyah, 1313/1896.

Ibn Kathír. *Tafsír al-Qur'án al-'Aẓím*. 4 vols. Cairo: Dár at-Turáth al-Arabí, 1385/1965.

Ibn Májah, Muḥammad. *Sunan*. Ed. Muḥammad Fu'ád 'Abd al-Báqí. 2 vols. Cairo: Dár Iḥyá al-Kutub al-'Arabiyyah, 1372–3/1952–3.

Muslim ibn al-Ḥajjáj. *Ṣaḥíḥ*. Trans. 'Abdul Hamid Siddiqi. Lahore: Sh. Muhammad Ashraf, 1975.

al-Muttaqí al-Hindí, 'Alá ad-Dín 'Alí. *Kanz al-'Ummál*. 16 vols. Aleppo: Maktaba at-Turáth al-Islámí, 1389–97/1969–77.

as-Suyúṭí, Jalál ad-Dín. *Ad-Durr al-Manthúr fí't-Tafsír bi'l-Ma'thúr*. 6 vols. Beirut: Muḥammad Amín Damaj, n.d. (facsimile of Cairo, 1314/1896 ed.).

al-Ṭabarání, Sulayman ibn Aḥmad. *Al-Mu'jam al-Kabír*. Various editons.

at-Tirmidhí, Muḥammad. *Ṣaḥíḥ* (together with the Sharḥ of Imám Abú Bakr ibn al-'Arabí al-Málikí). 13 vols. Cairo: Maṭba'ah as-Ṣáwí, 1353/1934.

General

'Abdu'l-Bahá. *Selections from the Writings of 'Abdu'l-Bahá.* Haifa: Bahá'í World Centre, 1978.

— *Some Answered Questions.* Wilmette, IL: Bahá'í Publishing Trust, 1981.

Bahá'í International Community. 'Global Action Plan for Social Development'. Contribution to the first substantive session of the Preparatory Committee for the United Nations World Summit for Social Development. New York, 31 January–11 February 1994.

Baig, Khalid. *First Things First: For Inquiring Minds and Yearning Hearts.* Stanton, CA: Open Minds Press, 2004.

bin Bayyumi, Muhammad (comp.). *Smaller Signs of the Day.* Riyadh: Dar-Us-Salam, 2004.

Brewster, David. *Memoirs of the Life, Writings, and Discoveries of Sir Isaac Newton.* Edinburgh/London: Thomas Constable & Co./ Hamilton, Adams & Co., 1855; rpt. in 2 vols. New York/London: Johnson Reprint Corporation, 1965.

Budge, E. A. Wallis. *Egyptian Religion: Egyptian Ideas of the Future Life.* London: Arkana, 1987.

Capra, Fritjof. *The Tao of Physics: An Exploration of the Parallels Between Modern Physics and Eastern Mysticism.* London: Flamingo, 1983.

The Compilation of Compilations. Prepared by the Universal House of Justice 1963–1990. 2 vols. [Mona Vale NSW]: Bahá'í Publications Australia, 1991.

Esslemont, J. E. *Bahá'u'lláh and the New Era.* London: Bahá'í Publishing Trust, 1974.

Feiler, Bruce. *Abraham.* London: Piatkus, 2002.

Gandhi, Mohandas. *Gandhi An Autobiography: The Story of My Experiments with Truth.* Boston: Beacon Press, 1993.

Gibran, Kahlil. 'A Poet's Voice', in Gibran, *A Tear and a Smile.* New York: Knopf, 1950.

— 'Resurrection', in Gibran, *A Treasury of Kahlil Gibran.* London: Arrow Publishing, 1997.

Gilani, Abdul Qadar. *Futuh Al-Ghaib: Revelations of the Unseen.* Lahore: Muhammad Ashraf, 1949.

Ibn Kathír Ad-Damishqi. *Before and After the Last Hour.* Trans. Rafi Abdur Rehman. Karachi: Darul Ishaat, 2004.

— *The Signs Before the Day of Judgement*. London: Dar Al Taqwa, 2007.

Iqbal, Allama Muhammad. *The Reconstruction of Religious Thought in Islam*. Chicago: Kazi Publications, 1999.

Judaism Online, http://www.simpletoremember.com/articles/a/einstein/

Kepler, Johannes. *Mysterium Cosmographicum*. Various editions.

Lemesurier, Peter. *The Armageddon Script: Prophecy in Action*. Salisbury: Element Books, 1983.

Mbiti, John S. *African Religions and Philosophy*. Oxford: Heinemann, 1990.

Plato. *Apology*. Various editions.

— *The Republic*. Various editions.

Rumi, Jalal al-Din Muhammad. *Mathnavi*. Various editions.

Saddhatissa, H. *The Life of the Buddha*. Windsor, QLD: Mandala Books, 1976.

al-Sa'dí, Shaykh 'Abd al-Raḥmán. *The Exquisite Pearl*. Trans. Abu Aaliyah Surkheel Sharif. London: The Jawziyyah Press, 2002.

Sarwar, Hafiz Ghulam. *Muhammad the Holy Prophet*. Lahore: Ashraf Press, 1969.

Sears, William. *Thief in the Night, or The Case of the Missing Millennium*. Oxford: George Ronald, 1961.

Shoghi Effendi. *God Passes By*. Wilmette, IL: Bahá'í Publishing Trust, rev. ed. 1995.

— *The Promised Day is Come*. Wilmette, IL: Bahá'í Publishing Trust, rev. ed. 1980.

— *The World Order of Bahá'u'lláh*. Wilmette, IL: Bahá'í Publishing Trust, 1991.

The Universal House of Justice. *The Promise of World Peace*. London: Bahá'í Publishing Trust, 1985.

Vidyarthi, Maulana Abdul Haq. *Muhammad in World Scriptures*. Delhi: Adam Publishers, 1994.

The World Book Encyclopedia. Chicago: World Book Childcraft International, 1982.

Yahya, Harun. *Signs of the Last Day*. New Delhi: Adam Publishers, 2002.

REFERENCES AND NOTES

Chapter 1: Rise and Shine

1. The egoic condition can be defined as the state of being identified with the ego or lower self, the motive force which seeks to defend and glorify the separate and separated self, works for separation, unhealthy autonomy or dogged independence, pleasure seeking, personal power and self aggrandizement, obscuring the divine Light.
2. Sarwar, *Muhammad the Holy Prophet*, p. 132.
3. ibid.
4. Yusuf Ali, *Holy Qur'an*, Appendix 8, p. 921.
5. Gilani, *Futuh Al-Ghaib*, discourse 58.
6. Gibran, *Treasury of Kahlil Gibran*, vol. 3, p. 242.
7. Yusuf Ali, *The Holy Qur'an*, note 1389, p. 484.
8. ibid. note 3632, p. 1092.
9. ibid. note 3634, p. 1093.
10. Abú Dáwud, *Sunan* 4336.
11. Yusuf Ali, *Holy Qur'an*, note 6148, p. 1742.
12. Vidyarthi, *Muhammad in World Scriptures*, p. 36.
13. Ibn Májah, *Sunan*, 4077; Ibn Ḥanbal, vol. 2, p. 319 and vol. 2, p. 482.
14. Sarwar, *Muhammad the Holy Prophet*, p. 129.
15. al-Bukhárí, *Ṣaḥíḥ*, 3611, 5057, 5058.
16. al-Ṭabaráni, *al-Mu'jam al-Kabír.*
17. Yahya, *Signs of the Last Day*, p. 33.
18. Ibn Májah, *Sunan*, 224.
19. Yusuf Ali, *The Holy Qur'an*, Appendix 8, p. 921.
20. ibid. note 6127, p. 1735.
21. Muslim, *Ṣaḥíḥ* 2891R1, 2892; Abú Dáwud, *Sunan* 4228.

Chapter 2: The Passage of Time

1. Mbiti, *African Religions and Philosophy*.
2. ibid.
3. ibid.
4. ibid.
5. ibid.

6. Budge, *Egyptian Religion*.
7. ibid.
8. ibid.
9. ibid. p. 110.

Chapter 3: Spiritual Revolutions

1. Saddhatissa, *Life of Buddha*, p. 73.
2. Zend Avesta Farvardin Yasht, 28:129, in *Sacred Books of the East*, vol. 23, Zend Avesta, part 2, p. 220.
3. Zend Avesta Zamyad Yasht, 16:95, in ibid. p. 308.
4. Vidyarthi, *Muhammad in World Scriptures*, ch. Zoroastrian Scriptures. Some prophecies are found in Farvardin Yasht 13:17 and 28:129; Zamyad Yasht 95; and Atash Nyayish 9.
5. Lao Tzu, *Tao Te Ching*, in *Tao Te Ching and Hua Hu Ching*, p. 29.
6. ibid. p. 66.
7. ibid. p. 17.
8. ibid. p. 41.
9. ibid. p. 45.
10. ibid. p. 44.
11. Hua Hu Ching, in *Tao Te Ching and Hua Hu Ching*, p. 38.
12. ibid. p. 43.
13. ibid. p. 75.
14. ibid. p. 77.
15. ibid. pp. 79–80.
16. Confucius, *Great Learning*.
17. Confucius *Analects*.
18. Plato, *Apology*.
19. Capra, *Tao of Physics*, p. 26.

Chapter 4: The Prophets of the Desert

1. Feiler, *Abraham*, p. 4.

Chapter 5: Muhammad

1. Abú Dáwud, *Sunan*, 4266/7/8.
2. Muslim, *Ṣaḥíḥ* 157R5; al-Bukhárí, *Ṣaḥíḥ*, vol. 13, p. 81; Abú Dáwud, *Sunan* 4239, 4319.
3. Ibn Májah, *Sunan*, 3992.
4. al-Bukhárí, *Ṣaḥíḥ*, 100 (V1 B3), 7307.
5. Ibn Kathír, *Before and After the Last Hour*.
6. al-Bukhárí, *Ṣaḥíḥ*, 65, 2938; Muslim, *Ṣaḥíḥ*, 2092R4.

Chapter 6: The Perfection of His Light

1. Yusuf Ali, *Holy Qur'an*, note 2285, p. 719.
2. Saddhatissa, *Life of Buddha*, p. 73.
3. Gandhi, *Story of My Experiments with Truth*, p. ix.
4. Kepler, *Mysterium Cosmographicum*.
5. Isaac Newton, quoted in Brewster, *Memoirs of . . . Newton*.

6. Judaism Online, http://www.simpletoremember.com/articles/a/einstein/
7. at-Tirmidhí, *Ṣaḥíḥ*, 2443.
8. Al-Ṭabarani, in *al-Mu'jam al-Kabír*, 8/187.
9. al-Bukhárí, *Ṣaḥíḥ* 3448, 2222; Muslim, *Ṣaḥíḥ*, 155.
10. Ibn Májah, *Sunan*, 4075.
11. al-Bukhárí, *Ṣaḥíḥ* 4918.
12. Abú Dáwud, *Sunan* 3658; Ibn Májah, *Sunan*, 4122; at-Tirmidhí, *Ṣaḥíḥ*, 2353.
13. Gibran, 'A Poet's Voice', in Gibran, *A Tear and a Smile*.
14. Confucius, *Great Learning*.
15. at-Tirmidhí, *Ṣaḥíḥ*, 2629; Ibn Májah, *Sunan*, 3986, 3988; Muslim, *Ṣaḥíḥ*, 145.
16. Sharif, Introduction, in al-Sa'dí, *Exquisite Pearl*, p. xii.
17. Ibn Májah, *Sunan*, 4077; Ibn Ḥanbal, *Musnad*, vol. 2, p. 319 and vol. 2, p. 482.
18. Ibn Májah, *Sunan*, 3986.
19. Ibn Bábúya.
20. Baig, *First Things First*, p. 321.
21. ibid.
22. Al-Haythamí.
23. Yahya, *Signs of the Last Day*, pp. 44–5.
24. ibid.
25. ibid.
26. al-Bukhárí, *Ṣaḥíḥ* 3611, 5057, 5058.
27. Al-Ṭabarani, in *al-Mu'jam al-Kabír*.
28. 'Imrán Ibn Ḥusayn, in Ibn Ḥanbal, *Musnad*; and at-Tirmidhí, *Ṣaḥíḥ*.
29. Ibn Májah, *Sunan*, 4048.
30. Ibn Bábúya.
31. al-Bukhárí, *Ṣaḥíḥ* 2059.
32. Abú Hurayrah, in at-Tirmidhí, *Ṣaḥíḥ*.
33. ibid.
34. Al-Haythamí.
35. Abú Dáwud, *Sunan* 448, 449; Ibn Májah, *Sunan*, 739.
36. Abú Hurayrah, in Ibn Májah, *Sunan*, 2278.
37. al-Bukhárí, *Ṣaḥíḥ*, 3606; Muslim, *Ṣaḥíḥ*, S1-1837, 1847; Ibn Májah, *Sunan*, 3979.
38. bin Bayyumi, *Smaller Signs of the Day*.
39. al-Bukhárí, *Ṣaḥíḥ*, 59.
40. ibid.
41. Ibn Májah, *Sunan*, 52; Muslim, *Ṣaḥíḥ*.
42. Ibn Ḥanbal, *Musnad*, vol. 2, p. 210.
43. ibid. 7319, 7320.
44. Abú Dáwud, *Sunan*, 4246; Ibn Májah, *Sunan*, 3961.
45. Ibn Kathír, *Before and After the Last Hour*.

Chapter 7: The Day of Sorting

1. Gibran, 'Resurrection', in Gibran, *Treasury of Kahlil Gibran.*
2. al-Bukhárí, *Ṣaḥíḥ*, 3448, 2222; Muslim, *Ṣaḥíḥ*, 155.
3. al-Bukhárí, *Ṣaḥíḥ*, 238, 876.
4. Muslim, *Ṣaḥíḥ*, 1978.
5. Ibn Májah, *Sunan*, 4290; Ibn Ḥanbal, *Musnad*, 2/49, 1/282.
6. Yusuf Ali, *Holy Qur'an*, note 2040, p. 660.
7. ibid. note 5044, p. 1433.
8. See Yahya, *Signs of the Last Day.*
9. Yusuf Ali, *Holy Qur'an*, note 4344, p. 1257.

Chapter 8: Clearing Away the Confusion

1. Ibn Ḥanbal, *Musnad*, 482; as-Suyúṭí, *Ad-Durr al-Manthúr* 2 (242).
2. Feiler, *Abraham*, p. iv.
3. Ibn Májah, *Sunan*, 4068.
4. ibid. 4082.
5. Abú Dáwud, *Sunan*, 4271, Ibn Májah, *Sunan*, 4086; al-Muttaqí al-Hindí, *Kanz al-'Ummál*, 38662.
6. Abú Dáwud, *Sunan*, 4270, at-Tirmidhí, *Ṣaḥíḥ*, 2231.
7. Abú Dáwud, *Sunan*, 4272.
8. Ibn Májah, *Sunan*, 4088.
9. Ibn Májah, *Sunan*; Ibn Ḥanbal, *Musnad*; al-Ḥákim, *Al-Mustadrak.*

Chapter 9: The Break of Dawn

1. Yusuf Ali, *Holy Qur'an*, p. 1730.
2. ibid. note 6108, p. 1731.
3. Ibn Ḥanbal, *Musnad*, 22 (1/2); *Majma' al-Zawá'íd* 10/410.
4. at-Tirmidhí, *Al-Dani, Al-Mahdi and the End of Time*, p. 44.
5. Ibn Ḥanbal, Aḥmad. *Musnad*, vol. 4, p. 110; Abú Dáwud, *Sunan*, 2476/7).
6. at-Tirmidhí, *Ṣaḥíḥ*, vol. 12, p. 146.
7. al-Muttaqí al-Hindí, *Kanz al-'Ummál*, vol. 14, p. 161, no. 38234.
8. Muhyi ad-Dín Ibn al-'Arabí, *Al-Futúḥát al-Makkiyyah*, vol. 3, pp. 166–8.
9. Muslim, *Ṣaḥíḥ*, 2137; Abú Dáwud, *Sunan*, 4307; Ibn Májah, *Sunan*, 4075.
10. Ibn Kathír, *Before and After the Last Hour*, p. 137.
11. Sears, *Thief in the Night*, p. 74.
12. Selections from the Dalá'il-i-Sab'ih, in The Báb, *Selections*, pp. 124–6.
13. The Báb, *Selections*, p. 104.
14. ibid. p. 106.
15. Bahá'u'lláh, quoted in Shoghi Effendi, *God Passes By*, p. 101.
16. Bahá'u'lláh, *Gleanings*, p. 10.
17. Bahá'u'lláh, *Tablets*, p. 118.
18. Bahá'u'lláh, *Kitáb-i-Íqán*, pp. 3–4.
19. Bahá'u'lláh, *Gleanings*, pp. 249–50.

20. ibid. p. 11.
21. Bahá'u'lláh, in *Compilation*, vol. 2, p. 157.
22. Bahá'u'lláh, *Kitáb-i-Íqán*, p. 97.
23. Bahá'u'lláh, *Gleanings*, pp. 79–80.
24. ibid. p. 97.
25. 'Abdu'l-Bahá, *Some Answered Questions*, ch. 12, pp. 62–6.
26. 'Abdu'l-Bahá, *Selections*, p. 174.
27. ibid. pp. 31–2.
28. Shoghi Effendi, *World Order*, pp. 42–3.
29. Shoghi Effendi, *Promised Day is Come*, p. 116.
30. The Universal House of Justice, *Promise of World Peace*, paras. 1, 2, 10 and 11.
31. Bahá'í International Community, 'Global Action Plan for Social Development', paras. 6 and 7.
32. The Báb, *Selections*, p. 217.
33. 'Abdu'l-Bahá, quoted in Esslemont, *Bahá'u'lláh and the New Era*, p. 99.
34. 'Abdu'l-Bahá, in *Bahá'í Prayers*, p. 114.
35. Bahá'u'lláh, *Tablets*, p. 111.
36. Bahá'u'lláh, *Gleanings*, pp. 60–2.
37. Bahá'u'lláh, *Prayers and Meditations*, p. 314.
38. Bahá'u'lláh, *Tablets*, p. 186.
39. Bahá'u'lláh, *Hidden Words*, Arabic no. 6.

INDEX

This index is alphabetized word for word; thus *I Ching* precedes *Ibn Kathír*. Connecting hyphens, apostrophes and the letters al- and -i- are ignored; 'and', 'for', 'in', 'of' and 'the' in entries are ignored.